On Modern Literature

On
Modern Literature

LECTURES AND ADDRESSES

BY

W. P. KER

EDITED BY TERENCE SPENCER
AND JAMES SUTHERLAND

OXFORD
AT THE CLARENDON PRESS

Republished 1971
Scholarly Press, Inc., 22929 Industrial Drive East
St. Clair Shores, Michigan 48080

Library of Congress Catalog Card Number: 70-158500
ISBN 0-403-01299-6

ACKNOWLEDGEMENTS

We are indebted to University College, London, for permission to use the manuscript material from which this volume has been compiled, and to Mr. C. P. Ker for allowing us to make use of one passage ('A Postscript on the Humanities') from a notebook in his possession. We are also grateful to one of Ker's old students, Lord Strang, for allowing us to look at the notes he took of several of Ker's courses. A more detailed statement of the provenance of the various lectures and passages included will be found in a Bibliographical Note on pp. xvii–xviii.

After we had done our best to trace Ker's allusions and identify the sources of his quotations, we were left with about twenty passages that still eluded us. Those have been reduced to a handful by the generous and erudite assistance of Professor Robert Dewar, Dr. J. R. Peddie, Professor W. L. Renwick, Professor D. Nichol Smith, and Dr. E. Stahl, and of our colleagues at University College.

91958

PREFACE

In the early years of this century W. P. Ker had become a formidable figure in English studies. It was a period when the Chairs of English Literature in England and Scotland were filled by such learned and lively men as Saintsbury at Edinburgh, A. C. Bradley at Glasgow, Grierson at Aberdeen, Oliver Elton at Liverpool, and Raleigh at Oxford, men who, in their different ways, were winning respect for this comparatively new discipline. In this scholarly company Ker occupied his own special place. Even among men of learning he was distinguished by the unusual range of his reading; and however much he read, he brought to it always 'a spirit and judgement equal or superior'. There were few great works in European literature, from Homer to his own time, that he had not read, and read in the language in which they were written. A man who can settle down comfortably to enjoy the *Iliad* and the *Aeneid*, *Beowulf* and the Icelandic sagas and the *Chanson de Roland*, Dante and Rabelais, Cervantes and Shakespeare, Molière and Goethe, and who can read those writers with no more difficulty than he reads Milton or Swift or Wordsworth, is not commonly to be found today. Most professors of English are, in his own happy phrase, less 'imprudently learned'. Ker began as a classical scholar, and for some years he taught in the Humanity department in the University of Edinburgh. The great classical authors were always at call when he turned to the literature of Modern Europe; for what was as remarkable as the extent of his learning was its availability. At what stage he became interested in the literature of the Dark Ages and of the medieval period it is impossible to tell; he belonged to an age when it had not yet become customary to contribute papers to learned journals (which, indeed, hardly existed), and he was forty-two when his first book, *Epic and Romance*, appeared in 1897. Before that, although he had been a professor at the University College of South Wales, and later at University College, London, for fourteen years, he had published almost nothing. We may conveniently suppose all that part of Ker's life which fell in the nineteenth century to have been filled with that wide reading which enabled him to discourse with such insight and authority on the whole literature of Europe.

Yet, wide as his reading was, it was far from being indiscriminate. He had no doubt read in many out-of-the-way places; but he can hardly be put among those omnivorous readers, such as Rabelais, Ben Jonson, and Butler, whom he once described as 'pedants with fire inside them'. Rabelais, he tells us, is 'the father of all the scholars who choose their own way of study and find the heaviest reading the most amusing thing in the world'; and he contrasts such learned autodidacts with Sterne, who 'was attracted by the humorous pedantry of Rabelais', but who 'managed to get the variegated effect of enormous learning by more commodious means'. In his own reading Ker was not one of the gross feeders, rooting among the mast and potato parings of literature. He seems, indeed, to have been no great believer in 'all such reading as was never read', the sort of reading that editors have to do if they are to provide satisfactory annotations for the works they edit; nor was he ever one of those who 'fished the murex up' at the Public Record Office. Ker took his turn at editing, and his *Essays of John Dryden* has remained standard for more than half a century; but it is a fine edition more on account of its introductory material than for the exhaustiveness of its notes. Ker, in fact, liked to keep good company in literature as in life; he was not prepared to waste too much valuable time (and here, perhaps, he may be contrasted with his learned contemporary, George Saintsbury) in reading what has been deservedly forgotten. 'Had we but world enough and time'—but we hadn't, and he stuck to the best, or, at any rate, to the good. Lecturing on Hazlitt towards the end of his life, he remarked, almost blithely, 'I have never read his *Principles of Human Action, an Argument in favour of the Natural Disinterestedness of the Human Mind*'; and we may be sure that he was not haunted by any fear that he had thereby lost the key to Hazlitt's mind.

Ker's wide reading enabled him to make many interesting observations in the field of comparative literature. To take only one example, he was unusually well informed on poetic forms, and some idea of his range may be obtained from the *Rhythmorum Exempla*, which, as Professor Chambers tells us, he printed and distributed to his class. The map of European poetry lay spread out before him; he had been everywhere, and everything fell into place in his mind. Yet, while he was fully alive to the value of historical criticism, a natural tact kept him from talking too much about 'tendencies' and 'influences'; he liked to remind his students that what they had to deal with was poets and poems, books and authors. Lecturing to them in 1889, he summed up the business of criticism in words which perhaps show the influence of Walter Pater:

Not to confound things different; to reckon every author as one individual, with his own particular story to tell, his own individual manner, his own value—that is the essence of it. Not to judge abstractly, but to see concretely, is the end and aim of it.

Ker was a literary historian in the sense that his mind was constantly alive to tradition and environment; his criticism was controlled, and to some extent initiated, by his awareness of the past. A man with Ker's reading will naturally—almost unconsciously—fall to comparing one thing with another; his memory is working for him all the time, and his criticism is in effect a crystallization of his knowledge and past literary experience. Indeed, we might apply to the critical process of such a scholar the words of one of Ker's favourite authors: his memory is continually 'moving the sleeping images of things towards the light, there to be distinguished, and then either chosen or rejected by the judgement'. Sometimes he will bring together two authors—Milton and Butler, Burns and Boethius, Plato and Jane Austen, Petrarch and Sterne— who seem to have little or nothing in common, making the sort of implausible comparison that would almost certainly earn a mild rebuke if it were put forward by a young beginner. But with Ker we can be sure that the relevance has been pondered, and that there is a genuine area of contact, even if it lies beneath the surface.

It is now more than thirty years since he died, and the passage of years has made it easier to recognize the characteristic qualities of his work. If we try to compare him with the greatest names in English criticism, we shall only draw attention to his shortcomings. He had always a tendency to substitute quotation for criticism. No doubt the *explication de texte*, so much in favour today, has made us more conscious of his apparent reluctance to place the poem on the dissecting table. If he approved of such proceedings at all, he probably thought them more suitable for schoolboys than for the adults to whom he normally addressed himself. When, in an Oxford lecture on *Samson Agonistes*, he permits himself what is, for him, a particular analysis of the action, he checks himself almost at once. 'I will not consider too curiously', he tells his audience, 'I will read the last speech of Manoa. . . .' And read it he does, fifty lines of it, and then passes on without comment to other matters. He could have learnt this habit of extensive quotation from Hazlitt, or possibly from Thomas Warton; but most probably it was forced upon him by the needs of several generations of students who were less well supplied with texts of English authors than their grandchildren are today. Lecturing on Warton's *History of English Poetry*, he told his students: 'Warton's is an excellent book to dip into, because, through its long extracts, it brings one into actual contact with the things themselves, and that, after all, is the main thing.' This is all very well; but too often in Ker, as in Warton, we ask for bread and are fed with a quotation.

His unwillingness to analyse the effect of poetry, to take the poem to pieces and put it together again, was undoubtedly due to some kind of romantic inhibition, common enough in his own day, but not likely to recommend him to the present-day reader. More reputably, he seems to have been reluctant to do the reader's work for him. Yet he appears at times almost too anxious to depreciate the sort of historical knowledge that he himself had in such full measure and to emphasize the unpredictability of genius and the ultimate mystery of great poetry. 'Great poems are miraculous', he told the Literary Society of University College in

1895, and there was always something of this reverent suppression of curiosity in his criticism. It is significant that some of his most delicate analysis occurs in his remarks on prose style, when, perhaps, he felt freer to 'peep and botanize' because the thing itself was not so sacred. It is clear, at all events, that he himself was deeply moved by great literature, and that he was more concerned that his students should experience it freshly and spontaneously than that they should grow learned about it. His lectures constantly helped his students to know and appreciate the natural magic of great literature, but he preferred to work unobtrusively by way of stimulating suggestions rather than by the method of formal analysis.

What strikes one today is his absolute integrity, his deep sense of responsibility to the writers he is discussing. He belonged to a generation in which the critic was still thought of as a relatively humble person, who stood to the creative writer in the same sort of relationship as a chairman to a lecturer. It is the lecturer we come to hear, and any unnecessary display or loquacity on the part of the chairman is an offence against decorum. But this tradition can hardly be said to be in fashion today. What Hazlitt observed of Beaumont and Fletcher—'They thought less of their subject, and more of themselves, than some others'—is more often applicable to present-day critics than to those of Ker's generation. Ker, at least, always put his subject first; his business was not to be exciting or original or profound, but to be right. His aim was to talk pleasantly and instructively about literature. He had the disinterestedness that Matthew Arnold looked for in the critic; no axes to grind, no importunate topics. As a man and a scholar he was far from being indifferent or neutral, but he rarely allowed his feelings to impair the steadiness of his vision. Occasionally, under great provocation, he would gore and toss a Mark Pattison; but such self-indulgence is comparatively rare. With undivided attention he kept his eye fixed steadily upon the object; his learning was not allowed to meander into irrelevant digression, but was brought to bear at the point where it would be most effective. His calm, imperturbable habit of turning things slowly over in his mind enabled him, time after time, to seize upon the obvious that everyone else had missed, as in the following passage on Corneille and Dryden:

> There is, in spite of many similarities, a great difference between Corneille and Dryden, a difference that marks very clearly the eighteenth-century strain in the latter. Corneille, in the collected edition of his works in 1660, is writing of what he has done, explaining the intentions and changes of intention in his past life. His life is not yet ended, his work is not yet at an end, but the greater part is finished; the French drama is prospering, and prospering in a way Corneille understood and had very much influenced.... Racine and Molière are following in his footsteps; the drama is in its great age, in the time of glory corresponding to the Elizabethan age in England. The critical essays of Corneille are a record of what is going on, of a process of dramatic creation still flourishing.
>
> Dryden, on the other hand, is writing of what he wants to do, of ideal forms of literature which he is at the time meditating and doing his best to realize. He has, so to speak, nothing like the treasury of Corneille, the secured and hoarded savings all to the good. He is a speculator in more senses than one. . . .

Such passages do not 'startle and waylay'—Ker's criticism rarely does that—but the cumulative effect of such rightness on page after page presses on the mind. When we notice particularly something that Ker has said, it is usually because just at that point the pitcher which has been quietly filling begins to brim over. There can rarely have been a less demonstrative, a more persistently undramatic critic; his lectures normally began and ended on a minor key. He expressed himself on all occasions, as a speaker and a writer, with precision and restraint; if he had any mannerism, it was a Scots habit of understatement. How well he could write may be seen in a passage where he is himself considering certain unpleasing developments in nineteenth-century prose:

> Now, it requires great skill to be imaginative or metaphorical or sentimental in prose. Since poetry became poetical again some eighty or ninety years since, prose has not been quite so sure of its balance. Prose practising short flights of poetry from one rafter to another is very far from politeness. All emphasis, all forcing of the tone, is alien to polite literature.

And then, after quoting an embarrassingly lush passage from John Addington Symonds:

> Now that sort of thing is either too good or too bad for ordinary prose, and in either case it is corrupting and licentious. It is bad form, like a masquer going home by daylight. Good prose is not written in this way. Good prose may be imaginative, may be lofty and dignified; it does not flutter into poetry like this.

The discussion ends with the suggestion that they did those things better in the eighteenth century. Ker himself had a good deal of that century in him: its good taste, its dislike of over-emphasis, and (it would seem) its general attitude to literature and the arts. So, at least, it has seemed to one of his old students, the Provost of University College:

> His appreciation of literature was rather the enjoyment that comes from a world of good taste, the ideal of the world of the eighteenth-century gentleman who had leisure to read, and had time to maintain discernment among the things that he had read. He would sometimes speak of literature as an idle study, and he was very aware of the world of action, of the practice of law, of medicine and the sciences. He would sometimes almost admit their strength as objects of study, as if they had ampler justification than literature. Yet the magic of the idle studies appealed to him overwhelmingly, and they were pursued with discipline and with an unrelenting energy.

In his own lifetime Ker's reputation rested mainly on his studies in the earlier literature of Europe, for he had, in fact, published little else. The appearance of his Oxford Lectures on Poetry in the year of his death (*The Art of Poetry*, 1923), of *Collected Essays of W. P. Ker* (2 vols., 1925), and of *Form and Style in Poetry* (1928), gave a much better idea of the range of his interest in modern European literature. Not all of the lectures in *The Art of Poetry* or in *Collected Essays*, however, show him at the height of his powers; it is perhaps permissible to see in some of them what Mark Pattison was so soundly castigated for seeing in *Samson Agonistes*—'a flagging of the forces, a drying up of the rich sources from which had once flowed the golden stream of suggestive phrase'. In this volume we offer Ker as generations of his students knew him, talking vigorously from day to day on modern English Literature. From all accounts he spoke to them slowly and carefully, without a note, but quite obviously from careful preparation. Few students can ever have been better served by their professor than those who attended Ker's courses at University College between the years 1889 and 1922.

> The modest wants of ev'ry day
> The toil of ev'ry day supply'd,

and here, if ever, was 'the power of art without the show'.

CONTENTS

BIBLIOGRAPHICAL NOTE

THE material from which this volume is compiled has been drawn from two sources: (*a*) unpublished lectures in Ker's own hand, and (*b*) lectures on the literature of the seventeenth, eighteenth, and nineteenth centuries delivered by him to his students at University College, London, and reported verbatim by the late Dr. Elsie Hitchcock.

From Ker's own manuscripts we have taken the passages on Sidney (p. 211), Butler (p. 1), Milton (pp. 13 and 17), Wordsworth (p. 86), 'Literature and Philosophy' (p. 271), and 'A Postscript on the Humanities' (p. 175), and the lectures on 'Criticism', 'Culture', 'Polite Literature', 'Progress in Poetry', 'Comedy', William Gilpin, Jane Austen, and Trollope.

The rest of the volume consists of passages taken from the University College lectures already mentioned. In 1928 Ker's colleague, the late Professor R. W. Chambers, edited a volume called *Form and Style in Poetry*. The series of lectures which gave that volume its title was taken in the main from a course delivered by Ker to his students at University College, and in his Preface Professor Chambers explained how they came to be preserved.

In 1911, and for some six years after, Professor Ker asked Dr. Elsie Hitchcock to attend his lectures at University College, London, and to let him have a report, as nearly verbatim as possible, of what was said. This was done, and the fair copy of these lectures was handed back to him. It was clearly Ker's intention to revise these manuscripts for publication, but this was never done.

The lectures on Form and Style were published by Professor Chambers in their entirety. With so much material at our disposal, we have chosen to select only such passages as seemed to us to show Ker at his best, as a scholar and critic. After some hesitation we decided not to indicate meticulously by dots every occasion on which we have made a cut, but to let the text run on if the transition was not too abrupt.

It is only fair to Ker, however, to make it clear that the transitions are not always his own.

A few other editorial changes have been made silently. Phrases such as 'the other day' or 'as Mr. George Meredith has recently reminded us' have been eliminated. Dr. Hitchcock's report has impressed us as being remarkably accurate, but once or twice, when a word was undoubtedly misheard, we have substituted the one that the context clearly demands. On such occasions we have had the benefit of a collation made about fifteen years ago by Professor Geoffrey Tillotson of several other reports of the same lectures. A few grammatical changes were necessary. Ker, who lectured slowly, habitually expressed himself with enviable precision, but occasionally we have had to correct small slips in syntax. We have sometimes had to correct his quotations—often, it would seem, made from memory. Finally, on a number of occasions we have relegated some observation of Ker's to a footnote, and have identified it as his by the letters 'W.P.K.' All other notes are editorial.

So far as we are aware, nothing in this volume has been previously published. One or two passages touch on points already treated in Ker's published work, and where the resemblance seemed close enough to warrant some acknowledgement we have drawn the reader's attention to it.

I. APPRECIATIONS

Samuel Butler

To speak of the author of *Hudibras* is to touch on one of the gravest parts of English history, and one which has left its effects so obviously on modern England that even at this day people may be found to take sides about it and to lose their tempers. At the same time no part of English history is so difficult to understand; and the more one tries to learn about it the harder it is to have any fixed opinions. When one was young things were easier—when the authorities were *Old Mortality*, *The Legend of Montrose*, and *Woodstock*, supported by *The Three Musketeers* and *Twenty Years After*. It is true that the matter was complicated for some of us, at least, in the north by *Scots Worthies*[1] and the *Tales of the Covenanters*;[2] but then it was possible to be Cavalier and Covenanter alternately or even in a sort of way simultaneously—before S. R. Gardiner's *History*. It is still possible for the old sympathies to be reawakened, but in a different and a painful way. Montrose on the one side, and Milton on the other, may still have power to call up a reflection of the old enthusiasms. But the historian's commentary leaves it more and more certain that for us it is no longer possible to take sides and very hard indeed to understand how things actually appeared to the several disputants in the thick of the debate.

Hudibras puts one side strongly, and that is its value and its title to fame. But *Hudibras* does not express the whole mind of its author. *Hudibras* is known by the quotations:

> Ay me! what perils do environ
> The Man that meddles with cold Iron![3]

[1] By John Howie (1735–93). *Scots Worthies* (1774) contains short biographies of Scottish reformers and martyrs.
[2] 1833. By Robert Pollok (1798–1827).   [3] I. iii. 1.

and so on. But one longer quotation, one of the most familiar,
must be given, because it is the most important part of Butler's case:

> For his *Religion* it was fit
> To match his Learning and his Wit:
> 'Twas *Presbyterian* true blew,
> For he was of that stubborn Crew
> Of Errant Saints, whom all men grant
> To be the true Church *Militant:*
> Such as do build their Faith upon
> The holy Text of *Pike* and *Gun;*
> Decide all Controversies by
> Infallible *Artillery;*
> And prove their Doctrine Orthodox
> By Apostolick Blows and Knocks;
> Call Fire and Sword and Desolation,
> A *godly-thorough-Reformation,*
> Which always must be carry'd on,
> And still be doing, never done:
> As if Religion were intended
> For nothing else but to be mended.[1]

That is the chief thing that Butler has to say, in *Hudibras*;
and it is enough to explain why the book was popular with
King Charles II—'Our Covenanted King', as he was called
at one period of his history by his friends, who implored him
to suppress 'the impious monster of Toleration'.

The misfortune of *Hudibras* is that the quotations are so
very much the best of the book; that the unquoted, the unfamiliar, passages are so uninteresting. The king apparently
had a different opinion, and it may be rash to disagree on a
question of wit with Charles II; but most people who have
read *Hudibras* through will be inclined to believe that the first
thoughts of his faithful servant Samuel Pepys have a good
deal to say for themselves:

Dec. 26. 1662: Hither come Mr Battersby; and we falling into discourse of a new book of drollery in use called Hudebras, I would needs
go find it out, and met with it at the Temple—cost me 2s. 6d. But
when I come to read it, it is so silly an abuse of the Presbyter Knight

---

[1] I. i. 189.

going to the warrs, that I am ashamed of it; and by and by meeting at Mr Townsend's at dinner, I sold it to him for 18*d*.

Feb. 6. 1663: And so to a bookseller's in the Strand, and there bought Hudibras again, it being certainly some ill humour to be so against that which all the world cries up to be the example of wit; for which I am resolved once more to read him, and see whether I can find it or no.

Dec. 10. 1663: ... Hudibras, both parts, the book now in greatest fashion for drollery, though I cannot, I confess, see enough where the wit lies.

Even Dr. Johnson, who says that the name of Butler can only perish with the language, admits that his poem is monotonous. I quote a sentence from W. E. Henley's essay:

Fashions change; the bogies of one epoch become the heroes of the next, and what yesterday was apt and humorous is balderdash and out of date tomorrow. That which we praise in Butler now is that for which two centuries ago no man regarded him. He is tedious, trivial, spiteful, ignoble, where he once was sprightly, exact, magnanimous, heroic.[1]

Butler, however, wrote much more than *Hudibras*, though the mass of his other writings remained unprinted till after his death and has had very little share in his fame. Even if *Hudibras* were as poor a thing as it appeared to Mr. Pepys, his other writings would make Butler remarkable; and if he had written nothing but *Hudibras*, his life and his character would still be memorable, for he was a man with a mind of his own. He lived through the most exciting times in English history and he formed a very distinct opinion or set of opinions about his age and about some of the influences by which the age was governed. As it is, we are not left to judge of him from his poem alone. Some of his most significant work is to be found elsewhere.

The theory got about, and became a commonplace of literary history, that Butler was very poor. He was evidently not rich or very prosperous, and he was disappointed if he ever hoped for much from the favour of the King or Lord Clarendon.

[1] *The English Poets*, ed. T. H. Ward, 1887, ii. 399.

Dr Sp[rat]'s Dedication of his Book to Cl. is not unlike what Marco Polo relates of the Tartars, that they never eate, nor drinke, but they spill some of it on the Ground as an offering to the Devil.[1]

There is no proof, however, that he was a starving scholar—which is the common legend: Dr. Johnson and Goldsmith (who speaks with sympathy of Butler's misfortunes)[2] both suffered more in their hungry days than anything reported of Butler. Yet although the history of his life has not so much of the interest of distress and of martyred genius as has sometimes been given to it, it leaves the impression very distinctly of a character that was not born to be prosperous and that very early had chosen its own way apart from the rest of the world. Butler is one of the eccentric and lonely scholars of whom there are many in the history of European learning—one of the humorists who had a craving for all kinds of knowledge, partly for the sake of knowledge and partly for the fun of the thing, the amusement or the dissipation of seeking about the back-streets of the universe. He is one of the sons of Rabelais. Rabelais is the father of all the scholars who choose their own way of study and find the heaviest reading the most amusing thing in the world. It is a type that does not become commoner after Butler's time. Burton of *The Anatomy of Melancholy* and the great Ben Jonson himself were the chief men of that school before Butler. After Butler, as a general rule, the learned men were not wits, and the wits were not imprudently learned. Sterne was attracted by the humorous pedantry of Rabelais, but he managed to get the variegated effect of enormous learning by

[1] Butler, *Characters and Passages from Note-Books,* ed. A. R. Waller (Cambridge, 1908), p. 401.

[2] In a letter to Mrs. Jane Lawder of 5 August 1758 Goldsmith wishes that he could 'forget that ever he starv'd in those streets where Butler and Otway starv'd before him' (*Collected Letters of Oliver Goldsmith,* ed. K. C. Balderston (Cambridge, 1928), p. 46). He reviewed Thyer's edition of the *Remains* in *The Critical Review,* viii (1759), lamenting the 'indigence in which the poet lived and died', and protesting 'at the want of discernment, at the more than barbarous ingratitude, of his contemporaries'. Cf. also *The Citizen of the World,* letter lxxxiv. 'The sufferings of the poet in other countries are nothing when compared to his distresses here, the names of Spencer and Otway, Butler and Dryden, are every day mentioned as a national reproach, some of them lived in a state of precarious indigence, and others literally died of hunger.'

more commodious means. There is many a sign of true Pantagruelist descent in Browning. The medley of learning in Browning's poems from *Pauline* to *Asolando*—the learning worn not lightly as a flower but ostentatiously with a swagger and bravado like a dress at a masquerade—all this is a mark of that family of the insatiable scholars who are never over-laden, with all their reading; who seem occasionally to get into a sort of drunken exhilaration of learning; but who never grow stupid over it, like common pedants. Pedants with fire inside them—Rabelais, Ben Jonson, Butler, Browning—this order of man is not so common or so widely diffused over the earth that it is hard to recognize when one meets it.

Butler was an isolated worker, a self-made scholar. It is not from such a man that one expects well-balanced views or a coherent philosophy. His style in many respects is old-fashioned. He was almost as far apart from the favourite literary ways of his time on the one side as his contemporary Milton was on the other. He is a kind of inverse Milton, almost as much alone, and quite as self-reliant—following, in a different way from Milton, old-fashioned traditions of literature, and bringing out new results of his own from methods which appeared to be worn out and had been generally abandoned by the smart contemporary authors. *Paradise Lost* was not composed till long after blank verse had been generally voted a stale, intolerable way of writing. Pope and Dr. Johnson could not understand why Milton chose that form, why he did not make it rhyme. Butler's *Hudibras*, which is a sort of diabolical counterpart of Milton on the minus side of the scale, is written in a style which follows the literary fashions of fifty years before, and gives them a new turn, a new meaning. Butler lived at a time when the tricks of the 'metaphysical school', as Dr. Johnson called it, were beginning to be found out; when the fashion of per-petual similes and conceits was becoming or had become a general nuisance, and poetry was settling down into different courses, into the steadier and less excitable movement of the great satirical poets.

Butler, however, keeps to the old ways. *Hudibras* is full of conceits of all kinds, not always burlesque, though the poet generally gave a new turn to the old methods of wit by making the comparison intentionally ludicrous:

> The Sun had long since in the Lap
> Of *Thetis* taken out his *Nap*,
> And like a *Lobster* boyl'd, the *Morn*
> From *black* to *red* began to turn.[1]

Not all of his comparisons are grotesque:

> The *Sun* grew low, and left the Skies,
> Put down (some write) by *ladies'* eyes.
> The *Moon* pull'd off her veil of Light,
> That hides her face by day from sight,
> (Mysterious Veil, of brightness made,
> That's both her lustre, and her shade).[2]

His prose writings are made up of an enormous mass of conceits in the old taste.

The Genuine Remains in Verse and Prose of Mr Samuel Butler were published in 1759 from Butler's manuscripts by Mr. Robert Thyer, Keeper of the Public Library at Manchester. About two-thirds of the first volume is in verse, miscellaneous poems. Most of the second volume is taken up with a series of Characters, a work on which Butler seems to have spent a great deal of time, and another proof of his old-fashioned tastes in literature. The writing of Characters, that is to say, descriptions of different types of human nature, generally bad, with as many smart things as the author could think of, had been a common thing for long past. Butler's are as good as the best; clever, and rather monotonous; full of observation of contemporary manners, full of surprising and ingenious comparisons. One of the essays, by the way, is the character of a publisher; it is not complimentary.

> He values nothing but as it is vendible, and would not greatly care what becomes of his own soul, but that he finds it will sell.[3]

Some of the original manuscripts of the Characters are preserved in the British Museum, written very carefully, num-

---

[1] Op. cit. II. ii. 29–32.
[2] Ibid. II. i. 903–8.
[3] *Characters*, ed. cit., p. 262.

bered, dated, and paged. The date of these sheets is 1667.
It is not clear why they were not given to the press.

It is from Butler's manuscripts that one learns to take
rather a different view of him than can be gained from *Hudibras*.
He is representative of his age; and, more than that, representative in a very remarkable way of the whole great intellectual movement of Europe from the first revival of learning
to the great achievements of rationalism in the eighteenth
century. He is old-fashioned in his manner, old-fashioned
among the practitioners of the new forms of polite literature,
old-fashioned when his style and his formulas are compared
with the manner of Cowley's essays or Dryden's prose. But
his ruling ideas, his philosophy of life, and his temper, are not
of the old school; on the contrary, they anticipate the character of much of the eighteenth-century view of life. (Swift in
many things is the exponent of the ideas and the sentiments
of Butler.) The bottles are old, but the wine is new. It was
Butler's defect or his misfortune that he never found any perfectly adequate form of expression for what he had in his
mind. It is perhaps on this account that he is interesting. It
is curious that he should never have used in any published
work the very clear and natural language in which he wrote
his unpublished reflections.

To make a man into a representative of the Spirit of his
Age is a common process among historians and critics. 'The
Spirit of the Ages, as you call it, turns out to be the mind of
the good gentlemen who interpret the Ages for us.'[1] The
warning is a timely one. But it is one thing to pretend to have
discovered the secret of history, it is another thing and a more
discreet and possible thing to discover, in the writings and
characters of authors, the common ideals, hopes, illusions,
fallacies, that belong peculiarly to their time; to trace their
gradual appearance, the growth of their influence, their decline or their transformation into the fashions of a new
generation.

[1] A loose translation of Goethe's
      Was ihr den Geist der Zeiten heisst,
      Das ist im Grund der Herren eigner Geist,
      In dem die Zeiten sich bespiegeln.
                            (*Faust*, Pt. I, 577-9.)

Butler is something more than the satirist and the scourge of the fanatical sectaries. He is one of the company of thinkers whose aims and work are denoted by the convenient titles 'Revival of Learning' or 'Renaissance'. His ideal is that for which generations of scholars and moralists had laboured, from the days of Petrarch to the days of Erasmus, of Rabelais, of Bacon; the ideal which was in all essentials the same, however different in its mode of operation, in the minds of Swift and of Voltaire.

Reason—a reasonable and sound judgement of human affairs and a consequent opposition to all extravagance, hypocrisy, and nonsense—this is what Butler worked for, in the spirit of his great forerunners. The odd thing is that he should have used in general such extravagant forms of expression to carry out his design; that, being as he was an admirer of simplicity, he should have used such variegated forms of expression, a dialect often as Babylonish as that of his hero himself. In this he is like Rabelais, whose preaching of simplicity and sanity is not itself either plain or sober. Rabelais, however, is more easily understood than Butler. He had the enthusiasm, the Dionysiac rapture of the great age at its beginning, when all things seemed possible to the adventurous, all knowledge attainable. The inexhaustible nonsense and confusion of his great book is the natural expression of his untamed belief in the new ideas. He is in his element, and you must not expect good manners or conventional rhetoric. 'By his neesings a light doth shine. . . . He maketh the deep to boil like a pot.'[1]

One of the most remarkable things in modern history, wider in its significance than any political fact, is the change of mind that gradually took place between the sixteenth and the eighteenth centuries—the cooling down of the vast enthusiasm of the Renaissance into a sober painful conviction of the limitations of humanity, of the very small amount of freedom available for the work of reason, the very slow rate of progress attainable in the education of the human race. 'Mostly fools': the formula is of later invention,[2] but it

[1] Job, xli. 18, 31.

[2] 'Twenty-seven millions mostly fools'; Carlyle, *Latter-Day Pamphlets* (1850), No. vi. 'Parliaments', *passim*.

expresses the sentiments of some of the greatest moralists of the eighteenth century, of the optimists as well as the others.

It is the difference between Rabelais and Swift, put shortly by Coleridge in his phrase describing Swift, *anima Rabelaisii habitans in sicco*.[1] The rationalism of the eighteenth century is summed up in that phrase. The ideal of Swift is the ideal of the Renaissance: the faith is the same, the faith in reason and good sense, but it has lost its hopefulness; the hope is too like despair, the forces of dullness are too many, and their armoury is too strong. What Rabelais and Swift have at heart is a theory of culture, and they agree in essentials (also with Bacon)—at any rate as to the sort of things that are to be excluded: sophistry, pedantry, superstition, false science. But in details how great is the difference! In Rabelais's scheme of an ideal education almost everything is included except the scholastic philosophy. Swift takes a very much lower estimate of what is suitable for such a creature as man in such a world as this. The learning that he thinks desirable is no more than enough to give a man power to understand the practical affairs in which he has to move, and he rejects as inconvenient and superfluous not only the useless knowledge of the medieval schoolmen, but all science and all study which is so complicated as to require special devotion and the sacrifice of the ordinary business of life. The studies of Newton are included in the useless science of Laputa.

This dispirited and disheartened estimate of human powers is shared and anticipated by Butler. 'In Religion and the Civill life, the wisest and Ablest are faine to comply and submit to the weakest and most Ignorant, for their own Quiet and convenience.'[2] But not less than this low estimate of their powers, Butler shares with Swift the unhesitating belief in the rightness of their cause. One may apply to the intellectual perseverance of Butler and Swift what is beyond a doubt the noblest passage that Butler wrote:

> For Loyalty is still the same,
> Whether it win or lose the Game;

[1] *Table Talk*, 15 June 1830.
[2] Butler, *Characters*, ed. cit., p. 420.

True as a Dial to the Sun,
Although it be not shin'd upon.[1]

'All the Business of this World is but Diversion, and all the
Happiness in it, that Mankind is capable of—anything that
will keep it from reflecting upon the Misery, Vanity, and Non-
sence of it; and whoever can by any Trick keep himself from
thinking of it, is as wise and happy as the best Man in it.'[2]

The spirit of that sentence is more common in the eighteenth century, even among those who were doing their best
to take the sting out of it, than is perhaps commonly supposed.
There was a recovery from this depression at the end of the
century; most notably in the eloquence of Burke, and in the
preaching of Wordsworth, not to speak of the revolutionary
thinkers and their ideals. But it is not too much to say that
for more than a century the prevalent temper among the
moralists and humanists was that expressed by Butler for
his own behoof in the notes which he never worked up for
publication.

If this is a sound interpretation of the character of Butler's
life, then it gives him, if not a higher rank among English
writers (for that must be determined mainly by his one
poem), at any rate somewhat more significance than is commonly assigned to him as a representative man. It is no
longer possible to take him merely as the satirical voice of the
reaction against Puritan tyranny and extravagance. He escapes from the controversy between Cavaliers and Round-
heads. He is something more than a Cavalier partisan (it may
be noted, by the way, that the satire in his prose Characters
as well as in *Hudibras* includes many things besides the particular vanities of the Puritans). He is the champion of an
intellectual ideal much older than the questions debated in
the English Civil War, and one that retains its meaning long
after the fashions of that age have passed away. He is the
inheritor of the principles of More and Erasmus, while the
spirit in which he holds these principles is much more in
harmony with the succeeding age, especially as represented
by Swift, than with anything that had gone before.

[1] *Hudibras*, III. ii. 173–6.   [2] *Characters*, ed. cit., p. 271.

The paradox of his work, then, is that while his spirit and temper are like those of the unenthusiastic century that was to follow, his methods of expression are in his own time already rather antiquated. Swift expresses his views in the clear, unaffected, undecorated prose which is exactly fitted to render their searching and pitiless force. His place can never be challenged by Butler, though Butler shared in many of his ideas. Only occasionally and only in notes which he never made public was Butler able to use the clear, unemphatic, colloquial prose which would seem to be the natural form for the thoughts of a man who has nothing important to tell the world except the simple and obvious things which the world can never be persuaded to remember. The conceited style, full of surprising comparisons, which he uses in his *Characters* and in *Hudibras* was a style which came into vogue in different languages of Europe as an accompaniment of the great imaginative work of the sixteenth and the early seventeenth centuries. It was one of the symptoms of the energetic, exuberant fancy of an age that took naturally to poetry. It has its place as decoration in the work of the great Elizabethans, thrown out by the same unresting vigour of the imagination as produced the more substantial and organic parts of the drama of Shakespeare and his contemporaries. It is not out of keeping, and it is scarcely noticed as anything extravagant, in the fluent and rapidly written plays of Calderón. In the English metaphysical poets, or in most of them, it was already becoming rather laboured and losing the natural grace it had when it was employed by more productive and less cogitative artists. It was abandoned by some of Butler's contemporaries, even by Cowley, the most practised wit of them all, when he took to prose. Dryden began by writing what might well be taken as the most shocking example of this kind of work, his elegy 'Upon the Death of the Lord Hastings'; and he still kept to the old devices even in his *Annus Mirabilis*, but he saw that it would not do, that its day was past. Yet Butler, who in many things was nearer to the eighteenth century than any of them, was never able to find the proper form for the things he wished to say. To the last he was a humorist, in the old sense of the word, that is, a man who would follow his own bent, and choose his own mode of behaviour, making a law for himself—and preaching moderation, to the tune of *Hudibras*. His manuscripts show that he made many experiments in the new forms of verse—the forms that were to show themselves in their full power in Dryden and Pope, the most perfect forms in the world for poems of moralizing and preaching, for *sermones*, to use the Latin name that includes both satires and moral epistles.

One of Butler's pieces, 'On Rhyme', is a translation of one of the satires of Boileau[1] in heroic couplets; and he made some way with a satire on pedantry and all the vices of education, 'Upon the Imperfection and Abuse of Human Learning', in the same form. But his experiments never came to anything, at least as far as the public was concerned. In prose also, as may be seen in his notes and aphorisms, he had a very effective weapon at command, and enough material for a number of prose essays which might have had a place along with Cowley's and Dryden's among the first specimens of the new unaffected natural way of writing, while the originality of his reflections would have kept him distinct from all his contemporaries. What prevented him? There is no explanation except that it was so. With all his gifts he was never quite at home in the forms of literature which seem to have been made for him. His star was an unlucky one, for though, as Dr. Johnson says, his name can only perish with the language, his reputation is founded on a book that does not do him full justice. In speaking of him one is naturally led to take the tone of an advocate: the interest of Butler's case is that it needs defence and explanation. He is one of the writers who have an attraction for students of literature on account of what they have failed to do; and the failures of Butler are in some respects even better worth study than his one successful book.

[1] Satire ii, addressed to Molière. Cf. Ker, *The Art of Poetry*, pp. 118–20.

John Milton

THE poetry of Milton is not the sort of poetry that is written in the first outbreak of enthusiasm, at the beginning of a new age. It is not youthful. The youth of Milton's poetry is to be found in Marlowe, Lodge, and Peele, in *The Shepheardes Calender*, in the poets of the reign of Elizabeth. He is their successor; he stands to Marlowe as Virgil stood to Lucretius. He has got rid of the wildness, the harshness, and his work is perfect. At the same time it has lost the freedom, the fierce and untamable grace of youth; it is not so quick, though it is sound and strong. Milton's poetry recalls very often the doctrine of Browning's poem: 'What's come to perfection perishes'.[1] After Milton there was no more poetry of the Elizabethan sort. The cycle of a hundred years was complete. The promise of *The Shepheardes Calender*, the expectation of Sidney, had been realized; the poets had entered the house that was strewn for them (in Sidney's beautiful phrase);[2] all that had been hoped for in the strivings of Marlowe might seem to have been gained; *Samson Agonistes* was the epode, and the listeners departed with their ears and souls fully satisfied. Marlowe, Shakespeare, Jonson even, died before the fulfilment of the promises. Twenty years after Marlowe's death, as twenty years after Shakespeare's, there was still prevalent a hopeful temper about poetry. Young men were drawn in by the eager and confident spirits of their elders to join in the search for the absolute Beauty. Milton himself was one of the young men who, contemporaries of the old age of Jonson, were full of the same kind of ideas as had already possessed two generations of poets. But when Milton died he was alone in the poetic house; another sect had been formed with other ideas, a sect whose representative,

---

[1] *Old Pictures in Florence*, xvii.

[2] 'For heertofore Poets have in England also florished; and, which is to be noted, even in those times when the trumpet of *Mars* did sounde loudest. And now, that an over-faint quietnes should seeme to strew the house for Poets, they are almost in as good reputation, as the *Mountibancks* at *Venice*.' 'An Apologie for Poetrie', in *Elizabethan Critical Essays*, ed. G. Gregory Smith (2 vols., Oxford, 1904), i. 194.

Mr. John Dryden, was courteously enough received by the
old poet, with permission to 'tag his verses' if it so pleased
him.[1] The young men had gathered round other masters and
the great Elizabethan tradition came to an end.

Milton as a representative poet represents the Elizabethan
age and the ideas of the Renaissance. These are beautiful
names; it might be wished that they were somewhat more definite, but there can be no doubt that they do stand for something. One fails to comprehend Milton unless one can asso-
ciate him with the revival of scholarship and with the Italian
school of poetry which drew its education from the classics.

Milton's reverence for Greek and Latin poetry is part of
himself, is of the essence of his mind. The effect of this on his
poetry is such as to make him perhaps unequalled in all
European literature for command over the classical resources.
I do not mean the material resources, the treasuries of myth
and legend, but the resources of style, the classical secrets of
literary workmanship. There are other English poets who
come near him in learning—Jonson and Chapman. There
are others, like Spenser and Sidney, who are as fervent in
their admiration for Greece and Rome. But none like Milton
had got the quintessence of classical poetry, the secret of
finished and harmonious poetical composition. Spenser and
Jonson are barbarians compared with Milton: Spenser with
his labyrinthine epic, Jonson with his perverse *satura*, his
unwieldy masses of ancient learning wedged in among the
vanities of Bartholomew Fair. In mastery of all the classical
rhetoric of poetry, in fidelity to classical ideals of style, Milton has no rival among the English. Ariosto among the
Italians, though his fabric is different from Milton's and his
artistic method different too, is perhaps of all other poets the
one who made the most successful use of classical learning;
who discarded the most wisely what was unessential and
pedantic, and kept the central and vital truth of the classical
schools, the counsel of perfection in style.

A good deal of the history of sixteenth-century literature
in England as in other countries is taken up with the conflicts
between medieval and classical ideas—sometimes opposed as

---

[1] Aubrey, *Brief Lives*, ed. A. Clark (2 vols., Oxford, 1898), ii. 72.

the passwords and war-cries of opposing factions, but more often, and in a more interesting sort of contest, dividing the being of a man against himself. Thus Sidney's *Apologie for Poetrie* lets us see how the students of Seneca and the Italian dramatists looked at the improvisations of the popular stage; how there were two sets contemptuous of each other, one of the vulgar thronging to see the battles, shipwrecks, knights, ladies, and dragons of the popular stage, another pondering in dignified retirement on problems of the unities and the employment of a chorus in modern drama. That is interesting, but it is more interesting to find Sidney himself divided in his allegiance between the rigid proprieties of Seneca and the rhymes of Astrophel or the changing adventures of Arcadia; to see Spenser rebuked by his uncompromising and learned friend for betraying Apollo and the Muses and following Hobgoblin and the Elvish Queen.[1] This division, of which the life of Spenser gives some of the most striking examples, is sometimes left out of sight; and naturally enough too, when, for instance, one is reading Spenser and finding in him, on every page, analogies to Titian or Ariosto, proof of his share in the common adventure of all Europe at that time, and in the riches of the new world of art. But one ought not to forget altogether that *The Faerie Queene*, in which we find so much that is characteristic of the great times of the revival of learning, was not to its author anything like a faithful following of the truest principles; that Spenser's strictest literary conscience would have obliged him—at one time, at any rate—to forswear the rhyming stanza of romance and take up with English senarians, sapphics, and hexameters. Spenser apparently must have known that he was doing wrong when he wrote *The Faerie Queene*; or, at any rate, that he was deliberately renouncing the highest ideals of poetry and giving himself up to an inferior kind that might play the bankrupt with him, as Bacon said about the English and modern

---

[1] 'If so be the *Faerye Queene* be fairer in your eie than the *Nine Muses*, and *Hobgoblin* runne away with the Garland from *Apollo*: Marke what I saye, and yet I will not say that I thought, but there an End for this once, and fare you well, till God or some good Aungell putte you in a better minde.' Gabriel Harvey in *Three Proper, and Wittie, familiar Letters* (1580); *The Poetical Works of Edmund Spenser*, ed. J. C. Smith and E. de Selincourt (Oxford, 1912), p. 628.

languages generally.[1] Spenser stifled his conscience and stopped his ears against the upbraidings of Harvey. Doubtless like other sinners he grew to forget his trespasses, and not to care. But at one time there must have been a wrench, and that there should have been, is curious.

⌁

Milton is a classical scholar using his classical scholarship in original English poetry, but, besides the Greek and Latin authors, he chiefly respects the Italians; he is in many ways of the Italian school. Dryden belongs to a later stage in the history of the Renaissance. His authorities, the people whose ideas he borrows and whom he respects, are French. Their prose style is also different. Milton's is the old-fashioned, magnificent, pompous prose, displaced by Cowley and Dryden. Dryden's is lighter in gait; he is trying to explain, and is more on a level with his readers.

The difference between the Italian allegiance and the French really amounts to this: the older school to which Milton belonged did not attend to the needs and capacities of readers in the same way as the later school did. The eighteenth-century writers and the forerunners of the eighteenth century, among whom Dryden is to be reckoned, are distinguished from the Elizabethan age by their social qualities. They feel that they are in communication with living society, with contemporary minds. The Italian school are not addressing anything like what in Dryden's time and later was known as 'The Town'. They often strike one—Milton does in particular—as writing for a republic of learned and intelligent men. They no doubt wrote very definitely for a certain social group; they were court poets; but although they might belong to particular courts or patrons, they did not write solely for them, any more than Goethe wrote exclusively for the society of Weimar. They wrote for educated people anywhere. Milton writes not only for the literary society of

[1] 'For these modern languages will at one time or another play the bank-rowtes with books: and since I have lost much time with this age, I would be glad as God shall give me leave to recover it with posterity.' Letter to Sir Toby Matthew in 1623. *The Letters and the Life of Francis Bacon*, ed. James Spedding (7 vols., 1861–74), vii. 429.

London but for any intelligent person, any fit audience in any quarter. The literary ideal of the great authors of the Italian period of the Renaissance is not much conditioned by contemporary approval. The aim is to do good things and leave them to take their chance, to be judged by right judges wherever they may be.

❧

Lycidas and *Paradise Lost* in different ways force one to consider the problem of the relation of Poetry to Truth. Some people are disturbed by the intrusion of Greek divinities on the shores of the Irish Sea, and the appearance of St. Peter, keys and all, among the Greek divinities. It is no excuse for this—if .this is wrong—to say that it was the poetical fashion of that time, or rather of all the times since the beginning of vernacular literatures in Christendom. Virgil and Ovid were sacred books in the Middle Ages; and Dante finds Centaurs and Harpies among the more orthodox devils. If Dante was wrong it is no excuse for Milton that Dante preceded him. That will not make the contradiction less monstrous—if it be a contradiction.

To try to bring out a contradiction here is to confuse poetical with literal truth. St. Peter, it is true, belongs to a different order of existence from the nymphs and the god of the sea. He is an historical character for one thing; for another, he is closely connected with facts of infinite importance. The mind in dwelling upon 'the fair humanities of old religion'[1] is not compelled to realize its own individual concerns and there may be a shock in passing from this region of pure 'theory' (in the original sense of the word) to a region of momentous and absorbing real interest. That is the case against the *Lycidas*.

There are very strong arguments, however, on the other side. It may be said that Milton has practically shown that the mind which can entertain the thought both of the Greek gods and St. Peter, can also represent that thought or combination of thoughts in a work of art. Further, it may be pointed out that a great amount of solemnity is given to the heathen

---

[1] Coleridge, *The Piccolomini*, II. iv. 124.

deities in *Lycidas*, by the solemnity of the occasion. They are not allowed to retain the half-frivolous character that they have in many of the Renaissance writings and paintings. They have something of the same dignity that they possess for Sophocles, or at any rate for Virgil. They are not the conventional and decorative deities that sprawl on the canvases of Rubens. They are the *numina magna Deum*. What is the good of prosing about poetical and literal truth, when the literal truth is there, in the poem—that is, in the mind of the author who knows and of the readers who know after him—that the gods are not dead, and not even exiled, but keep their old supremacy, in the imagination?

John Dryden

In Dryden's work it is not very easy to find the classical strain which we are led to expect by historians of literature who make so clear a distinction between the Elizabethan age and the eighteenth century. The incorrectness, the variety, the confusion of Dryden's work are very commonly disguised to those who have no knowledge of the plays. Dryden is commonly known through favourite pieces, like *Absalom and Achitophel*, in which he agrees with Pope and the eighteenth century, and so Dryden and the age of Dryden are commonly misjudged; people think of a change in literature about the time of the Restoration, a new fashion lasting almost unvaried down to the end of the eighteenth century. This view is as right as such things ever are with regard to the *aim* of literature. The ideal of polite writing revealed in Cowley's essays, just about the time of the Restoration, is much the same as the ideal of literature of the time of Pope, Johnson, and Goldsmith, of the time of Scott even, if one takes not the romances or lyrics of Scott but his discourses.

But in imaginative, original literature correctness was very long in declaring itself. There is hardly anything in the Elizabethan authors, hardly anything among the romantic authors of the nineteenth century, more extravagant, more capable of ridicule than most of the plays of Dryden. In these dramas there are great varieties of absurdity—absurdities of theme chosen, of plot, of sentiment, of dialogue, of description, of moralizing, and greater absurdities of what in different senses is called 'machinery', as in the astral spirits of *Tyrannic Love*[1] or in the patriotic opera-pageant of *Albion and Albanius*, and in many more. These are absurdities according to different standards of taste; absurdities for the age of Pope and also for the age of Scott and Byron.

There is a very strange contrast between all the confusion and variety, the disorderly production, the random energy of such things as the heroic plays, and the sane, clear, often

[1] IV. i.

humorous arguments of Dryden's critical essays, or the irony of the great satiric poems. The romantic parts of Dryden's poems show how the temper of the generation, the spirit of the age, was against romance; the critical, saner parts show the age's strength. 'Romantic' and 'spirit of the age' are questionable and dangerous terms which need explaining. 'Romantic' here is used in the rough and ordinary sense to denote the particularly adventurous things in Dryden's poetry: the heroic plays, the paraphrases of Chaucer and Boccaccio, the supernatural things which he and the writers of the time generally called 'machinery'. 'The spirit of the age', the bent of the men of genius of the time, was against romantic effects; these were the mark and aim of the age about one hundred years after Dryden's death, of the beginning of the nineteenth century.

In the Dedication of the opera of *King Arthur* Dryden describes the romantic spirit in a peculiar and beautiful phrase, 'that fairy kind of writing'. It was this spirit that recommended the opera to his 'first and best patroness', the Duchess of Monmouth; but Dryden's 'fairy kind of writing' is always impeded by Dryden's strength. He brings in Merlin and two contrasted spirits, Philidel, the spirit of air, the fallen angel, the least guilty of those that fell, and Grimbald, an earthly dæmon—such elements as might have been well used by a writer of fairy-tales one hundred years later. But Dryden, however he may imagine the spirits of the elements, cannot prevent their reasoning and arguing like the personages in the plays. Again, in the admirable work of the *Fables*, the passages of terror and wonder make nothing like the effect which very inferior artists and rhymers who live in more favourable times can produce.

Dryden and other writers of his time are not afraid of romantic methods, but their genius is not such as to use them rightly. Probably part of the explanation is that the artists made a mistake in their artistic use of romance. They did not understand that the thrill of terror and wonder, so peculiarly belonging to what we call romance, comes best of all when it is not calculated. In Dryden's 'fairy kind of writing', with all his good-will and strength, there is too much striving after effect, too much calculation. Romance comes by the way, often in unexpected places. How did Dryden come to allow the astral spirits in *Tyrannic Love*, which spirits are exactly repeated in *The Rehearsal*—not so much burlesqued and parodied as actually repeated, so as to make the original absurdity more obvious? These things are hard to understand. One does not get over them by the ordinary allowances for differences of taste and time, because these absurdities, these unhappy things, are in contradiction to Dryden's mind as explained in the prose essays, and revealed and expressed in the best poetry.

Part of the explanation must be that the drama (observe that these things are in the theatrical work) had passed the stage of natural growth and come to a time where the dramatic authors were looking about for new devices and were borrowing where they could. 'Natural growth' of literary form is a rather dangerous way of speaking, but one is obliged in literary history to think of the evolution and progress of types. With the drama, undoubtedly, there was after the Elizabethan age a time when the progress was interrupted, when the aim of the dramatic authors was confused, when they picked up ideas from books and the French stage, and tried to make them work in the English theatre. It is through this want of independence in the English drama of the time of Charles II that the absurdities come in.

The astral spirits, for example, were from the French spectacular opera. One could not have such spirits on the stage without a good deal of machinery, in the ordinary sense of the word. In France there had been, and still was, a taste for elaborate stage effects, transformation scenes; vast contrivances were necessary and were used in two of Corneille's plays, one *La Toison d'or*, or *Golden Fleece*. Such machinery had been used in the English masques, but Dryden's spirits were probably not the result of the masques of fifty years before, but were due rather to the suggestion of the French theatre. They are experiments in stage-effect, bringing into the ordinary play such things as better fitted more spectacular creations.

There is, in spite of many similarities, a great difference

between Corneille and Dryden, a difference that marks very clearly the eighteenth-century strain in the latter. Corneille, in the collected edition of his works in 1660, is writing of what he has done, explaining the intentions and the changes of intention in his past life. His life is not yet ended, his work not yet at an end, but the greater part is finished; the French drama is prospering, and prospering in a way Corneille understood and had very much influenced. He was a writer of comedy as well as tragedy, though his comedies, with the exception of *Le Menteur*, are now generally neglected. Racine and Molière are following in his footsteps; the drama is in its great age, in the time of glory corresponding to the Elizabethan age in England. The critical essays of Corneille are a record of what is going on, of a process of dramatic creation still flourishing.

Dryden, on the other hand, is writing of what he wants to do, of ideal forms of literature which he is at the time meditating and doing his best to realize. He has, so to speak, nothing like the treasury of Corneille, the secured and hoarded savings all to the good. He is a speculator in more senses than one. And while much of his work is thus visionary and future, he looks back to the past Elizabethan age with varying degrees of respect at different stages, always, however, with reverence, always feeling he is a successor and not one of the first conquerors. With all Dryden's lightness and freshness and spirit, there is all through his works a certain want of courage, an inability to plunge impulsively into what he has to do. His resolution is a little 'sicklied o'er with the pale cast of thought', with reflection and analysis, and critical comparison with the great English authors of the olden times. Whether praising Shakespeare, Fletcher, and Ben Jonson, or finding fault with their style and manners, he is always thinking of them, and is always aware that they accomplished things of which he and his contemporaries were incapable.

Can one compare Racine and Dryden? There is outward similarity in part of their work. Dryden's *All for Love* has some of the qualities found in French tragedy, but the difference is still immense and absolute. Racine has the dramatic spring in him; he thinks in tragic situations and characters; he is helped by reading, by history of different sorts, but he does not need that to conceive a tragic problem, to place a tragic plot, to give his characters appropriate tragic language. With Dryden one feels that anything in his dramatic plots might have been used for narrative, and that almost always he is thinking much less of the conflict of characters than of placing them upon the stage and distributing eloquent poetry among them.

Dryden's heroic plays are artificial, literary products obedient to literary precepts, not written like Shakespeare's to amuse, take, and instruct the audience, but to give the audience as much poetry as they could stand. Although Dryden is satirized in *The Rehearsal* and elsewhere for seeking the popular favour of 'pit, box, and gallery', he is in the heroic plays only partly moved by this motive. He thinks both of popular success and of conformity to rule, obedience to the ideal of poetry. In *All for Love*, which he says was the only thing he ever wrote to please himself,[1] there is a dignified kind of beauty, the beauty of strong construction, that kind of dramatic beauty dangerously near the undramatic play, the play written to be read.

Dryden was attracted all through his life by different literary ideals—the epic, the perfect heroic play, the correct tragedy, &c. But for all that, the main ideal was that of freedom. It was his own energy, more than any formal pattern to be filled out in detail, that urged him onwards. The very correctness and preciseness which he occasionally practises are emancipation from hindrances. The unities are sometimes respected because they do away with the clogging absurdities of the older, ill-calculating drama. The new numbers of Waller and Denham are freedom from the harshnesses and discords of Elizabethan verse. Dryden had no such enduring belief in correctness as Pope. What he wanted was not any one sort of perfection, but freedom from bad and encumbering fashions of literature, so that he might express himself in the best way, whatever the subject. To the end of his life he knew he had it in him to deal with a great number

---

[1] *Essays of John Dryden*, ed. Ker, ii. 152.

of things in a great number of ways. *The Spanish Friar*, one of his most successful things, is an Elizabethan play, written about the same time as the satiric poems.[1] At the very end of his life he plunges into narrative poetry; after his very heavy (and yet very spirited) work on Virgil, he takes up another kind of narrative work, shorter epic pieces, romantic tales adapted from Chaucer and Boccaccio.

The great difference between Dryden and Pope is that Pope generally knew what he wanted and intended to do, while Dryden had an immense undefined power and genius which might be applied in a great number of ways, and which Dryden was always ready to venture, often at great expense to himself, in kinds of expression where the profit was doubtful, both as regards material and artistic success. It is not in the actual poetic work of Dryden that his devotion to the epic comes out most clearly, but in his critical writings, as the determining influence that forms his ideas and gives them definite direction. The idea of epic poetry implies dignity, regard for proportion, for magnificence along with simplicity and order. If this is forgotten Dryden is misunderstood. With all the great variety of Dryden's writings, with all his concessions to popular taste, with all his freedom and absence of pretence, there is in much of his style somewhere present a controlling influence—the ideal of poetic magnificence, or in other words the ideal of the heroic poem. Sometimes Dryden calls this tragedy, but there is not much difference. He changes his opinion, at one time making tragedy, at another, epic, the highest form of poetic art. Either means a kind of greatness and glory beyond the reach of common poetic artificers, the ideal of a living poetic thing, at once great and comprehensible, containing the virtues of sublimity and clearness.

◦

The Hind and the Panther is the most extraordinary contradiction of everything one is told about the classical spirit, the ideal of correct literature, the age of good sense. It is a most disorderly poem; the plan of it seems utterly absurd, the

[1] Cf. Ker, Introduction to *Essays of John Dryden*, I. lxiv.

contradictions perpetual. Yet it is undoubtedly one of the great poems of the age and of the school of argumentative, satiric, or debating poetry. What is one to think of the form? Is it a lapse of Dryden into the old recklessness, the old want of proportion such as is commonly found among English authors before the French types of literature came to be known and studied? Undoubtedly there is a strong resemblance between *The Hind and the Panther* and *Annus Mirabilis*; the former is indeed the more irregular of the two. But one cannot truly say that Dryden has relapsed into an earlier fashion. For *The Hind and the Panther* is a very strong poem, magnificent in language, and in mere energy beyond anything else of Dryden's. It needs a good deal of interpretation before one can get over the absurdities, the pictorial contradictions, the folly of the Hind and the Panther going together to rest in a cottage, to have a meagre cold supper, and to debate on theology.

The best solution seems to be this. The poem is what it professes to be without the allegory. Taking it simply, it is a debate between the Church of Rome and the Church of England. This is what Dryden means, and he does not much trouble himself about anything else. This is his real aim. The argument and substance are disguised in different ways, first through the beast-allegory, and secondly through the allegory of the two ladies. The device of the comic beast-epic, partly Aesop, partly the old medieval Reynard the Fox, was well known in Dryden's time, and he, of course, knew Spenser's *Mother Hubberd's Tale*. The aspect of the disputants as two ladies arguing is really much more consistently held to than the allegory of the beasts. *The Hind and the Panther* will never be made out as a successful allegory comparable to *The Pilgrim's Progress* or *The Faerie Queene*, where the story is intelligible in itself, and where, as Hazlitt says, if people 'do not meddle with the allegory, the allegory will not meddle with them'.[1] But it accomplishes its purpose, and one can understand it pretty well if one attends first of all to the real debate about Church theology, and then takes the allegorical things as merely subsidiary and occasional, like nicknames. One

[1] *Lectures on the English Poets*, ii; *Works*, ed. P. P. Howe (1930–4), v. 38.

may think of Bishop Burnet as the Buzzard and find satisfaction therein, and yet not be inclined to work out thoroughly the life-history of the Buzzard with the real history of Burnet, Bishop of Salisbury. Satire often finds allegory useful, but often inconvenient; and Dryden, quite rightly though very irregularly, held to the main business and used the associations with Reynard, Aesop, and *Mother Hubberd's Tale* as occasional associations of ideas, as flashes of metaphor coming now and then, but not consistently worked out. The other allegory of the two dames is not so troublesome. It is simply a personification of the two sides, an easy abstract device, in order to enable Dryden to utter what is in his own mind on one side or the other.

❧

The author before Dryden's time who seems to have impressed him most is Oldham, a satiric poet who 'came out' just a little earlier. He was on the other side in politics, and believed in the Popish plot, but this did not make any difference to Dryden's admiration for him. There was nothing particularly novel in the style of Oldham's poetry, but, as often happens, the last-comer who adds just a little more, just something different of his own, has a conquering effect on his contemporaries. One finds this in many points of literary history (as, for instance, in the production of the novel). Oldham took hold of Dryden through some additional brightness and sharpness which we nowadays, wearied by the regular satiric manner, find hard to detect. Dryden was much affected, however, and warmly praises Oldham in the memorial verses,

Farewell, too little and too lately known,

as the 'young . . . Marcellus of our tongue'. This may seem to us exaggerated, but the tone of Dryden's speech shows us he was quite sincere, and that his admiration was really keen and strong. For Dryden, insincere though he may be in complimentary poems and dedications, is never guilty of fulsome flattery when speaking of poets and poetry.

❧

Dryden had an immediate motive for his *Mac Flecknoe*, as well as a general, and wrote it off in high spirits, with no loss of time, and with so much enjoyment of his work that one can almost imagine the victim himself enjoying the thing. Yet even *Mac Flecknoe*, with all its severity and success in hitting the object, has something of the insincerity of the old comic railings and 'flytings'—the abuse for the glory of it.

Although occasional poetry is hardly distinguishable from satire in the wide sense, the satiric poetry of Pope and Dryden, particularly of Pope, takes on a different quality through the intention of the writers to make it as good as possible. In the earlier part of the seventeenth century there is plenty of occasional verse of the nature of satire, of *sermones*. Towards the end of the seventeenth century and all through the eighteenth the new and definite ambition of poets shows itself in a kind of bracing or intensifying of this sort of verse. It is taken more seriously by people more ambitious as artists, and by people who keep their attention more closely on Roman models.

Many doubt whether satiric poetry is poetry at all. One sometimes hears 'rhymed prose' as a contemptuous description for it. The eighteenth century is classed as an 'age of prose',[1] a term including poetry of 'discourse' like Pope's *Epistles* and his *Essay on Man*. Now, we may allow that satire is not the most poetic kind of poetry. We do not find in its class anything to compete with 'Lycidas' or the great odes of Wordsworth and Keats. It is less exacting in construction than long narrative poems like the epic. It almost excludes such imagination as makes dramatic character, whether in drama or novel; the most brilliant pieces of character-drawing in satire are analytic descriptions.[2] The satiric method is

[1] 'We are to regard Dryden as the puissant and glorious founder, Pope as the splendid high priest, of our age of prose and reason, of our excellent and indispensable eighteenth century' (Matthew Arnold, 'The Study of Poetry', in T. H. Ward's *English Poets* (1880), vol. i, reprinted in *Essays in Criticism*, Second Series).

[2] The point is admirably brought out by Macaulay in his essay on Byron, where he considers Dryden's Zimri in comparison with Byron's Sardanapalus: 'Sardanapalus is more coarsely drawn than any dramatic personage that we can remember. His heroism and his effeminacy, his contempt of death and his dread of a weighty helmet, his kingly resolution to be seen in the foremost ranks, and the anxiety with which he calls for a looking-glass, that he may be seen to advantage, are contrasted,

easier, nearer the capacities of ordinary men. To make what is called 'a living character' in a play or novel requires a gift of the imagination not ordinarily shared by spectators or readers. But almost anyone with any wits at all can describe with the satiric method of the Zimri and Achitophel, can take point after point in character and build with a certain amount of success. But to make characters live, to make them speak and act naturally, is beyond even the ambitions of most people. They gaze in wonder at the miracle, and that is why plays and novels have such an attraction beyond that of mere descriptive writing, however brilliant.

But this inferiority, this comparative easiness of the satiric method, does not prove poetical satire impossible. Poetry does not always imply a different mode of thinking from prose. An epic may be translated into prose and much of its substance still preserved. A good deal of the *Iliad* is thought out in the same way as a novel. Poetry is not due to a different kind of thinking from prose, but to a heightening, a quickening of utterance, a difference in degree that changes, so to speak, the speaking into the singing voice. The qualities of poetry are not to be distinguished as peculiar ways of expression and thought, but rather as higher degrees of passion and energy. And in this way Dryden is a poet, and Pope also. Coleridge applies to Dryden the phrase, the idea, that Pope uses of Homer:[1] 'Dryden's genius was of that sort which

it is true, with all the point of Juvenal. . . . A dramatist cannot commit a greater error than that of following those pointed descriptions of character in which satirists and historians indulge so much. It is by rejecting what is natural that satirists and historians produce these striking characters. Their great object generally is to ascribe to every man as many contradictory qualities as possible: and this is an object easily attained. By judicious selection and judicious exaggeration, the intellect and the disposition of any human being might be described as being made up of nothing but startling contrasts. If the dramatist attempts to create a being answering to one of these descriptions, he fails, because he reverses an imperfect analytical process. He produces, not a man, but a personified epigram. . . . Sir Walter Scott has committed a . . . glaring error of the same kind in the novel of Peveril. Admiring, as every judicious reader must admire, the keen and vigorous lines in which Dryden satirised the Duke of Buckingham, Sir Walter attempted to make a Duke of Buckingham to suit them, a real living Zimri; and he made, not a man, but the most grotesque of all monsters.' (Review of Thomas Moore's 'Life of Byron' in the *Edinburgh Review* (1831), reprinted in *Critical and Historical Essays*.)—W.P.K.

[1] 'It is . . . remarkable that his Fancy, which is everywhere vigorous, is not discover'd immediately at the beginning of his Poem in its fullest Splendor: It grows

catches fire by its own motion; his chariot wheels *get* hot by driving fast.'[1] One might say he gathers speed as he goes till the increase makes a change in quality. The change from prose to poetry is really incalculable, indescribable. It will not do to speak of the verse of Dryden and Pope as an imitation of poetry or a substitute for poetry. It certainly is not prose, though there may be prose in it, and there is no other convenient name for it except poetry.

in the Progress both upon himself and others, and becomes on Fire like a Chariot-Wheel, by its own Rapidity.' Pope, Preface to *Iliad* (1715).

[1] Coleridge, *Table Talk*, 1 November 1833.

Edmund Burke

BURKE is more of an innovator in the eighteenth century than any other prose author. He brings in a method of thinking in which he agrees with Wordsworth and with Coleridge and, in many respects, with Carlyle. There is an exhaustion, a want of substance, in the education of the beginning of the eighteenth century, a want of history, a want of science. This is true of Addison and Steele, and of a good deal of Swift and Johnson. A change came somehow with the increase of historical studies, as is shown in the difference between Berkeley and Hume, men who resemble each other in their philosophical genius and method, but who differ in the range of their studies—Hume taking to the study of concrete things, of history, of political economy, subjects which require a large amount of facts. If the culture of the time be represented by Hume, then it is no longer simply a business of fine and elegant thinking and expression; it is no longer merely polite literature. It is still elegant in expression, fine in style; but it is solid, well nourished on facts and more immersed in matter.

Gibbon, too, with a style and thought purely eighteenth-century (as the eighteenth century is commonly understood), is without any of the vagueness, the trouble, the uncertainty, the aspiration, which comes to be the spirit of the next age. His was a clear and complacent mind, satisfied with itself and its powers and its range, working easily on very difficult matters, working happily with an infallible power of expression, with a perfect command of the instrument of language, without any desire to go further, to innovate, to find out new forms. It was a sceptical mind, a worldly mind, a perfect wit, but engaged in laborious study, in a kind of work for which neither Addison nor Swift nor Johnson would have felt inclined. One ought, of course, to consider the possibility of these men behaving differently in different circumstances. It is probable that neither Addison nor Swift under any conditions would have liked the work Gibbon liked. It is rather different with Johnson. Johnson had a low opinion of industry, but not of literary industry. Perhaps in his own way, in the work that he did on the *Dictionary* and on Shakespeare, he came nearer to the policy of Gibbon than one might at first think. However, the fact is that Gibbon composed a great historical work, one of the greatest works of historical art, and that this sort of work was not favoured two or three generations before. In Gibbon there is a change of study, but not otherwise a change of mind; the mind is still sceptical and rationalist.

But a real change of mind is found in the life and writings of Burke. Here is a new mode of thinking, unlike that of almost anyone in the eighteenth century, unlike Addison or Swift or Johnson or Berkeley or Hume or Gibbon. Not that the eighteenth-century mode of thought is absent in the writings of Burke; in the *Sublime and Beautiful*, an early work, there is a good deal of the superficial cleverness which is so common in the eighteenth century. But in the political speeches and in tracts like the *Reflections on the Revolution in France* and the *Letters on the Proposals for Peace with the Regicide Directory* the prevailing ideas are unlike those of Burke's predecessors and contemporaries and like those of Wordsworth and Coleridge.

What Burke hates most is the kind of rationalism common in almost all departments of study in his time; clear, abstract, analytic reasoning is what he detests. That is because he is dealing with politics, and because he understands politics as a business, not of argument or mere understanding, but of feeling, of sentiment, of instinct, of prejudice. To many Burke appears obscure, an 'obscurantist'. One perhaps is not quite sure of the meaning of this; but those who use the term 'obscurantist' are apt to find Burke 'obscurantist' and Coleridge 'obscurantist' and Carlyle 'obscurantist'. The explanation of this is, of course, that these three men put trust in sentiment and prejudice, which is offensive to people whose ideal of reasoning is a clear succession of positions, a kind of reasoning like Euclid's.

Burke is most acutely touched, most strongly provoked, when the political problem comes to be concerned with 'rights'. It was that which provoked him in the dealings with the American colonies. He did not deny the right of the government to tax the colonies. But the assertion and the exercise of that right seemed to be what he is fond of calling 'metaphysics', an ignoring of realities. Burke is so far from being foolishly mystical that he tries always to keep before his mind, as far as possible, the reality of the situation. The obscurity in Burke is the obscurity of things as they are, the complexity of the real world; and where he seems to be objecting to clear thinking he is really merely pointing out that clear thinking in politics is apt to be abstract thinking, in its not taking into account the variety of what is real.

One can see the likeness between Burke's way of thinking and Wordsworth's. Wordsworth in one sense distrusts the human mind; the human mind is fond of dissecting, and sometimes murders to dissect. The human mind is most to be trusted when it trusts to what Wordsworth calls 'Nature', when it takes in what Nature will give. As Wordsworth thought of Nature, so Burke thought of humanity, of history, of the life of the world, of the life of nations. You do not get, he says in effect, the right principle of philosophy by metaphysical or *a priori* reasoning. You get the right principle, which you may not be able to state, by understanding history, by seeing that the nation has a continuous life of its own, which you may not be able to understand in every particular, but which must be simply accepted and trusted for the sake of what our ancestors have done in the past and what our descendants will do in the future.

This philosophy, or mode of thought, of Burke is the beginning of the prevailing nineteenth-century fashions of thought, which are not limited to history or politics. Perhaps in the beginning they are historical or derived from history. At any rate they mark a difference from the earlier, eighteenth-century view of history (a view which is held even by Gibbon), of history as a mere succession of scenes with different personages, different costumes, but all the same kind of business, whether it be in the fifth or the fifteenth century. In Gibbon there is little sense of the different motives in different ages, although Roman Law and Christianity and the teaching of

Mahomet are all described in his pages. In the modern view, which is first explained by Burke, 'the great mysterious incorporation of the human race' (as he phrased it)[1] lives by a force of life descending and changing while it remains one and the same. Burke, indeed, begins in England the teaching of a theory of historical evolution. It is one of the strange things in history that Goethe in Germany, at the same time as Burke in England, was opposed to the same kind of limited rationalism, and in the same sort of way was studying the laws of life, though he studied those laws not so much in the political field of Burke, as in what we call science —botany chiefly. It is in the *Reflections on the Revolution in France* that Burke's ideas are most clearly expressed; he is there most clearly in opposition to the expounders of the particular kind of thought he hated.

One of the great admirers of Burke was Hazlitt; this fact may be rather surprising to those who remember Hazlitt's own politics—for example, his admiration of Napoleon. The truth seems to be that Burke does not make an appeal to party politicians. Of course, he is conservative in the sense in which the word was used before it became the name of a political party. But, as is often said, Burke has been quoted like Scripture for all purposes and in contradictory senses; and those who appreciate him may be found in any political party. Many admire his political philosophy who do not approve of his politics.

The history of Burke's political life cannot be separated from the history of his political writings, but one may get a good deal of profit from his writings even if one does not know everything about his life. In order to get advantage from what he has written one need not approve all his political action. In the American dispute it seems probable that he was led away by some enthusiasm, that he did not fully appreciate the coolness of certain of the colonial politicians, the craft of their plot against Great Britain.[2] With regard to

---

[1] *Reflections on the Revolution in France* (*Select Works*, ed. E. J. Payne (Oxford, 1874–8), ii. 39).

[2] This aspect of the case is brought out clearly by John Andrew Doyle, the historian of the American colonies, in his review of Sir George Trevelyan's book, *The American Revolution*, in the *English Historical Review*, xiv (1899), pp. 596–604;

India, there is little doubt that Burke was misled, perhaps self-deceived, in a way not uncommon among people of enthusiastic temper. The case against Warren Hastings, as argued by Burke, is more or less the case as stated by Macaulay in his essay on Hastings,[1] and that essay has been refuted in every important point. We know that Sheridan, Burke's colleague in the prosecution, went through the business with a good deal of hypocrisy. A story, probably true, is told that Sheridan, meeting Hastings in private company long after, assured him that all the hard language he had used in his famous speeches was not seriously intended. Hastings replied 'I wish, Sir, that I had earlier been informed of this'.[2] Old Mr. Thomas Grenville,[3] the brother of Lord Grenville, who survived most of his contemporaries and lived on into the forties of the nineteenth century, said that Burke was made an instrument by the regular politicians who wanted the case brought against Hastings in order to divert attention.[4] The prosecution of Hastings was used politically; it held the attention of the public and gave the managers a good reputation for patriotism and righteousness, the sort of reputation explained in Macaulay's essay.

All this sort of thing, all these detracting considerations, of course tell against the character of Burke as a politician; and, as the politician and the political philosopher are really inseparable, they take something from the value of Burke's political theories. If Burke's own judgement can be shown to have failed, that surely tells against his intellectual character. For the essence of Burke's political theory is that the statesman should judge particulars rightly, should have instinct,

xix (1904), pp. 367–73. For example: 'There was . . . a section of the American patriots headed by [Samuel] Adams who were fully determined to thwart any attempt at conciliation. This section was not numerous, but it was able, influential, well organized, and unscrupulous.' (J. A. Doyle, *Essays on Various Subjects*, ed. W. P. Ker (1911), p. 139.)—W.P.K.

[1] In the *Edinburgh Review* (1841), reviewing G. R. Gleig's *Memoirs of the Life of Warren Hastings*; reprinted in *Critical and Historical Essays*.

[2] J. W. Fortescue, *British Statesmen of the Great War, 1793–1814* (Oxford, 1911), p. 54.

[3] Thomas Grenville (1755–1846), the bibliophil whose collection forms the Grenville Library of the British Museum.

[4] Cf. *Memoirs, Journal, and Correspondence of Thomas Moore*, ed. Lord John Russell (8 vols., 1853–6), ii. 191–2.

talent, and imagination enabling him to read aright the appearance of things, all the variety of political life. But it does not tell against the theory, against the mode of thought, for obviously he may be right in his reading and his interpretation of the political mind, although he may make mistakes himself in particulars.

The *Reflections on the Revolution in France*, as already noted, brings out most clearly the leading principles in Burke's mind, namely the contrast between false abstract thinking in politics and that kind of imagination in which Burke resembles Wordsworth, the imagination that comes from life, from living in the system, which the mind interprets through its own life. In many of the earlier works you find the ideas that are expressed in the *Reflections*; for example, the objection to what Burke calls 'metaphysics' appears in the *Thoughts on the Cause of the Present Discontents* (1770):

No lines can be laid down for civil or political wisdom. They are a matter incapable of exact definition. But, though no man can draw a stroke between the confines of day and night, yet light and darkness are upon the whole tolerably distinguishable. Nor will it be impossible for a Prince to find out such a mode of Government, and such persons to administer it, as will give a great degree of content to his people; without any curious and anxious research for that abstract, universal, perfect harmony, which while he is seeking, he abandons those means of ordinary tranquillity which are in his power without any research at all.[1]

But the *Reflections* shows his ideas best. The French Revolution gave Burke his chance, because the French politicians were, as he says, most of them lawyers, men without political experience, acute minds with the faculty of reasoning but without the substantial experience to which Burke trusted in himself and others. There is a phrase of John Morley, in the earlier of his books on Burke, describing the French politicians as 'finished novices'.[2] This perfectly expresses in the most pointed form what Burke means in his *Reflections*. The French politicians are 'finished', accomplished, in the art of reasoning, but they are 'novices' in political experience; they are representative of eighteenth-century rationalism.

[1] Payne, i. 39.   [2] *Edmund Burke: a Historical Study* (1867), p. 233.

Burke, as the opponent of such shallower culture and argument, may be compared to Bacon opposing the vanities of science in the *Novum Organum* and *The Advancement of Learning* and elsewhere. There is between the two a great likeness, one might almost say there is an identity, of principle and mode of thought. Their adversaries are the same sharp, analytic people, who, as Bacon says, break up the substance by subtlety of words; they are keen and active reasoners, but they are not in communication with 'Nature', and, according to Bacon, 'Nature is only won by obeying'.[1] What Nature is to Bacon, the realities of human affairs are to Burke. Burke's field of science, his Nature, is all the political, all the moral life of humanity. And the problems of Burke's Nature cannot be solved except by those who will trust themselves to it, who themselves have lived in the thick of it, who know by experience, by their own life and habits, what moral decision really is. In passage after passage of the *Reflections* this sort of doctrine is expounded.

'Nature' is one of Burke's ideas; he speaks of it much as Bacon does, in the same way as Aristotle. He believes that Nature is a law, that in truth and right, where found, there is right and true following of Nature.[2] This seems a little strange when his argument generally is so much against all abstract terms. But it is not difficult to get over that seeming inconsistency. The word 'Nature' is used by Burke, as by his friend Sir Joshua Reynolds and very commonly by the eighteenth-century thinkers, to mean both that which is ideal and that which is alive, the infinite source of variety of life. There is one curious passage in the *Letters on the Proposals for Peace with the Regicide Directory* where Nature and the ideal are brought together and seem to mean much the same:

Never, no, never, did Nature say one thing and Wisdom say another. Nor are sentiments of elevation in themselves turgid and unnatural. Nature is never more truly herself, than in her grandest forms. The

[1] 'Natura enim non nisi parendo vincitur.' *Novum Organum*, I. iii; cf. also I. cxxix.

[2] 'By a constitutional policy, working after the pattern of nature, we receive, we hold, we transmit our government and our privileges, in the same manner in which we enjoy and transmit our property and our lives' (*Reflections*; Payne, ii. 39).

Apollo of Belvedere (if the universal robber has yet left him at Belvedere) is as much in Nature, as any figure from the pencil of Rembrandt,
or any clown in the rustic revels of Teniers.[1]

'To love the little platoon we belong to'[2] is the beginning
of political life. You do not begin in large abstract ideas,
but by living with the people next you. The attachment to
our 'little platoon' in political life is not unlike Wordsworth's
attachment to the countryside where he was born, to his own
neighbours among the fells. The criticism of the abstract
reasoners of the French Revolution is only one part of Burke's
argument. The 'finished novices' are met in two ways: first,
by the insistence on ordinary political experience, for want of
which they misjudge realities; secondly, by the lofty imaginative view of the universe which transcends the clever, sharp
opinions of Burke's opponents. Burke resembles Wordsworth
in two ways at least: by his trust in ordinary experience, and
by a form of worship like that of Wordsworth's 'Ode to
Duty', where Duty, a moral idea, is found to be the same as
the physical law of the universe. Compare Wordsworth's

Thou dost preserve the stars from wrong

and Burke's passages in the *Reflections* on 'the great mysterious incorporation of the human race'[3] and 'the inviolable
oath'.[4]

[1] Payne, iii. 165–6.
[2] 'One of the first symptoms they discover of a selfish and mischievous ambition,
is a profligate disregard of a dignity which they partake with others. To be attached
to the subdivision, to love the little platoon we belong to in society, is the first
principle (the germ as it were) of public affections. It is the first link in the series
by which we proceed towards a love to our country and to mankind.' *Reflections on
the Revolution in France* (Payne, ii. 54–55).
[3] 'The institutions of policy, the goods of fortune, the gifts of Providence, are
handed down, to us and from us, in the same course and order. Our political system
is placed in a just correspondence and symmetry with the order of the world, and
with the mode of existence decreed to a permanent body composed of transitory
parts; wherein, by the disposition of a stupendous wisdom, moulding together the
great mysterious incorporation of the human race, the whole, at one time, is never
old, or middle-aged, or young, but in a condition of unchangeable constancy, moves
on through the varied tenour of perpetual decay, fall, renovation, and progression'
(Payne, ii. 39).
[4] 'Society is indeed a contract. Subordinate contracts, for objects of mere occasional interest, may be dissolved at pleasure; but the state ought not to be considered
as nothing better than a partnership agreement in a trade of pepper and coffee, callico

Burke's style differs from that of the other writers of his time in the same way as his thought differs from theirs. The manner of his thought is distrust of mere reasoning, of mere argument, of logical success—distrust which comes from knowledge of the complexity of life, knowledge that many things are known through experience which cannot be fully analysed. In style of writing Burke expresses that same fashion of mind. His arguments are clearly worked out; he knows the art of exposition; but he does not insist upon divisions, does not try for obvious clearness or symmetry. He pours out his argument, and, as it runs along, it is accompanied and illustrated in all sorts of ways; it is full of allusion, of quotation, of historical examples, of names used often in the manner of Milton. His works are full also of a great deal that was considered 'low' by the sort of people who thought Goldsmith 'low'; the same accusation was brought against Burke as against Socrates, that he was fond of vulgar illustrations; such things as calico and tobacco are found in the same context as 'the inviolable oath'.

In the use of particular terms Burke may be said to belong to the new age, to the age of Carlyle and Macaulay and Dickens and Browning. The respect for general terms which you find expressed so often in the eighteenth century is gone, and any passage of Burke might be mistaken for Macaulay from the way in which particulars are brought in. The principle of Burke's concrete method seems unlike that of Johnson, yet it is really very like the principle of *one* of Johnson's ways of writing. Johnson does not stick to the rule that general terms are the most magnificent; he uses when he

---

or tobacco, or some other such low concern, to be taken up for a little temporary interest, and to be dissolved by the fancy of the parties. It is to be looked on with other reverence; because it is not a partnership in things subservient only to the gross animal existence of a temporary and perishable nature. It is a partnership in all science; a partnership in all art; a partnership in every virtue, and in all perfection. As the ends of such a partnership cannot be obtained in many generations, it becomes a partnership not only between those who are living, but between those who are living, those who are dead, and those who are to be born. Each contract of each particular state is but a clause in the great primeval contract of eternal society, linking the lower with the higher natures, connecting the visible and invisible world, according to a fixed compact sanctioned by the inviolable oath which holds all physical and all moral natures, each in their appointed place' (Payne, ii. 113-14).

pleases particular terms. Burke's phrase, 'The Sultan gets such obedience as he can',[1] is very like Johnson, especially if one puts 'No, Sir' before it. There is again a likeness in Burke's method to Macaulay's. Burke and Macaulay share in the liking for particulars, especially for historical names used in the Miltonic manner. Johnson is sometimes like Macaulay in the pointed use of particulars, and in Burke too you may find many passages which look like anticipations of Macaulay's style. In the first of the *Letters on a Regicide Peace* one of the perorations, the concluding paragraph of a section, is almost exactly in Macaulay's manner, especially in the contemptuous and satirical allusion at the end to the fable of Captain Jenkins's ears:

For any thing which in the late discussion has appeared, the war is entirely collateral to the state of Jacobinism; as truly a foreign war to us and to all our home concerns, as the war with Spain in 1739, about *Guarda-Costas*, the Madrid Convention, and the fable of Captain *Jenkins's* ears.[2]

The fourth[3] *Letter* contains some of Burke's most telling passages of vivid particular allusions and also one of his most glowing praises of that mode of thinking. It is one of the liveliest of Burke's writings, equal to the *Letter to a Noble Lord* in contemptuous eloquence, and containing the best and clearest statement of Burke's hatred of 'the hocus-pocus of abstraction'.[4] The tract is an argument against a pamphlet of Lord Auckland's which tried to make out a case for peace with France—Lord Auckland not being a Jacobin and seeing clearly all the objections to French policy, but thinking it convenient for England to make peace. Here Burke was not arguing with such an opponent as in the *Reflections*, not arguing, say, with Dr. Richard Price, but with a clever and responsible politician. The passage on the French Directory

---

[1] *Speech on Moving his Resolutions for Conciliation with the Colonies*, 1775; Payne, i. 184.

[2] Payne, iii. 55.

[3] 'Fourth' because published after the others, but really the first, written at the end of 1795 and corrected for press, but never published till long after, because events hurried on too quickly and the letter was antiquated before it was ready.—W.P.K.

[4] Payne, iii. 267.

and the individuals who make it up shows Burke letting himself go with real enjoyment and comic zest:

> Are they not the very same Ruffians, Thieves, Assassins, and Regicides, that they were from the beginning? Have they diversified the scene by the least variety, or produced the face of a single new villainy? *Taedet harum quotidianarum formarum.* Oh! but I shall be answered, it is now quite another thing—they are all changed—you have not seen them in their state dresses. This makes an amazing difference. The new Habit of the Directory is so charmingly fancied, that it is impossible not to fall in love with so well-dressed a Constitution. . . .[1]

The spirit of the old Athenian comedy is very strong in Burke, and does not appear for the first time in these last years of his life. He was not afraid of the reproach of vulgarity and fully understood the rhetorical value of 'low' terms, as when he describes the Chatham ministry of 1766, 'who had never spoke to each other in their lives, until they found themselves, they knew not how, pigging together, heads and points, in the same truckle-bed'[2]—an example of vulgar language comparable to the railing of the old comedy, and used by Burke in the same way as the railing of Aristophanes. He harmonizes the 'low' with anything else he wants to say and even with the most magnificent lyric passages of eloquence.

Burke's early parody of Bolingbroke, *A Vindication of Natural Society*, published in 1756, is important as bringing Burke into relation with Bolingbroke, from whom he learned so much in the art of prose, while he was provoked by all Bolingbroke's teaching. *A Vindication of Natural Society* brings out in an ironical way a number of commonplaces which one hardly expects to find so soon, but which became very common as the influence of Rousseau spread abroad. The parody is noteworthy for its extraordinary art, so subtle that it must often have failed in its effect. 'A knavish speech sleeps in a foolish ear'; and many ears not exceptionally foolish may well have been taken in. The sophistry is so plausible that unless one is prepared one may take it for sound reasoning.

[1] Payne, iii. 293.
[2] *Speech on American Taxation*, 1774; Payne, i. 145.

The style of Burke, in the narrow sense of the term, his grammatical art, his syntax, is not easily described; it cannot be summed up in the same way as, say, Johnson's or Gibbon's. The style of Johnson is more varied than people think; but, still, there is a common tune in Johnson's prose. There is no such common tune in Burke, or, if there is, it is much more difficult to seize and note. Burke was a great student of rhetoric in the proper sense of the word, not merely of figurative eloquence, but simply of the art of expression. He knew all there is to know about grammar, about the value of different types of clause and phrase, about rhythm of sentence and period. There is no fixed pattern; the effects vary from one page to another. What is most regular is the effect of climax or culmination, the working up into some telling and sonorous close to the period. The effect of Burke's prose would be nothing without the varied diction, varying from the 'truckle-bed' to 'the inviolable oath', from the lowest bass string of the language to the sublimity of the loftiest lyric ode. Part of the richness comes from the poetic allusions. Burke builds occasionally a paragraph out of reminiscences of Shakespeare, and is full of quotations, particularly from Latin and English poetry. The quotations are sometimes commonplace, and come in, even when commonplace, with effect, as, for example, the quotation from 'Lycidas',

> That strain I heard was of a higher mood,

in the fourth of the *Letters on a Regicide Peace*.[1]

[1] Payne, iii. 272.

Robert Burns

BURNS is so often spoken of as making a great change in literature, as leading the way to the new poetry, that it is as well to notice the old-fashioned things in him. Burns is 'old-fashioned', 'eighteenth-century', in much of his sentiment and in his rhetoric. His rhetoric varies greatly both in prose and verse; his taste is uncertain; he can be direct and clear, and at other times he uses the falsest kind of ornament and most affected sentiment. The chief examples of false rhetoric occur in the letters to 'Clarinda' ('O Love and Sensibility, ye have conspired against My Peace! I love to madness, and I feel to torture!').[1] The opening paragraph of the Edinburgh edition (1787) of the poems is old-fashioned in character:

To the Noblemen and Gentlemen of the Caledonian Hunt.

My Lords and Gentlemen,—A Scottish Bard, proud of the name, and whose highest ambition is to sing in his Country's service—where shall he so properly look for patronage as to the illustrious Names of his native Land; those who bear the honours and inherit the virtues of their Ancestors? The Poetic Genius of my Country found me, as the prophetic bard Elijah did Elisha—at the *plough*, and threw her inspiring mantle over me. She bade me sing the loves, the joys, the rural scenes and rural pleasures of my natal Soil, in my native tongue: I tuned my wild, artless notes, as she inspired. She whispered me to come to this ancient metropolis of Caledonia, and lay my Songs under your honoured protection: I now obey her dictates. . . .

Later on the fashion is not improved, bringing in that curious abstract personification which was in favour all through the century and later, and which is sometimes found in Burns's great contemporaries,[2] Wordsworth and Coleridge:

When you go forth to waken the Echoes, in the ancient and favourite

---

[1] 25 January 1788; *The Letters of Robert Burns*, ed. J. de L. Ferguson (2 vols., Oxford, 1931), i. 174.

[2] 'Contemporaries' because, though the dates are often forgotten, there were only eleven years between Wordsworth and Burns, and Coleridge was born very little later.—W.P.K.

amusement of your Forefathers, may Pleasure ever be of your party; and may Social-joy await your return! When harassed in courts or camps with the jostlings of bad men and bad measures, may the honest consciousness of injured Worth attend your return to your native Seats; and may Domestic Happiness, with a smiling welcome, meet you at your gates! May Corruption shrink at your kindling, indignant glance; and may tyranny in the Ruler, and licentiousness in the People, equally find you an inexorable foe!

'The Vision' is Burns's 'Poet's Confession', the statement of his ambitions and poetic aims. The poem is divided into two 'duans', and by that slight trace Burns shows he had read *Ossian*. There is very little of Ossian in Burns's poetry, save this and a humorous reference in 'The Twa Dogs',[1] and Burns seems to have been little affected by Macpherson. The substance of 'The Vision' is the visit paid to the poet by the Muse of his native land. The idea of Coila is taken from the Scota of Alexander Ross, who under that name invokes his Muse at the beginning of *Helenore, or The Fortunate Shepherdess*, a pastoral narrative poem written in imitation of Allan Ramsay's *Gentle Shepherd* and first published in 1768. Burns's Coila is the goddess not of Scotland, not even of Ayrshire, but of Kyle, a third part of Ayrshire, the limited region in which Burns was born and to which he properly belonged.

In 'The Vision' should be noted the changes of language and the changes of imagination as the mind passes from one theme to another. People speak sometimes as if Burns were able to write interesting verse only in his vernacular, as if he were a failure in English. But when is his language vernacular, and when English? In this poem one can easily see there is no consistent language; some of the stanzas are in English, some in the vernacular, and some in English with more or less Scottish forms.

The beginning of 'The Vision' is in the best style of Burns's short verse.

[1]
> And in his freaks had Luath ca'd him,
> After some dog in Highland sang,(a)
> Was made lang syne—Lord knows how lang.
>
> (a) Cuchullin's dog in Ossian's *Fingal*. (R.B.)

The sun had clos'd the winter day,
The curlers quat their roarin' play,
And hunger'd maukin ta'en her way,
    To kail-yards green,
While faithless snaws ilk step betray
    Whare she has been.

The thresher's weary flingin-tree
The lee-lang day had tired me;
And when the day had clos'd his e'e,
    Far i'the west,
Ben i'the spence, right pensivelie,
    I gaed to rest.

There, lanely by the ingle-cheek,
I sat and ey'd the spewing reek,
That fill'd, wi' hoast-provoking smeek,
    The auld clay biggin;
An' heard the restless rattons squeak
    About the riggin.

The language is difficult, but interesting. The play of the
curlers is 'roaring play', not because of the merry voices, but
from the sound of the stones travelling along the ice: this is
one of the definite, exact descriptive words picked up by
Burns from the common dialect. 'Maukin' is the 'hare':
Burns uses that name, not in the conventional way in which
we speak of Reynard or Chanticleer, but because 'maukin'
was commonly adopted in Burns's country, in the same way
as we accept 'robin' for the 'redbreast'. The 'flingin-tree' is
the 'flail', another example of vivid vernacular diction. 'Hoast-
provoking smeek' is 'cough-provoking smoke'.

The goddess enters with much liveliness and brightness
of description:

When, click! the string the snick did draw;
An' jee! the door gaed to the wa';   .
And by my ingle-lowe I saw,
    Now bleezin bright,
A tight, outlandish hizzie, braw,
    Come full in sight.

Ye need na doubt, I held my whisht;
The infant aith, half-form'd, was crusht;
I glowr'd as eerie's I'd been dusht
    In some wild glen;
When sweet, like modest Worth, she blusht,
    And steppèd ben. . . .

Her mantle large, of greenish hue,
My gazing wonder chiefly drew;
Deep lights and shades, bold-mingling, threw
    A lustre grand;
And seem'd, to my astonish'd view,
    A well-known land.

Here, rivers in the sea were lost;
There, mountains to the sky were toss't;
Here, tumbling billows mark'd the coast
    With surging foam;
There, distant shone Art's lofty boast,
    The lordly dome.

'The Vision' comes by some strange untraceable way from the old allegorical, didactic form. There is some connexion between Burns's 'Vision' and the vision of Boethius—a strange proof of the way in which certain devices of the imagination have survived; and, curiously, there are other points in the description of the 'Vision' that touch Boethius. In the *Consolation of Philosophy* will be found the same ignoring of what is properly visible as in Burns. In allegory, writers vary much regarding the allegorical dress and accoutrements of the beings they describe. When Boethius describes Philosophy he is thinking not of the picture before him, but of Philosophy's allegorical meaning. When Burns describes the mantle of his visitor he, too, is not really thinking of Coila's actual pictorial representation; he wishes her to be emblematic of his native country, her mantle is to have pictures on it of his native landscape, but he is thinking more of meaning than of presentment. Again, one of the doctrines in Boethius is that men never pursue evil, but always what they regard as good—a doctrine, of course, derived from Aristotle. When they go wrong it is not from desire to do evil, but from mistaking

the nature of the good, from error not design. The address
of Burns's visitor to him shows this same belief.

> I saw thy pulse's maddening play,
> Wild-send thee Pleasure's devious way,
> Misled by Fancy's meteor-ray,
>   By passion driven;
> But yet the light that led astray
>   Was light from Heaven.

There is no inference to be drawn from these resemblances
except that traditions of literature, often through very intri-
cate lines of descent, often seemingly through accident, affect
the minds of writers in different generations.

'The Vision' contains Burns's view of Nature, and it is
significant that the winter view comes first, and is described
with much more liveliness. Burns does not often speak of the
sea, although he lived close to it, and his references are almost
always to wintry or stormy seas. There is, of course, the
suggestion of the calm sea in the wonderful phrase quoted
by Carlyle:

> The wan moon sets behind the white wave,
> And Time is setting with me, O![1]

But generally it is the 'sounding shore' and the 'dashing roar'
that Burns paints for us. The summer scene in Coila's speech
is much less vivid, almost tame by comparison.

The theory of poetry in 'The Vision' is not revolutionary.
Burns was always reverent to established reputations, speaking admiringly of Pope, Steele, Beattie,[2] Thomson, Gray,
and Shenstone.[3] There is nothing really in his theory of

---

[1] 'Open the door to me, O!' See Carlyle's review of Lockhart's *Life* in the *Edinburgh Review* (1828), reprinted in *Critical and Miscellaneous Essays*, ii. 17.

[2]
> I've scarce heard ought describ'd sae weel,
> What gen'rous, manly bosoms feel;
> Thought I, 'Can this be Pope or Steele,
>   Or Beattie's wark?'   ('Epistle to John Lapraik', 19–22.)

[3]
> Thou canst not learn, nor can I show,   .
> To paint with Thomson's landscape glow;
> Or wake the bosom-melting throe
>   With Shenstone's art;
> Or pour, with Gray, the moving flow
>   Warm on the heart.   ('The Vision', 247–52.)

poetry except the desire to be true to his own country, to deal with the life he knows, and to live up to the eighteenth-century, old-fashioned, dignified morality of the true poet, with his solemn, exalted idea of his true vocation:

> Preserve the dignity of Man,
> With soul erect;
> And trust the Universal Plan
> Will all protect.[1]

Burns is sometimes spoken of as the poet of a new democracy, a poet of liberty, and is sometimes condemned as a Jacobin by the strict Tories. One of the best descriptions of the poet is 'Jacobin and Jacobite', for it brings forcibly to one's mind the contradictions in his poetry. His politics cannot be neglected, for the substance often determines the poetical form. It is quite clear that he has no great respect for his fellow creatures; he does not think of the Kilmarnock weavers as ideal citizens of an ideal republic. He sometimes idealizes the simple country life, but where he does so he is clearly less true than in such poems as 'Halloween' or 'The Holy Fair'. Burns is a lyrical satirist of the old sort; as he told some adversaries of his once, he would hang his opponents up as 'tattie bogles', that is, like scarecrows among the potatoes. This was the old office of that kind of poetry whose technical name was 'iambic', and Archilochus was really the founder of the school to which Burns belongs.

Burns had a hatred of tyranny, which was partly due to his hatred of mismanagement; he hated tyranny partly because it was cruel, and partly because it was wasteful and untidy. He was pleased at the news of the French Revolution, and got into trouble through expressing his sympathy with the revolutionaries at a time when he was in the service of the British government as exciseman. But he was a Jacobite by sentiment, feeling the beauty and the spell of the old devotion to the unhappy royal house; he is never better than in the song made out of old traditions and ballads:

> It was a' for our rightfu' King.

[1] 'The Vision', 267–70.

But he shares in that tradition as we share in it; it thrills us to this day, but it is not a practical thing and has nothing to do with present politics. And Burns in dealing with present politics is remarkably rational and independent, discussing them with great vigour and clearness and without attaching himself to any particular political party, his hero being the great-minded Chatham.

Those who have dealt with Burns have noted his Jacobite songs, his poems of republican sentiment, his sympathy with the French Revolution and so forth. But they have not valued properly his study of contemporary history and his distinct views on the happenings of his own times. They have not taken into account Burns's versatility, his literary faculty for taking up different points of view. The apparent contradiction between

> It was a' for our rightfu' King

and

> A man's a man for a' that

is not really a contradiction; it is superficial to say the one song is Jacobite and the other a poem of equality. Burns was able to take the one point of view at one time and the other at another, and we ourselves, as readers of Burns, can easily do the same. Burns speaks of 'A man's a man for a' that' as a good specimen of his prose;[1] he knew it was not poetry, but the versification of such respectable moral ideas as

> The rank is but the guinea's stamp,
> The man's the gowd for a' that.

This is very different from the true poetry of

> Now a' is done that men can do,
> And a' is done in vain.

Burns is a citizen of the United Kingdom. The birthday-

---

[1] 'The following . . . will be allowed, I think, to be two or three pretty good *prose* thoughts inverted into rhyme.—

> Is there for honest poverty . . .

I do not give you the foregoing song for your book, but merely by way of vive la bagatelle; for the piece is not really Poetry.' Letter to George Thomson, January 1795 (*Letters*, ed. cit. ii. 284).

address to His Majesty (entitled 'A Dream') and 'When Guilford good our pilot stood' are the political poems of a man in whom there was nothing limitedly and locally Scottish.[1] In the birthday-address he agrees with a good deal of the enlightened political opinion of his time. He is not over-respectful to His Majesty: no one at that time did show much respect for the Crown. Jacobite sentiment which, though not practical, still remained, had naturally no respect for the House of Hanover, and, on other grounds, there was very little respect on the other side. But Burns is in no way seditious in his satire; he addresses the king for the sake of the kingdom, and the advice he gives, using the licence of the comic poet, is for the good of the whole state and still at this day worth noting. Burns has discovered the value of the Navy, and one thing he dwells on is the danger of reducing the naval strength of Great Britain:

> But, God sake! let nae saving fit
> Abridge your bonie barges
> An' boats this day.

'When Guilford good our pilot stood' is a comic historical poem to the tune of 'Gillicrankie', following the pattern of an old poem of 1689 and another poem on the 'Forty-Five'. It is curious to think how Burns picked up all the information; he must have attended very carefully to the contemporary history in the newspapers. This comic history does not seem at first to have any particular meaning, except that of stringing facts together in comic rhyme—a fashion of historical lyric used in Scotland before. What Burns's sympathies are one cannot at first decide. The first stanza

> When Guilford good our pilot stood,
>   An' did our hellim thraw, man;
> Ae night, at tea, began a plea,
>   Within Americà, man:
> Then up they gat the maskin-pat,   [tea-pot]
>   And in the sea did jaw, man;
> An' did nae less, in full Congress,
>   Than quite refuse our law, man.

---

[1] Cf. Ker's essay on 'The Politics of Burns' in *Collected Essays*, i. 128 ff.

E

begins the history of the American War, the history of ten years, 1774–84. Guilford is Lord North. It is a curiosity of literature that Burns should be fond of calling people out of their usual names, following the old trick of poetry that likes to have its own vocabulary. Lord North is not commonly called Guilford; hence Burns calls him so. He has a still more curious 'kenning' (to use the Icelandic term for figurative language) for Chatham in 'The Author's Earnest Cry and Prayer', calling him 'Boconnock' after the Cornish house.

> Tell yon guid bluid of auld Boconnock's,
> I'll be his debt twa mashlum bonnocks:[1]

Burns seems to be on the American side in the second stanza, or, at any rate, the hero is General Montgomery, who was on the side of 'the Continentals' and fell attacking Quebec. After a stanza or two the American War is passed, and one gets to British domestic politics. Charles James Fox is not much respected by Burns. Burns was no severe censor of morals, but he seems to think mainly of Fox's gambling, and to find little political stuff to approve of in his policy.

> Then Montague, an' Guilford too,
>   Began to fear a fa', man;
> And Sackville doure, wha stood the stoure
>   The German chief to thraw, man:
> For Paddy Burke, like onie Turk,
>   Nae mercy had at a', man;
> An' Charlie Fox threw by the box,
>   An' lows'd his tinkler jaw, man.[2]

In 'A Dream' he tells how the Prince 'rattled dice wi' Charlie', and evidently regards such occupation for men in high and responsible posts with little favour.

Then there is a very vivid summary of the changes about 1782–4. The Marquis of Rockingham came in and held office for a short time—Rockingham whom Burke especially followed till he died. A confused time followed. First came the short ministry of Lord Shelburne, then the coalition of Fox and North, and then the failure of Fox's India Bill, and the advent of Pitt the younger.

[1] Stanza xxi.   [2] 'When Guilford good...', stanza v.

Lastly, the poet quickens up and deepens his tone, till the poem becomes a war-song, and a war-song for William Pitt the younger, whom Burns takes as his hero, because he is the son of his great hero, Chatham. The piece is marked as a 'fragment', but it really artistically ends here, with the burst of inspiriting war-music:

> ... An' Chatham's wraith, in heav'nly graith,
>   (Inspirèd bardies saw, man),
> Wi' kindling eyes, cry'd: 'Willie, rise!
>   Would I hae fear'd them a', man?'
>
> But, word an' blow, North, Fox, and Co.
>   Gowff'd Willie like a ba', man,
> Till Suthron raise an' coost their claise
>   Behind him in a raw, man:
> An' Caledon threw by the drone,
>   An' did her whittle draw, man;
> An' swoor fu' rude, thro' dirt an' bluid,
>   To make it guid in law, man.

Burns is not affected by any cant of politics. 'Hero' may not perhaps be the right title for him,[1] but he had found out all the essentials of what Carlyle preached fifty years or more later. It is difficult to find anyone in Great Britain (and impossible in Scotland) at this period with anything like Burns's good-humoured political judgement, with this rejection of the unnecessary and this choice of what is really important for the welfare of the country. If one looks at the opinions of Hume, who, of course, had much more time for thinking, and who was much more accomplished than Burns, one will find instances of limited and partial judgement against the English that one never finds in Burns.

In the Kilmarnock and Edinburgh editions of 1786 and 1787 there are some poems wanting which are part of the chief work of Burns. Some were wanting because Burns did not find it convenient to put them in, and some were as yet unwritten. 'Holy Willie's Prayer' is left out—that deadly satiric poem which says everything Burns meant with regard to the religion of his country; and so is 'The Jolly Beggars'.

[1] The fifth of Carlyle's lectures *On Heroes, Hero-Worship, and the Heroic in History* (1840) was on 'The Hero as Man of Letters. Johnson, Rousseau, Burns'.

Opinions differ about 'The Jolly Beggars', with its sentiment of

> Let them cant about decorum
> Who have character to lose.

Many people are disgusted at the brutality of life depicted
here; they think of the poem as Satanic, giving in spirited
verse the exaltation of mere lawlessness, even sin. It is interesting to compare the judgement of two moralists about
this and 'Tam o' Shanter', the notorious poems of Burns.
J. C. Shairp in his *Robert Burns* disapproves of 'The Jolly
Beggars'; he is sorry Burns should have written such a
thing.[1] On the other hand Wordsworth, who is seldom a
'Wordsworthian', praises 'Tam o' Shanter':

> Who, but some impenetrable dunce or narrow-minded puritan in
> works of art, ever read without delight the picture which he has drawn
> of the convivial exaltation of the rustic adventurer, Tam o' Shanter?
> The poet fears not to tell the reader in the outset that his hero was a
> desperate and sottish drunkard, whose excesses were frequent as his
> opportunities. This reprobate sits down to his cups, while the storm is
> roaring, and heaven and earth are in confusion;—the night is driven
> on by song and tumultuous noise—laughter and jest thicken as the
> beverage improves upon the palate—conjugal fidelity archly bends to
> the service of general benevolence—selfishness is not absent, but wear-
> ing the mask of social cordiality—and, while these various elements of
> humanity are blended into one proud and happy composition of elated
> spirits, the anger of the tempest without doors only heightens and sets
> off the enjoyment within.[2]

Now 'The Jolly Beggars' and 'Tam o' Shanter' have a close
resemblance in spirit to another work of genius, Diderot's
Le Neveu de Rameau, which has been also blamed for its
immorality and recklessness. The reason of these poems, and
of Wordsworth's praise of 'Tam o' Shanter', is the 'life' in
them, 'life' that has a meaning even when wicked. Words-

---

[1] 'In that cantata, if the genius is equal [to that shown in *Tam o' Shanter*], the
materials are so coarse, and the sentiment so gross, as to make it, for all its dramatic
power, decidedly offensive.' *Robert Burns* ('English Men of Letters' series, 1879),
p. 201.

[2] *A Letter to a friend of Robert Burns* [James Gray]: *occasioned by An intended
Republication of The Account of the Life of Burns, by Dr Currie* (1816); *Prose Works
of William Wordsworth*, ed. W. Knight (2 vols., 1896), ii. 269–70.

worth, with his lawless mind, finds what he can thoroughly praise and enjoy in this poem of the adventures of the drunken Ayrshire farmer. The contradiction is much more extreme in 'The Jolly Beggars' than in 'Tam o' Shanter', but there is nothing in Wordsworth's praise of 'Tam o' Shanter' that might not be easily adapted to 'The Jolly Beggars'. There is no doubt that art is frequently immoral, or, perhaps, one should rather say, art frequently uses a different standard from the law of right conduct, not because it recommends another law of right conduct, but because conduct is not that in which art is chiefly interested.

'Tam o' Shanter' is possibly Burns's most successful poem, though, of course, one may argue endlessly upon this point of success, if one compares the merits of things in different styles. Burns is not, as a rule, good at narrative; narrative is not the kind of artistic work he likes best. Neither is he particularly dramatic, although 'The Jolly Beggars' is dramatic in a way. In the narrative poem of 'Tam o' Shanter' Burns has, however, managed to bring in a great variety of moods and poetic imagery. There is the hilarity of the beginning that Wordsworth particularly praises. Then comes the 'movement' of adventure, of the ride home by night. There is the gathering upon the mind of the traveller and poet at the same time of all the associations of the world around. The poet himself knows the country and feels the meaning of such places as that

> Whare drunken Charlie brak's neck-bane.

Then comes all the supernatural element, the comic mixture of horror and of laughter—of 'romance', if you will, though there is no particular need to use that dangerous term. The whole thing is carried on with 'life' and 'energy', through the crash of the great contest between pursued and pursuers, to the quiet, affectedly sober ending,

> Remember Tam o' Shanter's mare.

'Energy', indeed, is the word one thinks of in connexion with Burns. 'Tam o' Shanter' is a great poem, not because it puts before the mind things ideal, things far-sought, things beautiful, but because of the 'energy' with which the poet works up into poetical sequence some quite ordinary memories and a very ordinary piece of local superstition. 'Beauty', it is said, is not to be found in Burns.[1] It depends on what one means by 'beauty'. The 'beauty' of Burns is not that of Wordsworth or Coleridge, not even of Cowper, though Burns is nearer that. It is not the 'beauty' of melody, for, like most of the Scots poets, he often uses clinking, staccato, metallic verse. Burns's 'beauty' is the attraction, the grace, of vivid perception, vivid feeling, and of clear language rightly used.

Burns in his Songs is again a follower of older examples. In his poetry he invents no new form; in his Songs he very often does not trouble about inventing new words. The Songs are not merely, like 'The Holy Fair' and 'Death and Doctor Hornbrook', exercises in established form, but the very songs themselves with the old phrases modified so as to produce a new effect. No telling work in poetry is less original than the Songs of Burns, and some of his best lyrics are made up of the oldest things, as for example,

> It was a' for our rightfu' King.

Of course, there are all degrees of originality. Some Songs are entirely Burns's words, some are adaptations of rough old songs, and in some he had to get rid of older adaptations and decorations, of the conventional language of earlier editors. The history of popular Scottish songs is difficult, because the popular songs were edited so very early. The new versions made by Burns are in continuation of the process begun at the commencement of the century. The songs, for example, in *Orpheus Caledonius* (1726 and 1733) are

---

[1] See Henley's essay appended to *The Poetry of Robert Burns*, ed. W. E. Henley and T. F. Henderson (4 vols., Edinburgh, 1896-7), iv. 275.

'Felicities he has—felicities innumerable; but his forebears set themselves to be humorous, racy, natural, and he could not choose but follow their lead. The Colloquial triumphs in his verse as nowhere outside the *Vision* and *Don Juan*; but for Beauty we must go elsewhither. He has all manner of qualities: wit, fancy, vision of a kind, nature, gaiety, the richest humour, a sort of homespun verbal magic. But, if we be in quest of Beauty, we must e'en ignore him, and "fall to our English": of whose secrets, as I've said, he never so much as suspected the existence, and whose supreme capacities were sealed from him until the end.'

edited and modernized versions. 'Auld Lang Syne' is an example of the way in which Burns restored, and gave new life to, a motive taken up rather heavily, in rather a conventional way, by Allan Ramsay.

Burns's strength is like the strength of Pope, and when Matthew Arnold dwelt on 'Scotch drink, Scotch religion, and Scotch manners'[1] he was led away by externals. The world described by Burns was in many respects a disagreeable one, but that is not the essential thing in, to use another phrase of Arnold's, his 'criticism of life'. The essential thing about Burns is that he was in his station, and that he took his station as the ground from which he was to compose his poetry, accepting the conditions of his station as a subject of, and material for, his poetry—in the same way as Pope accepts the 'town', London society, as the basis of his satires and epistles. Thus Burns is in many ways an aristocratic poet; he has the security of a noble order which does not trouble itself about its ways of living. His poetic life is full, and there is no need for him to range far after remote, 'romantic' things and themes. Of course, the life of Ayrshire, Burns's country, was not of the same rank as the life of the Noblemen and Gentlemen of the Caledonian Hunt, to whom he dedicated the Edinburgh edition of his poems. But the difference of rank, of which Burns was fully conscious, does not make much difference in the poems; the poems have throughout a sense of content with themselves and their own standards.

Burns must not be regarded simply as the poet of Ayrshire; he is the poet of all rustic Scotland that is not Highland or Gaelic. When he came out with his poems in the Scottish dialect, he was speaking in a style that could be understood through all the provinces of the kingdom, east and west, that understood the forms of poetry used by poets of previous generations. So he is not a mere utterance from and for his own countryside, but an artist admitted into a well-established and widely known school.

Scottish poetry of the eighteenth century is a revival, not poetry written by descent, inherited from tradition. The old

[1] 'The Study of Poetry' in *Essays in Criticism*, Second Series; reprinted from T. H. Ward's *English Poets* (1880), vol. i.

Scottish poetry had really come to an end with the sixteenth century. The revival is mainly due to Allan Ramsay, the contemporary of Pope, who may be called the founder of the later school of Scottish poetry which has lasted with varying success ever since. The chief of Burns's predecessors, after Allan Ramsay, is Robert Fergusson.

The history of the traditional Scottish stanzas is very important. Stanzas always are noteworthy things; they are never mere diagrams or patterns of lengths of line and order and recurrence of rhyming syllables. In this Scottish poetry it comes out how much of thought the different stanzas bring along with them; they are tunes setting the mind of the poet dancing in a particular measure. The forms of Burns's poetry were all of them inherited. There is scarcely anything of the innovating fashions and changes of form found in Coleridge and Scott and Byron. Of course, Burns's forms were generally unfamiliar in England, and so produced in England something like the effect of 'The Ancient Mariner' or *The Lay of the Last Minstrel*. But in the mind of Burns himself there was no wish to begin a new fashion. No great poet ever kept so close as Burns to the example of his predecessors. His forms of verse, his subjects, his modes of jesting were all authorized by Scots poets before him. He is very much nearer to his poetic 'fathers' than even Pope is to Dryden. If one compares the work of Burns and Fergusson one can easily see the truth of these statements.

Burns is sometimes spoken of as 'a poet of the poor', or as 'the voice of rustic Scotland'. Such a description is not altogether foolish; it is what Burns himself wished to be. But one must note that he does not 'render' or interpret the life of rural Scotland simply as one of the people. He stands apart. He is not the voice of the people, but the voice of a judge to whom the people are more or less indifferent, who is far above them, and who sees them as small creatures moved by slight and trivial motives. 'Halloween', the poem on country usages and superstitions, is the record made by one who is not simply and ingenuously one of the party. 'The Holy Fair' is a contemptuous poem, with contempt not merely of the particular form of religion to which Burns is opposed, but of almost all the people engaged. It is a poem whose energy is 'daemonic' in different senses of the word. Burns is not simply a ploughman writing verses about things he knows and on an equality with the people among whom he lives. He is a judge seated above them.

A proof of Burns's reputation in England is to be found in the writings of William Gilpin. Gilpin was a southern Englishman with surroundings and education as different as could be from those of Burns, but his book on the scenery of Scotland has quotations from Burns, often curiously brought in and not very relevant; as, for instance, in the passage about Killiecrankie and the death of John Graham of Claverhouse, Viscount Dundee, where Gilpin, the refined English tourist, quotes one of Burns's poems on drink.

> In the article of victory Dundee was mortally wounded. An old highlander shewed us a few trees, under the shade of which he was led out of the battle; and where he breathed his last with that intrepidity, which is so nobly described by a modern Scotch poet, in an interview between death and a victorious hero:[1]
>
>> Nae cauld, faint-hearted doubtings tease him;
>> Death comes, wi' fearless eye he sees him;
>> Wi' bluidy han' a welcome gies him;
>>> An' when he fa's,
>> His latest draught o' breathin lea'es him
>>> In faint huzzas.[2]

This poem of Burns is interesting in connexion with Wordsworth, who uses 'faint huzzas' in his line on the death of Dundee in *Descriptive Sketches*,[3] which shows he had been reading Burns, or rather Gilpin's quotation of Burns.[4]

The qualities in Burns's poetry, however, that touched English people were not very new qualities. Burns was educated in the same way as his English contemporaries, having the ordinary good education accessible to everyone. He had not very much knowledge of the tongues: no Greek, a very little Latin, and some French. But in English literature he

---

[1] *Observations on Several Parts of Great Britain* . . . (1789), i. 137.
[2] Postscript to 'The Author's Earnest Cry and Prayer'.
[3] l. 302. [4] Cf. Ker, *Collected Essays*, i. 133.

was a well-read boy and man, probably knowing as much of the good English authors as most young men at Oxford and Cambridge of his time. He read Shakespeare and Milton, but his favourite authors were those of the time of Queen Anne and later; he was a great admirer of Addison and Steele, and warmly appreciated Gray and Goldsmith.[1] For the literature of 'sensibility' he had a very strong bent, thinking highly of Henry Mackenzie's *The Man of Feeling*, a book that might be described as 'an extreme case' in the literature of 'sensibility'. Burns's praise of Mackenzie is significant as being characteristic of the old-fashioned taste:

M'Kenzie has been called the Addison of the Scots, and in my opinion, Addison would not be hurt at the comparison. If he has not Addison's exquisite humour, he as certainly outdoes him in the tender and the pathetic. His Man of Feeling (but I am not counsel learned in the laws of criticism) I estimate as the first performance in its kind I ever saw. From what book, moral or even pious, will the susceptible young mind receive impressions more congenial to humanity and kindness, generosity and benevolence—in short, more of all that ennobles the soul to herself, or endears her to others—than from the simple, affecting tale of poor Harley?[2]

One may detect here the difference between eighteenth-century 'sentiment' and the sentiment of the romantic age. Burns compares *The Man of Feeling* with moral and even 'pious' works; he does not actually find a didactic purpose in it, but judges it in comparison with didactic works, regarding the sentiment of it as obeying an indefinite but still recognized law of good behaviour. Thus the eighteenth-century 'sentiment' is quite a different thing from the reckless, lawless sentiment common in romantic writers of very different types. Burns made an impression partly through his share in this 'sensibility', through understanding such motives as are used by Gray in the *Elegy* and Goldsmith in *The Deserted Village*.

Beyond Burns's share in the common quality of 'sensibility', there is his extraordinary vividness. In this he is like the romantic authors; for part of the romantic scheme, or policy or method, was to make things much more definite

[1] Cf. p. 46 above.
[2] Letter to Mrs. Dunlop, 10 April 1790 (*Letters*, ed. cit. ii. 19–20).

and particular than was allowed by the classical rules and the numerous critics who praised the dignity of general terms.[1] Particularity or definiteness in description is not, however, a peculiarly romantic or modern thing; the literary virtue of ἐνάργεια, 'clearness', 'distinctness', 'definiteness', was recognized by the scholarly critics. Tasso, in one of his critical essays,[2] applies this technical term to Dante, in whom he finds definiteness of description. Some critics blamed Dante for this quality; Thomas Warton depreciates him for the use of particular terms against the principle generally recognized by modern authors.[3] Yet this prejudice against particular terms did not practically affect the work of poets; critics could not affect those whose minds led them to see things clearly and definitely and to seek for the right and particular word. What is the good of classic literature unless it finds the right word? Indeed the glory of Virgil, the most classical of classic poets, lies in his choice of the right word, so that his pictures spring at once to the mind. It is in this connexion of particularity that Carlyle's essay on Burns[4] is best worth remembering. Carlyle's literary criticism is unequal; he is apt to be led away from literature to some other motive of teaching. But, in dealing with Burns, Carlyle well brings out the power of Burns's language in fixing the idea of what he sees, in 'rendering' the moments of his experience. It is noteworthy that the passages chosen by Carlyle for quotation are wintry passages. It is even more in dealing with winter scenes than in what are commonly regarded as 'the beauties of nature' that Burns excels.

'Nature' is often in Burns's mind. In the passage where he

---

[1] See the principle stated by Buffon: 'A cette première règle, dictée par le génie, si l'on joint de la délicatesse et du goût, du scrupule sur le choix des expressions, de l'attention à ne nommer les choses que par les termes les plus généraux, le style aura de la noblesse.' *Discours sur le style* (1753) (quoted by Ker in the introduction to his edition of Dryden's *Essays*, i. xxxiv).—W.P.K.

[2] *Discorsi dell'arte poetica* (1587), p. 29.

[3] Warton remarks that Dante's prolixity is 'common to all early compositions, in which everything is related circumstantially and without rejection, and not in those general terms which are used by modern writers'. (*The History of English Poetry*, sect. xlix.)

[4] A review of Lockhart's *Life* in 1828, reprinted in *Critical and Miscellaneous Essays*, ii (especially pp. 15–17).

speaks of Cowper as the poet of 'God and Nature',[1] 'nature' is not simply pictorial nature. It is 'nature' in a large sense, including the life and principles of life, not merely what is seen and heard. Burns is not a descriptive poet in the same way as Cowper; he does not depend so much on description. But he agrees with Cowper, when he does describe, in not as a rule limiting himself to the 'beauties of nature', to picturesque landscape. Landscape in poetry is not merely, or should not be merely, pictorial; it is an atmosphere enveloping the world round about the human business.

To appreciate Burns properly, then, one must get away from the merely romantic; his poetry, as we have seen, is poetry through its energy, through the fire of it, not through the choice of subject or any fanciful grace. Burns is not very good when he embroiders, and it is there that the praise of him is so often exaggerated. He does not make anything out of folk-lore except in a comic way. He never, or hardly ever, touches upon the poetry of the old ballads, although he knew them well; his bogles and fairies come in, not for their value as bogles and fairies, but as parts of the people's mind. Thus they come at the beginning of 'Halloween' as necessary to the harmony. In 'Tam o' Shanter' Burns is very near to one kind of romantic game; it is, perhaps, the most 'romantic' of his poems, fusing together, like many avowedly 'romantic' works, the extravagant ridiculous motive and the motive of fear; there is the right sort of 'romantic' thrill in the 'devilish cantraips' of the ghosts and howlets of Kirk-Alloway. But Burns's main motive, after all, is the comic mind and life of Tam, and not the poetry of the witches.

Where Burns comes near the ordinary romantic pathos or 'sentiment' he is in danger of falsity. In 'The Cotter's Saturday Night', beautiful as the poem is, we are getting rather too near the region of *The Man of Feeling*. Burns is not on his own ground, not using his own strength, as he does in 'Halloween' and 'The Holy Fair'. It was 'passion', not 'sentiment',

---

[1] 'Is not the Task a glorious Poem? The Religion of The Task, bating a few scraps of Calvinistic Divinity, is the Religion of God & Nature; the Religion that exalts, that ennobles man.' Letter to Mrs. Dunlop, begun 15 December 1793 (*Letters*, ed. cit. ii. 225).

that made his name both in Scotland and England, and when one speaks of 'passion' one does not think solely of the love-songs, which show the same variations as the other poetry between truth and artifice. 'Passion' is used in a general sense, for that stress of the mind or being, whatever the motive may be, which increases the 'life' of poetry, and which is found, if not in every poem of Burns, at least in every subject Burns touches upon in some poem or other.

George Crabbe

IN the *Life* of Crabbe by his son there are interesting reminiscences of Crabbe's relations with Scott and Burke and other great men of the time. Lockhart saw Crabbe when Crabbe went to Edinburgh in 1822 to stay with Scott, and the letter of Lockhart to Crabbe's son eleven years later gives a more vivid impression of Crabbe from the life than many of the descriptions in more formal biography.

Dear Sir,—I am sorry to tell you that Sir Walter Scott kept no diary during the time of your father's visit to Scotland, otherwise it would have given me pleasure to make extracts for the use of your memoirs. For myself, although it is true that, in consequence of Sir Walter's being constantly consulted about the details of every procession and festival of that busy fortnight, the pleasing task of showing to Mr. Crabbe the usual *lions* of Edinburgh fell principally to my share, I regret to say that my memory does not supply me with many traces of his conversation. The general impression, however, that he left on my mind was strong, and, I think, indelible: while all the mummeries and carousals of an interval, in which Edinburgh looked very unlike herself, have faded into a vague and dreamlike indistinctness, the image of your father, then first seen, but long before admired and revered in his works, remains as fresh as if the years that have now passed were but so many days.—His noble forehead, his bright beaming eye, without anything of old age about it—though he was then, I presume, about seventy—his sweet, and, I would say, innocent smile, and the calm mellow tones of his voice—all are reproduced the moment I open any page of his poetry: and how much better have I understood and enjoyed his poetry, since I was able thus to connect with it the living presence of the man!

The literary persons in company with whom I saw him the most frequently were Sir Walter and Henry Mackenzie; and between two such thorough men of the world as they were, perhaps his *apparent* simplicity of look and manners struck one more than it might have done under different circumstances; but all three harmonised admirably together—Mr. Crabbe's avowed ignorance about Gaels, and clans, and tartans, and everything that was at the moment uppermost in Sir Walter's thoughts, furnishing him with a welcome apology for dilating on such topics with enthusiastic minuteness—while your father's countenance spoke the quiet delight he felt in opening his imagination to what was really a new world—and the venerable 'Man of Feeling', though a fiery Highlander himself at bottom, had the satisfaction of lying by and listening until some opportunity offered itself of hooking in, between the links, perhaps, of some grand chain of poetical imagery, some small comic or sarcastic trait, which Sir Walter caught up, played with, and, with that art so peculiarly his own, forced into the service of the very impression it seemed meant to disturb. One evening, at Mr. Mackenzie's own house, I particularly remember, among the *noctes cœnæque Deum*.[1]

Crabbe was among the English admirers of Burns, and in 'The Patron' (Tale V) puts Burns and Chatterton together, like Wordsworth in 'Resolution and Independence'. 'I much rejoice', exclaimed the Noble Patron of the young poet,

> 'such worth to find;
> To this the world must be no longer blind:
> His glory will descend from sire to son,
> The Burns of English race, the happier Chatterton.'

Crabbe also appreciated Dunbar, and the passage proving this liking is further interesting as showing Scott's admiration for this old poet:

It surprised me, on taking Mr. Crabbe to see the house of Allan Ramsay on the Castle Hill, to find that he had never heard of Allan's name; or, at all events, was unacquainted with his works. The same evening, however, he perused 'The Gentle Shepherd', and he told me next morning, that he had been pleased with it, but added, 'there is a long step between Ramsay and Burns'. He then made Sir Walter read and interpret some of old Dunbar to him; and said, 'I see that the Ayrshire bard had one giant before him.'

Crabbe was born in 1754, and died 1832, the same year as Scott. He comes into Wordsworth's elegy, the 'Extempore Effusion', on the death of the Ettrick Shepherd; there Scott, Coleridge, Lamb, and Mrs. Hemans are also remembered. It should be noted that Burns was born in 1759 and died in 1796, about ten years before Crabbe came out with really strong work; for, though Crabbe was known as a poet in the eighties, about the same time as Cowper's *Task* and Burns's

---

[1] Chapter ix.

poems, and so is contemporary with Cowper and Burns, it was not till he published *The Borough* (1810) that he showed what his genius could do. Crabbe's literary life is something like Cowper's in its want of continuity: there is a long interval between 1785 and 1807, between his earlier experimental time and the later period of steady poetical industry. The great difference between the experiences of Cowper and Crabbe is that Crabbe, although he did not publish, and was hardly thought of as a living poet between 1785 and 1807,[1] was yet writing (and burning) a great number of things for himself, and was so keeping his hand in and improving his talent.

Crabbe is the third poet who made a great impression in the eighties, who struck readers as giving them something fresh. Yet Crabbe is no more an innovator in form than Cowper or Burns. He keeps to the old rules and fashions of poetry, and there is not much in his variations that would be noted by the generality of readers who liked him. One can make out now the difference between Crabbe's method in the heroic couplet and that of his contemporaries, but there is nothing obvious, nothing sensational in him, nothing making any marked difference in his style from, say, that of Pope, Johnson, or Goldsmith, nothing anywhere like the novelty of 'The Ancient Mariner' or *The Lay of the Last Minstrel*.

Crabbe, of course, gave a new kind of matter. There was the interest of him as a story-teller, and stories had not been common in poetry for some time past, and are not among the valued things, when they are to be found, in eighteenth-century poetry. Dryden's *Fables* are, perhaps, the last great work of narrative poetry before the end of the eighteenth century. In the eighteenth century one may find narrative things (Parnell's 'Hermit' is a good example); but they are generally short, like Swift's 'Baucis and Philemon' or Gay's *Fables*.

It is easy to understand the effect of Crabbe's stories, for they are stories that are memorable and hold the attention

1 Crabbe published *The Newspaper* in 1785. His next volume of poetry, *Poems*, containing 'The Parish Register' and other pieces, did not appear till 1807.

still, in spite of all the riches of imagination found in the most vivid of modern writers. Yet in the early poems of the eighties Crabbe does not show much of this narrative work; he does not really come out as a narrative poet till the publication of *The Borough*.[1] So his success is not so very different from the success of Cowper; it is success well within the limits of the old fashions, gained by freshness and originality within the old rules.

The way Crabbe made his fortune is one of the most wonderful things in history. Crabbe himself, though he does not say so, was very nearly in the same tragic circumstances as Chatterton ten or eleven years before. Chatterton's year of adventure, of his 'attack' upon London, was 1770. Crabbe in 1781 was living in London in poverty with the same sort of anxieties. He had writings to dispose of, was full of literary projects; he had dealt with publishers and made little out of that business; he had tried to find patrons, had written to Lords Thurlow, North, and Shelburne, and all with no effect. Then he wrote to Burke, and in Lockhart's letter to Crabbe's son there is a touching reminiscence of the straits the poet was in.

Sir Walter, himself, I think, took only one walk with Mr. Crabbe: it was to the ruins of St. Anthony's Chapel, at the foot of Arthur's Seat, which your father wished to see, as connected with part of the Heart of Mid-Lothian. I had the pleasure to accompany them on this occasion; and it was the only one on which I heard your father enter into any details of his own personal history. He told us, that during many months when he was toiling in early life in London, he hardly ever tasted butcher's meat, except on a Sunday, when he dined usually with a tradesman's family, and thought their leg of mutton, baked in the pan, the perfection of luxury. The tears stood in his eyes while he talked of Burke's kindness to him in his distress; and I remember he said, 'The night after I had delivered my letter at his door, I was in such a state of agitation, that I walked Westminster Bridge backwards and forwards until day-light.'

Looking at the story of Crabbe's life in this year, one might be ready to look for an end like Chatterton's. He had been beaten in one attempt after another; his wares had no market;

---

[1] 1810.

and one would reckon, with ordinary chances, he could not last out much longer. His case was not quite so hard as Chatterton's. He was older and steadier-minded, and had a way of retreat back to Aldborough; but the stress upon his mind was of the same kind. Then came the wonderful rescue. There seems nothing in Crabbe's letter to Burke, which is preserved and printed,[1] so very different from the ordinary begging letter; but there was evidently something in it that caught the attention of Burke, and Burke answered Crabbe at once and saved him and made his fortune at a stroke. He took him into his house and introduced him to Fox, Reynolds, Johnson, and other friends. He found for him a richer patron, the Duke of Rutland. He advised him to take holy orders, and got the duke to provide for him as a clergyman.

Of course, the reason for this continued patronage was the merit of Crabbe's poetry, which was read by Burke, Fox, and Johnson, and found good enough by all. The fact that Johnson came down upon Crabbe for an innocent observation at their first meeting[2] means nothing with regard to Johnson's opinions of Crabbe's merits. Yet, in spite of Crabbe's real skill in poetry, it is difficult to get over one's amazement at Burke's insight and readiness to help. It was one of the busiest times of the politician's life, towards the end of North's ministry and of the American War. Burke, as a member of the Opposition, would seem to have little leisure for begging letters. Crabbe's venture and its success must be remembered as contradicting what is usually said about literary patrons. It is sometimes asserted that Johnson's letter to Lord Chesterfield was the death-knell to patronage, the beginning of a new order of things for literary men. Yet Crabbe, thirty years after, had his fortune made by Burke and Rutland. He did not depend later on patrons for the

---

[1] In the *Life* by his son, chapter iv.

[2] 'It was at Sir Joshua's table that he first had the honour of meeting Dr. Johnson. . . . My father . . . said, that, at this first interview, he was particularly unfortunate: making some trite remark, or hazarding some injudicious question, he brought on himself a specimen of that castigation which the great literary bashaw was commonly so ready to administer. He remembered with half comic terror the Doctor's *growl*; but this did not diminish Mr. Crabbe's respect and veneration. . . .' *Life*, by his son, chapter iv.

success of his books, but without patrons he would never have had a chance.

Johnson's early poem, *London*, was read and praised by Pope; and Johnson, in his old age, rendered a like service to Crabbe, the young poet of another generation. Crabbe and Johnson agreed very closely in some of their opinions. *The Village*, which Crabbe had in manuscript at the time of his adventure, and on which he relied to make his name, begins with sentiments like those of Johnson, and Johnson made them his own with a little modification, in the lines adopted by Crabbe and included in his work—just in the same way as Goldsmith adopted Johnson's suggestions in *The Traveller*.[1] Crabbe hit Johnson with his dislike of pastoral; both had had enough of the regular conventional imitation of Virgil. Crabbe voiced his dislike of pastoral in the beginning of *The Village*:

> In fairer scenes, where peaceful pleasures spring,
> Tityrus, the pride of Mantuan swains, might sing:
> But charmed by him, or smitten with his views,
> Shall modern poets court the Mantuan muse?
> From Truth and Nature shall we widely stray,
> Where Fancy leads, or Virgil led the way?

Johnson approved of the sentiment, but not of the expression, and 'translated' Crabbe, making statelier music out of Crabbe's slightly comic jingles and mild conceit—a passage very instructive for Johnson's poetry:

> On Mincio's banks, in Caesar's bounteous reign,
> If Tityrus found the Golden Age again,
> Must sleepy bards the flattering dream prolong,
> Mechanick echos of the Mantuan song?
> From Truth and Nature shall we widely stray,
> Where Virgil, not where Fancy, leads the way?

One curious thing should be noted. Crabbe had put Virgil and Fancy together as misleading, as giving the poet something different from truth. Johnson makes Fancy the same as poetical reason (and so, whether by accident or not, agrees with Wordsworth, for the Fancy of Johnson is Wordsworth's

---

[1] See Boswell, *Life of Johnson*, ed. Hill-Powell, iv. 175–6; ii. 5–7, 478.

Imagination) and takes Virgil simply as convention. Fancy is for Johnson the living power of the poetic mind working to find poetic truth.

At the time when Burke made the fortune of Crabbe, Burke was editor of the *Annual Register*, and printed there extracts from Crabbe's *The Village*, which were read by Scott and Wordsworth in their youth, and which made Crabbe widely known. *The Village* was published in 1783.

The Parish Register in manuscript was sent in 1806 to Charles James Fox, who was then very near the end of his life. Fox in his early days had made a promise to read and criticize the next poem Crabbe should write; he died in September 1806, and the story of Phoebe Dawson in the second part was one of the last things he read. *The Parish Register* was published in 1807, and was warmly received. It brought a letter from Scott, who did not know Crabbe then, telling of Scott's early admiration for the selections from *The Village* in the *Annual Register*. Crabbe had before that discovered *The Lay of the Last Minstrel*, having picked it up in a newspaper shop, and read it nearly all through as he stood.

The poetry of Crabbe rapidly became popular, though it was never so thoroughly accepted as the poetry of Cowper was for a very long time. The reputation of Crabbe is interesting for literary history, particularly for the history of fiction. Strange to say, one of the severest critics of Crabbe is Hazlitt in *The Spirit of the Age*—not that he dislikes Crabbe, not that he dispraises his poetry, but that he judges severely Crabbe's attitude towards life, refusing to find imagination in it. Now Crabbe was admired for his stories, and admired because he gave readers something besides description (though there is a good deal of description in them) and sentiment; he gave them what people look for in novels, making his effect through fiction which might have been effective in prose. One ought not to take Crabbe as a novelist writing with the wrong method, turning good prose stories into conventional rhyme. Yet much of Crabbe's effect is of a sort that might be made in prose; many of his stories make one think of the short stories of Thomas Hardy, and the comparison is good and relevant. Readers found in Crabbe harshness of experience and an unrelenting view of life. Some critics found fault with his unhappy endings, others with his love of disgusting things, unpleasant scenes with unpleasant people in them. Hazlitt takes Crabbe as a 'realist', for though that nickname was not in use then, Hazlitt thinks of Crabbe's method as 'realistic', in the sense we use it of modern novelists, as simple copying of nature without modification or imagination.

Crabbe defends his method in the Preface to the *Tales*, in the volume of 1812. The apology is not the strongest that might have been made, but is nevertheless interesting. He defends the particularity of his work by appealing to the authority of Pope, for example:

Pope himself has no small portion of this actuality of relation, this nudity of description, and poetry without an atmosphere; the lines beginning 'In the worst inn's worst room', are an example, and many others may be seen in his Satires, Imitations, and above all in his Dunciad.

Though he does not actually say so, he takes 'actuality of relation', 'nudity of description', and 'poetry without an atmosphere' as describing his own poetic attempts, but these expressions do not really do him justice. In his poetry, just because it is poetry, there is not 'nudity of description'. There is great particularity, and much unpleasantness, but not 'nudity' and not 'poetry without an atmosphere'. By 'poetry without an atmosphere' Crabbe means without idealizing touches such as you get in pastorals. But fancy and imagination are not wanting in Crabbe, and his trick of fancy ought not to have escaped the notice of so keen a critic as Hazlitt. Poetic or pictorial representation of unpleasant things need not be unpleasant. Many subjects which are in actuality unpleasant may be pleasant in art. Curiously enough, the critics are slightly offended by the 'dull' country Crabbe describes: they do not realize Crabbe's enjoyment in it. Take, for instance, the passage from 'Peter Grimes' in *The Borough*, describing the tidal water Crabbe knew so well. This, adopting the phrase of Lamb on Coleridge, is merely 'Mr. Crabbe's fun'. The scenes may be 'dull' dramatically for the mind of

Peter Grimes, but they are most interesting to Crabbe himself and to all who read him in the right way.

> Thus by himself compell'd to live each day,
> To wait for certain hours the tide's delay;
> At the same times the same dull views to see,
> The bounding marsh-bank and the blighted tree;
> The water only, when the tides were high,
> When low, the mud half-cover'd and half-dry;
> The sun-burnt tar that blisters on the planks,
> And bank-side stakes in their uneven ranks;
> Heaps of entangled weeds that slowly float,
> As the tide rolls by the impeded boat.
>
> When tides were neap, and, in the sultry day,
> Through the tall bounding mud-banks made their way,
> Which on each side rose swelling, and below
> The dark warm flood ran silently and slow;
> There anchoring, Peter chose from man to hide,
> There hang his head, and view the lazy tide
> In its hot slimy channel slowly glide;
> Where the small eels that left the deeper way
> For the warm shore, within the shallows play;
> Where gaping mussels, left upon the mud,
> Slope their slow passage to the fallen flood;—
> Here dull and hopeless he'd lie down and trace
> How sidelong crabs had scrawl'd their crooked race;
> Or sadly listen to the tuneless cry
> Of fishing gull or clanging golden-eye;
> What time the sea-birds to the marsh would come,
> And the loud bittern, from the bull-rush home,
> Gave from the salt-ditch side the bellowing boom:
> He nursed the feelings these dull scenes produce,
> And loved to stop beside the opening sluice;
> Where the small stream, confined in narrow bound,
> Ran with a dull, unvaried, sadd'ning sound;
> Where all, presented to the eye or ear,
> Oppress'd the soul with misery, grief, and fear.

Crabbe's 'fun' is brought out in the comic poem of 'The Lover's Journey'. Crabbe, with all his fondness for sad stories, is no pessimist, and has no consistent theory of human misery. By nature he is cheerful and fond of jokes of all sorts. He is a chronicler of human life without any prejudice in favour of misery. His mind is something like that of a medical doctor who has to deal with all kinds of pain and disease, but is not thereby depressed or made to think hopelessly of humanity. 'The Lover's Journey' is a cheerful light poem, clearly bringing out Crabbe's game. The point of the whole is that Orlando (born John) rides through changing landscape which appears to him beautiful or desert according to the feeling of the moment. Everything seems to him beautiful as he rides off to his adored lady. Then he comes to her house, and finds her gone to see a friend. He rides, sore-hearted, through a much richer country, and finds all drear. One can see clearly how Crabbe is distinguishing, not between the ugly landscape and the lover's opinion of it, but between the true beauty of the landscape and the false beauty in the mind of Orlando. The whole thing is ironical. While pretending to depreciate, Crabbe is thoroughly enjoying all he has before his mind's eye. The depreciation is incomparably higher praise than the trivial fancy of the lover. Consider again the difference between the gipsies as directly described by Crabbe, and the fanciful opinion of them in the mind of Orlando. It is strange that Hazlitt, who was a painter, should not have compared Crabbe with the Dutch landscape-painters or the English painters of that eastern country. When Crabbe indirectly described his poetry as 'without an atmosphere', he forgot 'atmosphere' as known to painters, which is suggested over and over again in his poems—that light and air which gives beauty to the barren heath and fen.

The style of Crabbe is criticized in *Rejected Addresses*. Parody is the most difficult, but the best kind of criticism, and this parody shows exact detection in the keenest way of the little tricks of style in Crabbe's poetry. The verse used by Crabbe is the heroic couplet, which he moulds in the old-fashioned way, with more of the triplet and alexandrine than Pope allowed, though Crabbe keeps pretty regularly to the stopped couplet. Compare the beginning of *The Frank Courtship*:[1]

> Grave Jonas Kindred, Sybil Kindred's sire,
> Was six feet high, and look'd six inches higher. . . .

[1] *Tales in Verse* (1812), No. vi.

with the parody in *Rejected Addresses:*

> 'Tis sweet to view, from half-past five to six,
> Our long wax-candles, with short cotton wicks,
> Touch'd by the lamplighter's Promethean art,
> Start into light and make the lighter start;
> To see red Phoebus through the gallery pane
> Tinge with his beam the beams of Drury-Lane,
> While gradual parties fill our widen'd pit,
> And gape, and gaze, and wonder, ere they sit. . . .

> John Richard William Alexander Dwyer
> Was footman to Justinian Stubbs, Esquire;
> But when John Dwyer listed in the Blues,
> Emanuel Jennings polish'd Stubbs's shoes.
> Emanuel Jennings brought his youngest boy
> Up as a corn-cutter, a safe employ;
> In Holywell Street, St. Pancras, he was bred
> (At number twenty-seven, it is said)
> Facing the pump, and near the Granby's Head.

One can easily see how the trick of false antithesis and the unscrupulous filling up of the lines are picked out in *Rejected Addresses.* Then there are the rattling rhymes and the fondness for rhyming on insignificant syllables—a device used by Milton for comic purposes in the sonnet on *Tetrachordon* (clogs, dogs, frogs, hogs). All these little vanities do not spoil Crabbe's real style, which is admirable for narrative poetry.

Hazlitt's criticism of Crabbe as a realist opens the debate on the old problem of the possibility of imitating nature. Hazlitt thinks the popularity of Crabbe was helped by those who found 'painting' in him. His criticism is fallacious in that he seems to think it possible to transfer reality to the page either of poetry or painting without any thought, any imagination.

Painting is essentially an imitative art; it cannot subsist for a moment on empty generalities: the critic, therefore, who had been used to this sort of substantial entertainment, would be disposed to read poetry with the eye of a connoisseur, would be little captivated with smooth, polished, unmeaning periods, and would turn with double eagerness and relish to the force and precision of individual details, transferred, as it were, to the page from the canvas. Thus an admirer of Teniers or Hobbima might think little of the pastoral sketches of Pope or Gold-smith; even Thomson describes not so much the naked object as what he sees in his mind's eye, surrounded and glowing with the mild, bland, genial vapours of his brain:—but the adept in Dutch interiors, hovels, and pig-styes must find in Mr. Crabbe a man after his own heart. He is the very thing itself; he paints in words, instead of colours: there is no other difference. As Mr. Crabbe is not a painter, only because he does not use a brush and colours, so he is for the most part a poet, only because he writes in lines of ten syllables. All the rest might be found in a newspaper, an old magazine, or a county-register. Our author is himself a little jealous of the prudish fidelity of his homely Muse, and tries to justify himself by precedents. He brings as a parallel instance of merely literal description, Pope's lines on the gay Duke of Bucking-ham, beginning, 'In the worst inn's worst room see Villiers lies!' But surely nothing can be more dissimilar. Pope describes what is striking, Crabbe would have described merely what was there. The objects in Pope stand out to the fancy from the mixture of the mean with the gaudy, from the contrast of the scene and the character. There is an appeal to the imagination; you see what is passing in a poetical point of view. In Crabbe there is no foil, no contrast, no impulse given to the mind. It is all on a level and of a piece.[1]

But the dullest copier must put something of his own mind into his work; he must select, and selection is a mode of the imagination, selection is idealism. A more striking fallacy still is to be found in Hazlitt's application of his doctrine. It is not so bad to have this easy-going theory of imagination, this belief in the possibility of exact imitation of nature; it is unphilosophical, uncritical, but it cannot do much harm. When, however, Hazlitt quotes as an example of mere copy-ing the description of the tidal water in 'Peter Grimes', he is painfully wrong. He takes it as a mere 'facsimile of some of the most unlovely parts of the creation',[2] and does not reckon on the dramatic value of the piece, does not apparently feel the zest of the whole thing. The description is not

[1] Hazlitt, *The Spirit of the Age*; *Works*, ed. P. P. Howe (1930–4), xi. 166.
[2] 'This is an exact *fac-simile* of some of the most unlovely parts of the creation. Indeed the whole of Mr. Crabbe's *Borough*, from which the above passage is taken, is done so to the life, that it seems almost like some sea-monster, crawled out of the neighbouring slime, and harbouring a breed of strange vermin, with a strong local scent of tar and bulge-water.' *The Spirit of the Age*, ed. cit. xi. 168.

description merely, but part of the story and of the soul of Peter Grimes. It is very strange that Hazlitt does not appreciate Crabbe's 'gusto', the enjoyment of the artist in his work, the gesture, the vividness, the spirit of the whole, for 'gusto' was one of Hazlitt's favourite words and ideas, especially in criticizing paintings, and he did more than anyone towards making it popular in literature.

Where Hazlitt is most wrong is in thinking of Crabbe as 'a sickly, a querulous, a uniformly dissatisfied poet'.[1] On the contrary, Crabbe seems always in good spirits. He is not 'sickly and querulous' because he tells sad stories; for he tells his sad stories with a temper that is not in itself melancholy, in an impartial sort of way so as not to pain the reader unnecessarily by the absurdities of life. In many ways he is an idealist; he is so in the ordinary sense of the word, in making out things better than they really are. The cruelty and misery of real life consist in accident, uncertainty, in what seems to be pure unreason; what makes the pain of the human race is not mere misery, but the inability to explain it, to see the end of it. Now Crabbe's stories, just because they are works of art, give, not indeed a reason for everything, but a view which is consistent and harmonious. What is pain in the story is so thought out by the poet that it becomes in a way harmonized.

Crabbe is indeed a tragic poet, and he does not leave the situation, problem, plot, without a 'conclusion', and this 'conclusion' is always that subtler poetic justice found in the great tragedies, and not the mere 'happy ending'. Crabbe's 'The Brothers'[2] may be compared with *King Lear*. The problem of *King Lear* has been used by different narrative authors in narrative fiction, and it is interesting to compare Crabbe's story with *A Lear of the Steppes* by Turgenev, *King Lear* reduced to modern Russian terms, and without the heroic personages of Shakespeare's drama. In 'The Brothers' there is a

[1] 'Mr. Crabbe's great fault is certainly that he is a sickly, a querulous, a uniformly dissatisfied poet. He sings the country; and he sings it in a pitiful tone. He chooses this subject only to take the charm out of it, and to dispel the illusion, the glory, and the dream, which had hovered over it in golden verse from Theocritus to Cowper.' *The Spirit of the Age*, ed. cit. xi. 168.

[2] *Tales in Verse*, No. xx.

similar sort of transposition of the problem of *King Lear* to the scenery and people Crabbe knew best. 'The Brothers' is a painful story, but it is not unfairly so, and not by any means 'sickly and querulous'. There is nothing in it that seems impossible, and in the painful feelings described or aroused there is nothing contrary to the laws of poetic beauty.

Much of Crabbe's poetry is cheerful, and he is cheerful over all sorts of ideas and inventions. His general policy is brought out in a letter to Sir Walter Scott, before the two had met. Scott had written to Crabbe telling of his clerkship in the Court of Sessions, and describing his life. Crabbe answers, eagerly asking for more information. He is by no means 'sickly and querulous', but is cheered by hearing of reports of human misery, and would enjoy reading them, so that he might get from them interesting plots for stories:

Law, then, is your profession—I mean a profession you give your mind and time to—but how *'fag as a clerk'*? Clerk is a name for a learned person, I know, in our Church; but how the same hand which held the pen of Marmion, holds that with which a clerk fags, unless a clerk means something vastly more than I understand—is not to be comprehended. I wait for elucidation. Know you, dear sir, I have often thought I should love to read *reports*—that is, brief histories of extraordinary cases, with the judgments. If that is what is meant by *reports*, such reading must be pleasant; but, probably, I entertain wrong ideas, and could not understand the books I think so engaging. Yet I conclude there are *histories of cases*, and have often thought of consulting Hatchard whether he knew of such kind of reading, but hitherto I have rested in ignorance.[1]

'The Brothers', 'Resentment',[2] and 'Delay has Danger' in *Tales of the Hall*[3] are certainly among the best of Crabbe's tragedies. Crabbe has already been compared with Thomas Hardy. The favourite miserable theme with both Crabbe and Thomas Hardy is the decay of love, of affection, of enthusiasm, of hope; and that is the sort of subject in which Crabbe proves his superiority to the ordinary dull realist. For the

---

[1] 5 March 1813. Lockhart, *Memoirs of the Life of Sir Walter Scott* (10 vols., Edinburgh, 1839), iv. 34. Cf. *The Letters of Sir Walter Scott, 1811–1814,* ed. H. J. C. Grierson (1932), pp. 279–80.
[2] *Tales in Verse,* No. xvii.   [3] No. xiii.

essence of that kind of story is Time—the triumph of Time defacing human nature—and that kind of subject cannot be taken by anyone without imagination. It is Time that keeps the sad stories of Crabbe alive; they are not merely painful, sensational things, but stories in which the movement of life is given, and therein lies their power.

'The Learned Boy'[1] is one of the best of the comic poems. The child is brought up and spoilt by his grandmother, and his early studies are of the pious, mechanical sort described by his grandmother after he has begun to read infidel writings. He gets into bad company, turns free-thinker, and strives to enlighten the minds of his elders. The passage describing the chastisement of the boy by his father brings out the poetry of Crabbe:

> 'Hold, in mercy hold—
> 'Father, oh! father! throw the whip away;
> I was but jesting, on my knees I pray—
> There, hold his arm—oh! leave us not alone;
> In pity cease, and I will yet atone
> For all my sin'—In vain; stroke after stroke
> On side and shoulder, quick as mill-wheels broke;
> Quick as the patient's pulse, who trembling cried,
> And still the parent with a stroke replied. . . .
>
> 'Oh! I shall die—my father! do receive
> My dying words; indeed I do believe;
> The books are lying books, I know it well,
> There is a devil, oh! there is a hell;
> And I'm a sinner: spare me, I am young,
> My sinful words were only on my tongue;
> My heart consented not; 'tis all a lie:
> Oh! spare me then, I'm not prepared to die.'

It is a mistake to think Crabbe would do as well in prose, or that his poetry is only prose with rhymes added. His great poetic achievement is that, while seeming to follow Pope on the whole, he gets over Pope's epigrammatic manner, restoring the heroic couplet as a form of narrative verse, using it as it was used in Dryden's *Fables*, but with much more variety,

---

[1] *Tales in Verse*, No. xxi.

and going back by his natural genius to the art of Chaucer. The distinctively poetic quality of the passage is not in the diction but in the style, in the simple relation of phrases and themes to one another, and in the unobtrusively varying melody—the restrictions of the verse being so disguised as to give the appearance of free, natural, prosaic speech, ordinary conversation, in spite of the definite art and artifice of the lines and couplets.

William Gilpin

SCOTT and Byron did not invent the taste for scenery; there were tourists before their day, and even without *The Lady of the Lake* and *Childe Harold's Pilgrimage* people would have gone to the Trossachs and to the Rhine to admire the beauties of Nature. But poets have increased the number of pilgrims beyond all reckoning; and they have much to be responsible for.

Long ago Carlyle in *Sartor Resartus* complained of scenery-hunting, and asked whether it might not be possible to find some inoculation against it.[1] It has not been possible; and though there may be some indications that the taste will not last for ever, it is still flourishing, a source of incalculable profit to a great host of tradesmen. Everyone knows the advertisements, the catalogues of wares, the tariffs, the incidental attractions by the way, including lectures. 'They pass both tropics and behold the poles'; or at any rate they go to the edge of the Northern Ice, with five days ashore in Spitzbergen. To look at the illustrated programmes of some of the chief firms is to see that the earth has at last been conquered; and the victory has been won mainly by the authors of *The Lady of the Lake* and *Childe Harold's Pilgrimage*, by their putting ideas into people's heads. What place is exempt?—if it be not the island of which Heine wrote: 'This Island lies hidden far in the quiet sea of Romance not to be reached except on the wings of Fable. Never does Sorrow harbour there, and there no steamboat brings its freight of Philistines, inquisitive, smoking tobacco.'[2]

---

[1] ' "Some time before Small-pox was extirpated," says the Professor, "there came a new malady of the spiritual sort on Europe: I mean the epidemic, now endemical, of View-hunting. Poets of old date, being privileged with Senses, had also enjoyed external Nature; but chiefly as we enjoy the crystal cup which holds good or bad liquor for us; that is to say, in silence, or with slight incidental commentary: never, as I compute, till after the *Sorrows of Werter*, was there man found who would say: Come let us make a Description! Having drunk the liquor, come let us eat the glass! Of which endemic the Jenner is unhappily still to seek." ' *Sartor Resartus*, II. vi.

[2]   Dieses Eiland liegt verborgen   Niemals ankert dort die Sorge,
        Ferne in dem stillen Meere   Niemals landet dort ein Dampfschiff
        Der Romantick, nur erreichbar   Mit neugierigen Philistern,
        Auf des Fabelrosses Flügeln.   Tabakspfeifen in den Mäulern.

                                                         Atta Troll (1843), Kaput xx.

Other motives, no doubt, besides scenery-hunting enter into the successes of modern tourism, but scenery is one of the chief inducements, and literature has been one of the chief agents in bringing about the prodigious development.

Literature has not done everything, even where scenery is what is looked for. Scenery is made obvious by other means, and perhaps in the eighteenth century most commonly by that kind of spectacle to which the name is most appropriate; by the scenery in theatres. That is the sort of picture which is most generally known, and it is that which probably helps most to interpret the descriptions in books. It is by that co-operative education that people are taught what to admire in the beauties of Nature. Thus, we can explain certain ways in which scenery is taken, which would be inexplicable if literature were the only educative source of the movement. Natural scenery in some places is felt to require the additional help that is given in the theatre; hence the additions to the beauty of Switzerland. Alleviations of the mountain gloom, auxiliaries of the mountain glory; illuminations for the waterfalls, and electric searchlights on the promontories; these plainly are nothing but magnifications of the old familiar limelight apparatus, supplying a felt want.

The historian of these fashions may be well advised to go back beyond the great romantic generations, to find some earlier ways of contemplating the beauties of Nature, before the popular excitement began to declare itself. One of the most instructive writers that he will come upon, just before the days of Wordsworth, Scott, and Byron, is the Rev. William Gilpin, who wrote a number of descriptive tours in different parts of Britain and is supposed to be the original of Dr. Syntax. One of his books is *Observations relative chiefly to Picturesque Beauty, Made in the Year 1776 on several Parts of Great Britain, particularly the High-Lands of Scotland*, published in two volumes octavo in 1789.

It is a pleasant book to go back to. Its mode of regarding the beauties of Nature is quite unlike that of *Childe Harold's Pilgrimage*, and it belongs to a time in which the roar of tourists and of competitive descriptions of scenery has not yet broken the stillness. After a hundred years of furious energy

in various kinds of romantic treatment of nature, after Byron
and Victor Hugo, it is refreshing to go back to the older
time, and to come upon a different mode of representation.

This eighteenth-century pilgrim knows what he is looking
for in Nature; and it is definitely the *picturesque*. Not picturesque in its common loose acceptation, but as meaning
that which is convenient for painting, that which is like a
good picture. He himself distinguishes it from *romantic*, and
he makes the distinction in talking of the view of Edinburgh
with which the epithet 'romantic' is perpetually associated
from its use in the famous description in *Marmion* ('Mine
own romantic town').[1] Gilpin says: 'A nearer approach did
not give us a more pleasing idea of the environs of Edinburgh. We had always heard it represented as one of the most
picturesque towns in Britain; but people often consider
romantic and *picturesque* as synonymous.' He thinks that
Arthur's Seat resembles a cap of maintenance in heraldry,
but admits that 'the town and castle indeed on the left, make
some amends, and are happily introduced'.[2]

One might expect him to be severely tried by the landscape of the Scottish Highlands, where 'romantic' views are
common, as everyone knows, but where there are said to be
difficulties about getting the views to compose well for pictures. It is the great interest of the book that it makes its way
through difficulties like these in a fresh and unexpected and
unpredictable manner, taking each problem as it comes and
treating it without prejudice. Contrary to what one might
have expected, Gilpin finds no excess of the romantic in the
Highland landscape.[3]

It is remarkable that there is a general agreement between
Mr. Gilpin and a later student who went over the same
ground with a widely different training, Sir Archibald Geikie,
in his book on *The Scenery of Scotland* (1865). One likeness
between them is that neither of them is untrained. Gilpin has
his principles of drawing and painting, Geikie has his geo-
logy. It is useful to have a science of some sort as a protection
against the fascinations of literature. In this case science has

[1] IV. xxx. 18.
[2] Op. cit. i. 59–60. Cf. Ker, *The Art of Poetry*, p. 73.   [3] Ibid. ii. 127.

come to the support of the poets with some effect. Geikie's geological analysis of the characteristic landscape in the Border country is a revelation of certain qualities which the romantic tourist is apt to mistake for defects (see the account of Washington Irving's impressions in Lockhart's *Life of Scott*).[1] The geological demonstration in general agrees with Gilpin, and is all to the honour of Teviot, Tweed, and Ettrick.

Gilpin, long before Wordsworth, and from a different point of view, discovered and described the beauty of that landscape in which the lines are simple. 'The mountains formed beautiful lines' is a phrase he repeats, and he gives very nearly full marks to a landscape which Scott knew better than anything else in the world—a view looking down the Tweed towards the Eildon Hills.[2]

It is a quaint old-fashioned way of treating the subject; it may seem thin and spiritless to those who are accustomed to more passionate and more eloquent observers with a more heavily charged vocabulary. We are not used to this kind of writing: 'On the right Ben Lomond, the second hill in Scotland, raised its respectable head', or, 'As the day was fine we had indeed a most amusing view over all the southern division of the lake', or to be told of the view at Inveraray that, 'Its skreens are everywhere equal to the expanse of its waters.'

Yet the discourse is rational and sincere. Gilpin brings to

---

[1] 'I gazed about me for a time with mute surprise. I may almost say with disappointment. I beheld a mere succession of grey waving hills, line beyond line, as far as my eye could reach, monotonous in their aspect, and so destitute of trees, that one could almost see a stout fly walking along their profile; and the far-famed Tweed appeared a naked stream, flowing between bare hills, without a tree or thicket on its banks; and yet such had been the magic web of poetry and romance thrown over the whole, that it had a greater charm for me than the richest scenery I had beheld in England. I could not help giving utterance to my thoughts. Scott hummed for a moment to himself, and looked grave; he had no idea of having his muse complimented at the expense of his native hills. "It may be pertinacity," said he at length; "but to my eye, these grey hills, and all this wild border country, have beauties peculiar to themselves. I like the very nakedness of the land; it has something bold, and stern, and solitary about it. When I have been for some time in the rich scenery about Edinburgh, which is like ornamented garden land, I begin to wish myself back again among my own honest grey hills; and if I did not see the heather, at least once a-year, *I think I should die!*" ' Washington Irving's account of his visit to Scott at Abbotsford in 1817, printed in Lockhart's *Life of Scott* (shorter edition, chapter ix), London, 1892, i. 374-5.

[2] Gilpin, op. cit. i. 51.

a conclusion the characteristic fashion of his century in the study of the beauties of Nature.[1] This study was determined generally by a regard for what was picturesque in the strict sense of the word. It was the century of landscape gardening, the art with which Pope and Shenstone were so much concerned. The vanities of landscape gardening were in that century the danger incident to the beauties of Nature. Capability Brown was the Vice attending on the Sublime and Beautiful in Landscape. Whereas now, the danger comes from the devastating rush of the tourist, in those days it was limited to the absurdities of a few landed proprietors who might take the advice of a landscape gardener to plant dead trees near the house in order to give a greater appearance of Nature to its surroundings.

One indication of the change is the disuse of the Claude Lorraine glass which once was necessary to the traveller in search of the picturesque—a mirror in which the landscape is toned down below the glare of reality. Gray took one with him on his travels,[2] and so did the young man who lost his life on Helvellyn.[3] The Claude Lorraine glass is of no value without the special training of the old schools of Fine Art, and it has been replaced by the snapping camera. Gilpin doesn't much approve of the glass:

The only picturesque glasses are those, which the artists call Claude Loraine glasses. They are combined of two or three different colours; and if the hues are well sorted, they give the objects of nature a soft, mellow tinge, like the colouring of that master. The only use of these glasses, (which have little, but in sunshine,) is to give a greater depth to the shades; by which the effect is shewn with more force. How far the painter should follow his eye, or his glass, in working from nature, I am not master enough of the theory of colouring to ascertain. In general, I am apt to believe, that the merit of this kind of modified.

[1] See his discussion of the sublime and beautiful, simplicity and variety, ii. 120–2.
[2] See Gray's journal of his tour in the Lake District, 30 September to 15 October 1769 (*Correspondence of Thomas Gray*, ed. Toynbee-Whibley (3 vols., 1935), iii. 1074–80, &c.). 'On the ascent of the hill above Appleby the thick hanging wood & the long reaches of the Eden (rapid, clear, & full as ever) winding below with views of the Castle & Town gave much employment to the mirror: but the sun was wanting & the sky overcast' (30 September).
[3] See Wordsworth's poem 'Fidelity' (1805) and Sir Walter Scott's poem 'Helvellyn' (1805).

vision consists chiefly in its novelty; and that nature has given us a better apparatus, for viewing objects in a picturesque light, than any the optician can furnish.[1]

Gilpin's work might be described as a closing of one chapter in the history of the beauties of Nature. It brings the characteristic eighteenth-century regard for Nature as near as possible to Wordsworth, without making the transition. Gilpin appreciates the things that Wordsworth appreciates. They would have admired the same landscape, and Wordsworth, if asked to describe it, need not have rejected Gilpin's terms. Gilpin's interpretation of the simple lines of the Border mountains is in no disagreement with Wordsworth's view of the subject. Only Gilpin did not go further; his landscape is distinctly one for the pictorial observer. The imagination and meditative interpretation of Wordsworth are not to be found in him.

He is in a similar relation to Scott. It is one of the most curious and attractive things in his book that it is full of that sort of interest in tradition and in history which was to pass into the romances of Scott. But in Gilpin they are not allowed to interfere with the picturesque. A strict line is drawn between the two sets of ideas. Here, you have your landscape and its commentaries, its screens, its middle distance, its composition, and so forth. There, in separate paragraphs you have the historical remarks, and there is little communication between them. What is meant for the eye is kept separate from the humanities of sentiment and from historical or literary association.

Gilpin was wonderfully open to the influences that told so strongly upon Scott. The quickness of his mind for local character, for traditions and reminiscences, is far beyond what is common even now, when the way is known. He notices many things which he might easily have passed over. His book was published in 1789, only two years after the Edinburgh edition of Burns—the first available edition—but Burns is quoted freely. His notes on the Highland character and customs are evidently made with zest and at first hand.

[1] Op. cit. i. 124.

In talking of the Border landscape he does not neglect the Border songs.

> It is no little recommendation of the rivers we met with here, that almost every one of them is the subject of some pleasing Scotch ditty; which the scene raises to the memory of those, who are versed in the lyrics of the country. The elegant simplicity of the verse, and the soothing melody of the music, in almost all the Scotch songs, is universally acknowledged.[1]

But all these things are kept in their own place. They are not allowed to run over into the landscape, when landscape is being discussed.

It is no longer the fashion as it once was to depreciate the eighteenth century. The eighteenth century is recovering from the romantic deluge; the declamatory surges have passed by and left the eighteenth-century wits not seriously damaged. The present value of Voltaire is something considerable. But while the great worldlings of the century are still appreciated, still unsurpassed in the quickness of their play, there is perhaps not enough recognition of the gentler and less combative spirits. Perhaps Wordsworth may be thought to have disqualified writers such as Gilpin. It may be, however, that this student of the picturesque has something independent in him. He is not, like Wordsworth's poetry, 'passionate, for the instruction of reason'. He is dispassionate, and he writes in prose. But there is something peculiarly attractive in his leisurely ways, and in the freedom of his contemplative life. In some respects, too, he had better fortune than Wordsworth. Wordsworth saw the beginning of worse days and had to fight against the Windermere railway.[2] In Gilpin's time it was not yet possible for gluttonous people to trade dishonourably on the love of natural scenery; the process of 'opening up' the beauties of Nature in those days stopped short of the present methods, where 'opening up' too often resembles evisceration. The quiet century, as Leslie Stephen called it, and its quiet lovers of the picturesque,

---

[1] Op. cit. i. 52.
[2] See his·sonnet (1844) 'On the projected Kendal and Windermere Railway'.
  Is then no nook of English ground secure
  From rash assault?

they do not need the intensity of Wordsworth's imagination. Their clear vision and their simplicity of motive are as far beyond our reach as the greatest things in Wordsworth. William Gilpin can never be of much importance to the modern world, but he has not yet lost his charm.

William Wordsworth

WORDSWORTH has suffered greatly from popular misconceptions and prejudices. Many think of him as the inventor of the 'beauties of nature', as a poet who made a revolution in taste by calling people to nature, by breaking up the town convention of poetry in the tradition of Pope, by giving a new mode, the virtue of which lay chiefly in regard for beauty of landscape. This is a flatly wrong opinion. 'The beauties of nature', by which is meant chiefly landscape beauty (though the phrase is not necessarily limited to beauty as appealing to the eye), were appreciated all through the eighteenth century. Indeed, they were often taken in too attentive a way, being studied and admired so that the pleasure often became affected and in danger of exaggeration. The taste for landscape gardening is evident at the beginning of the eighteenth century; the tours in search of 'the beauties of nature' become more and more common in the second half of the century; the works of Gilpin are widely read—altogether by about the third quarter of the century scenery was greatly attracting persons of leisure and good taste. Especial interest was taken in snow-mountains and glaciers before the literary use of that sort of scenery, before *Manfred* and *Prometheus Unbound*, though no doubt the taste had early literary encouragement from Rousseau. Then, coming to 'the beauties of nature' in English poetry, there are Thomson's *Seasons*, and Cowper's *Task*. Wordsworth in no sense invented 'the beauties of nature'. He had an original way of dealing with landscape, but he was not the first poet to whom 'beautiful things had seemed beautiful'.[1]

Then there is the prejudice, which the poet himself in his essays did a good deal to encourage, with regard to Wordsworth's diction. He is thought of by many of his admirers as

[1] Scott is often supposed to have made the reputation of the Highlands for tourists. This is a mistake, obvious to anyone who knows the life of Wordsworth. Wordsworth, his sister, and Coleridge went to the Trossachs, the scene of *The Lady of the Lake*, in 1803, before *The Lady of the Lake* was written, and they went there because it was already well-known as a place to be visited.—W.P.K.

abolishing the ornamental diction of the eighteenth century, and, by many of those who do not like him, as talking dully, flatly, monotonously, about uninteresting people and their furniture—their cloaks, tubs, &c. This wrong view comes from a wrong contrast between Pope and Wordsworth, a wrong estimate of eighteenth-century poetry in general, and particularly of the diction of Pope. Pope's diction is not generally the pompous, periphrastic language often put in opposition to Wordsworth's simplicity. Pope when he is most spirited, when on his own ground and happy, uses colloquial language no more ornamental than Wordsworth's own. Wordsworth, in his discussion of poetic language, exaggerated the amount of pretence and false ornament in eighteenth-century poetry. He had an argument to work out about poetic language; he wished to find for himself a thoroughly sincere language, in which nothing tricky, nothing false, nothing detachable, should come between the poet's mind and that of the reader. Who shall say he was wrong in trying to solve this problem? The fault lay in his thinking himself the first poet to attempt the task.

It is a great pity that *The Prelude* was not published as soon as it was written, in 1805. One result of its suppression was that Wordsworth was judged by many from *The Excursion*, and *The Excursion* misjudged for want of *The Prelude*. Wordsworth was misjudged for want of that explanatory biography that *The Prelude* contained. Shelley would have better understood his change of mind from early republicanism to the later Tory politics. Keats's judgement would not have been altered in essence, for he understood Wordsworth thoroughly and rightly, but *The Prelude* would have helped him to fill up and supplement his opinions. Byron and people like him—all the smart worldly folk who depreciated the 'Lakers' or 'Lakists'—would not have judged Wordsworth according to what Hood called his 'Betty foibles'.[1] *The Excursion*, as Wordsworth's deliberate, careful explanation of his life, is a book of authority, but it does not tell the truth about the poet as *The Prelude* does. It has too much, not perhaps of art, but of translation and paraphrase.

[1] Hood, *Works* (1870), ii. 369 ('Literary Reminiscences', No. iv).

Wordsworth, instead of telling directly what he has known, as in *The Prelude*, arranges his impressions, even altering the features of the landscape he has known.

Wordsworth's early ideas should be compared with Coleridge's. It is not unjust to say there is a great deal of twaddle in Coleridge's early blank verse, as in the *Religious Musings*, for example, and other pieces of the same tone and same kind of argument. One has to clear away the fallacies, the bad taste, the imperfect art, before one can appreciate the true poetry of Coleridge. Among what one may reckon the fallacies is the humanitarian republican sentiment. This is said without prejudice, for there is nothing in any form of political, moral, or religious belief that makes it unfit, or less fit than another form, for poetry. What one ventures to censure in Coleridge is the conventional, hackneyed, hypocritical delight in philanthropic humanitarian formulas. Although Wordsworth was always more sober in his flights of humanitarianism than Coleridge or Southey, he had the republican fervour in a form which is not thoroughly remembered in his reminiscences. If you go back to the actual documents of the time, to his early republican essay, *A Letter to the Bishop of Landaff* (1793), you can see that his thought was much more crude and violent than as represented and harmonized in *The Prelude*. Again, in Wordsworth, though you may detect sometimes a conventional mode of thought and speech about the natural dignity of man and so on, the republican ideas are drawn from actual experience. The contrast of the free, independent countryman, the simple man living upon the land, with the sophisticated townsman is an old commonplace, older than Rousseau who gave it a renewed currency in European literature. But Wordsworth derived his knowledge and notions of equality not from books, but from life, from mixing with the 'statesmen', the small freeholders of Cumberland and Westmorland, who had each a strong sense of independence and no fear of any mortal man. Yet, in spite of this sincere and natural origin of Wordsworth's republicanism, there is every now and again something of the conventional formulas of the friends of Rousseau.

Wordsworth in his writings, when talking of himself,

shows much more likeness to the enthusiastic authors than to the merely contemplative—particularly to Rousseau and Carlyle. Carlyle, with his tumultuous energy, his insistence, his outcries, seems at first very different from the quiet, grave Wordsworth. But, if one looks at Wordsworth's writings, one finds 'passion', 'passionate', coming again and again as a word summing up what he most admires. Wordsworth is misunderstood partly through neglect of his prose. The early republican tract was unpublished, perhaps fortunately for himself. But, long after that, long after the great crisis that changed his republicanism, there is the tract on *The Convention of Cintra* (1809), a curious flaming thing, and, like much of the writing on that subject, only partially informed, its indignation not being properly justified by the facts. The right or wrong of the subject does not here matter. What it is important to note is that Wordsworth, writing in sympathy with the popular indignation, makes the tract almost throughout a eulogy of 'passion'. The Spaniards are right in their resistance to the French tyranny, and Wordsworth seems to think they are most right where they are most 'impassioned'. He has that lawless sympathy with 'energy' which one finds in Blake in one form, and in another very questionable form in much of the literature of that time, particularly German literature—such things as are burlesqued in *The Anti-Jacobin*. Wordsworth seems to hold that 'passion', right or wrong, is self-justified—it is anyway 'life'. This is his habitual thought and very different from the tame sort of dull contemplation commonly attributed to him.

Wordsworth's earliest writings are in the eighteenth-century style, in couplets of the old fashion and with plenty of the old artifice. There is distinct value in *An Evening Walk* and *Descriptive Sketches*. They are not very like his later poems, but they have a good deal of his mind, particularly in the attention to particulars. Wordsworth had learned the aspects of nature from his own life in the proper way, not as a tourist coming to look at the country in the holidays, but as a country boy, living in the country. Yet he did not rely merely on the knowledge he got through his own life, but came to reflect seriously on landscape. One effect of this study was that he began to pride himself on his skill in finding new aspects in nature. In this respect his skill is something like Tennyson's—especially in the early work, for later there is less attention to minute things, less of landscape, more of the feeling, more of general impression. Tennyson picks out the obvious things that few people notice—such as 'black as ashbuds in the front of March',[1] which so impressed the old gentleman in *Cranford*.[2] Wordsworth in his early poetry does the same.

Descriptive Sketches ought to be compared with *The Traveller*. Goldsmith's poem is made up out of his own travels on the Continent, and *Descriptive Sketches* are the poetic result of the tour of Wordsworth and Robert Jones in the long vacation of 1790. Both poems go over much the same ground; Wordsworth and Jones walked through Calais, France, Switzerland, over the Simplon to Lake Como, and back again in fourteen weeks, and out of the memories of that time Wordsworth made his poem. The *Descriptive Sketches* are not very well arranged; they have too much art in one way, too little in another. Wordsworth was not content simply to make a rhyming diary of the journey, which would have been interesting. Yet he does not arrange his scenes sufficiently carefully to get a new ideal frame for the matter; he modifies and selects, but not enough. However, one can still find meaning and interest in the poem, and it is instructive to compare it with the same subjects as treated in *The Prelude*. Perhaps the best way to appreciate *Descriptive Sketches* is to compare them with other works about the same time in the same old verse—with Rogers's *Pleasures of Memory*, Campbell's *Pleasures of Hope*, and, perhaps, Hayley's *Triumphs of Temper*. The difference is made by the closer relation to experience: Wordsworth is talking about what he has seen, not simply compiling ideas.

Wordsworth in his various essays, the first important one being the Preface to the second edition of the *Lyrical Ballads* in 1800, had a great deal to say, and said very fine things, about the nature of poetry. But he had not cleared up his

---

[1] Tennyson, 'The Gardener's Daughter', 28.
[2] Mr. Holbrook praises this phrase in chapter iv of *Cranford*.

ideas, and certainly had not discovered the best line of attack against things he disliked, nor the best way of recommending, indeed of explaining, what he himself admired. Probably he was confused; probably the thing was complicated in his mind through the different sorts of poetry he was composing. Much of his argument applies to some of his poetry. When he speaks of rustic language, or the language of the common people, when he says there is not, and ought not to be, any difference between the language of poetry and of prose, he is probably thinking of such poems as 'The Thorn' and 'The Idiot Boy'. In 'The Thorn' he is dramatic, speaking through an imaginary person belonging to the class he is recommending as authority. In 'The Idiot Boy', though not exactly dramatic, he is in a way pretending, assuming a simple and childish language, not the direct expression of his own mind.

Now it was direct expression that Wordsworth wanted. The essence of his whole argument was to get rid of the merely ornamental in poetry, to find for poetry a language that should not interfere, come between the minds of the poet and his hearers. Wordsworth, in dealing with this subject, was himself under a sort of glamour. He knew something of what he meant by false diction, but he had not as a reader, a critic, worked out the history of diction. He began a theoretical exposition without enough previous study, taking the first examples that came into his head, and showing very little sign of any real study of Pope and Dryden.[1] And he does not

---

[1] In the 'Essay Supplementary to the Preface' of 1815 Wordsworth quotes an example of false language from Dryden's *The Indian Emperor, or, The Conquest of Mexico* (III. ii):

'A blind man, in the habit of attending accurately to descriptions casually dropped from the lips of those around him, might easily depict these appearances with more truth. Dryden's lines are vague, bombastic, and senseless. . . .'

But he did not necessarily get the well-known passage from Dryden himself. It was quoted in the same way by Thomas Warton in the first edition of his *Observations on the Faerie Queene of Spenser* (1754), p. 300:

'But what can we expect from a critic [Rymer] who confesses himself to be struck with this choice representation of the night in Dryden's conquest of Mexico?

All things are husht, as Nature's self lay dead;
The mountains seem to nod their drowsy head:
The little birds in dreams their songs repeat,
And sleeping flowers beneath the night-dew sweat.
Ev'n Lust and Envy sleep.—   [*Cont. on next page*

deal with the real adversaries to poetic simplicity—the company of poets of Wordsworth's own time who were using the old manner in a merely artificial way, with more ornament than Dryden and Pope, the great masters of the old school. If he had taken Erasmus Darwin as his example, he might have succeeded better in saying what he really meant. Darwin, in his *Botanic Garden*, is the great example in English literature of the periphrastic order of poetry, that takes any subject and turns it into poetry by the use of regular devices of amplification, of periphrasis, or ornament. It is a kind of literature which flourishes in the decay of classicist schools. It flourished about the same time in France, and the attack of the new romantic school in France, some of it a generation later than the *Lyrical Ballads*, was directed a good deal against the misuse of language by authors who attained a kind of magnificence by refusing to call things by their proper names.

Anyone who criticizes the poetry of the eighteenth century is bound to consider its variety, and this Wordsworth did not do. He did not take into account the poems of Pope where Pope refuses periphrastic phrases and unnecessary epithets. It is Pope, in *The Art of Sinking in Poetry* by Martinus Scriblerus, who shows up the vices of Amplification[1] in almost exactly the same language as Wordsworth in dealing with Dr. Johnson's version of 'Go to the ant, thou sluggard'.[2]

These lines are no bad burlesque; but it is their misfortune, that they are written without the least intention of producing a smile.'
It is possible that his reading of Warton gave Wordsworth this convenient stone to fling at the adversary and that he had not collected the ammunition for himself.—W.P.K.

[1] 'We may define *Amplification* to be making the most of a Thought; it is the spinning-wheel of the Bathos, which draws out and spreads it in the finest thread. . . . In the book of Job are these words, "Hast thou commanded the morning, and caused the day-spring to know his place?" How is this extended by the most celebrated Amplifier of our age? [Richard Blackmore who published his *Paraphrase on the Book of Job* in 1700]

> *Canst thou set forth th' etherial* mines on high,
> *Which the refulgent* ore *of light supply?*
> *Is the celestial* furnace *to thee known?*
> *In which* I melt *the golden* metal *down?*
> *Treasures, from which* I deal *out light as fast,*
> *As all my stars and* lavish *suns can* waste.'

Of the Art of Sinking in Poetry, chapter viii.
[2] In the Appendix to *Lyrical Ballads* (1802).

A careful, unprejudiced study of Milton will probably bring out better than Wordsworth everything Wordsworth really meant in his various discussions of poetic diction. Milton is one of the great sources of false taste in language, and also one of the best examples of simplicity. The passage in *Samson Agonistes*,

> My race of glory run, and race of shame,
> And I shall shortly be with them that rest.

has all the dignity and simplicity of diction that Wordsworth aimed at, and secured very often; the gravity, austerity, and freedom from everything merely ornamental and unnecessary that is brought out in Wordsworth's *Michael*.[1]

There is nothing very definite in the poems of the Scotch Tour of 1803 to distinguish them, or the spirit of them, from the *Lyrical Ballads*, but you may find in them, probably, a deeper, livelier feeling in the contemplation of Nature. There are two poems that should be noted particularly, 'The Solitary Reaper' and 'Rob Roy's Grave'.

'The Solitary Reaper' is not only one of the best of Wordsworth's best poems, but one of the most wonderful lyrics in the whole of literature. The occasion of it is not like that of 'Yarrow Unvisited', or 'Stepping Westward', or 'To a Highland Girl'. It is not directly from experience; Wordsworth did not see the Solitary Reaper, did not hear her song. The poem is imaginative in the ordinary trivial sense; he had got the idea from another man's record,[2] and recreated the reality for himself. The magic of the poem is not simple, and cannot be described in any one sentence. It is a poem that brings out

[1] Cf. Matthew Arnold: 'The right sort of verse to choose from Wordsworth, if we are to seize his true and most characteristic form of expression, is a line like this from *Michael*—

"And never lifted up a single stone".

There is nothing subtle in it, no heightening, no study of poetic style, strictly so called, at all; yet it is expression of the highest and most truly expressive kind.' (Preface to *The Poems of Wordsworth*, chosen and edited by Matthew Arnold (1879); reprinted in *Essays in Criticism*, Second Series).—W.P.K.

[2] 'Passed a female who was reaping alone; she sung in Erse as she bended over her sickle; the sweetest human voice I ever heard: her strains were tenderly melancholy, and felt delicious, long after they were heard no more.' Thomas Wilkinson, *Tours to the British Mountains* (read by Wordsworth in manuscript, eventually published in 1824), p. 12.

what was almost always in Wordsworth's mind, the communion between Man and Nature. Wordsworth is not a regular landscape-poet, not, as he is sometimes thought to be, a descriptive poet—at least, that is not his main interest. What he sees is not the landscape only, but the landscape as it is for the people who live in it. The Solitary Reaper, the Highland woman reaping and singing, is the voice of the whole land. And this comes out in the same way in the voice of the cuckoo, 'a voice so thrilling' being the voice of the spring time in a world which seems to be proof against the charm of spring; 'the silence of the seas'—what have the seas to do in renewing life? The voice of the cuckoo is the triumph of the new voice of the year over the desert of waters. This is the divination of Wordsworth. He had never been in the outer islands, never heard the cuckoo there; he did not know, what is true, how the cry sounds over that strange land, half moor, half water.

'Rob Roy's Grave' is a poem often neglected, with the consequence that people who do not read it think themselves entitled to a contemptuous opinion about Wordsworth. It seems at first a mere piece of rhyming sentiment, tourist's verses about an object of interest with historical associations. There is this in the occasion of it: Wordsworth was not proof against historical association, though he did not care particularly about it. But the real meaning of the poem is to declare Wordsworth's theory of action, and, by the way, to judge the character of Napoleon. The poet's mind was taken up at the time with many other things besides the beauties of Nature. He had come through the great ordeal described in *The Prelude*, but the trials of his mind were not ended; he was more than ever a fighting man, and here he utters his mind about the greatest practical and moral questions of the day. It is not sufficiently widely known now how much Bonaparte was admired in England at that time for his successes and for his greatness. Historians tell us how Fox persisted in his courtship of Bonaparte till disillusioned on coming into office after the death of Pitt. Many of the Whigs admired Bonaparte, partly, of course, to annoy the other side. But it is not generally known what sincere admiration there was for him

—in a land where he was for the general public a monster and tyrant. Wordsworth was by this time thoroughly convinced of the deadliness of Napoleon, of his danger to England and to the liberty of all the countries of Europe; but he understood his greatness, and has put that into the poem, 'Rob Roy's Grave'.

Wordsworth has also put into this poem the lawlessness of his own mind, which is strangely disguised through the moral platitudes of much of his duller writing. His moral philosophy, his practical theory of life, was really not very different from that of the Abbey of Thelème: 'Do what you like. If you don't like the right things, then you are a beast, and will perish like beasts. That is your own look-out.' Wordsworth's admiration for energy is seen everywhere. What is false or wrong, in his view, is dullness and deadness. The poem on Rob Roy's grave is a lyric in praise of energy, energy without law making its own law: the birds and beasts are happy because their lives are ruled by the law of might; they are kept in their proper places, and do not strive for what is out of their reach, beyond their proper world.

> The creatures see of flood and field,
> And those that travel on the wind!
> With them no strife can last; they live
>   In peace, and peace of mind.
>
> For why?—because the good old rule
> Sufficeth them, the simple plan,
> That they should take, who have the power,
>   And they should keep who can.[1]

What is good is powerful; power may be turned to bad ends, but in essence it is good.

At the same time the poem plays into Wordsworth's political ideas. To use the method of Blake, Wordsworth sees the spiritual form of Napoleon or Rob Roy working in the glorious heroic manner which Wordsworth discovers even in the enemy, the 'present Boast'[2] of France. It is an ideal vision and glorification of the power of the conqueror, who is also a reshaper of the kingdoms of the earth. Wordsworth has

---

[1] ll. 33–40.   [2] l. 95.

another poem in the same book, a satiric sonnet against the conventional flatterers of Bonaparte, the mean admirers of his power;[1] but he himself nobly admires what he discovers as noble in the great man who is his enemy. In many other poems of 1807 Wordsworth comes out as an 'heroic' poet, not in the old technical sense of maker of an heroic poem, but as a lyric poet for heroism, as in 'The Happy Warrior' and many of the political sonnets. There is a great likeness between the motive of 'Rob Roy's Grave' and the argument of the prose essay on the Convention of Cintra. The hero, who is not exactly Rob Roy, not exactly Napoleon, the idealized Rob Roy with the spiritual qualities of Bonaparte, is very like the Spanish people rising against tyranny, and justified in the same way, because of their energy. The idea is much the same as that of Blake, expressed most clearly in *The Marriage of Heaven and Hell*. The love of heroism is, of course, another aspect of the love of energy, but is not exactly the same thing. It is one of the great injustices of popular opinion that Wordsworth is not recognized for his heroism and energy. There was surely hardly ever a book more full of the true heroic spirit, of courage and passion, than those two volumes of 1807, with 'Rob Roy's Grave, 'The Happy Warrior', and the magnificent sonnets on the great contest then going on.

In 'Rob Roy's Grave' one should note Wordsworth's ironical humour, which is often so subtle that it escapes notice. There are many people who think Wordsworth could not see a joke. Two jokes of the poet's are recorded, but these do not prove anything one way or another about the irony in his poetry. The jokes are these. Wordsworth came in one day from a walk, laughing to himself. When asked what amused him, he said he had met a tramp who inquired of him, 'Sir, have you seen my wife?', to which he answered, 'My good man, I did not even know you were married.' The other was during Wordsworth's laureateship, on the occasion of a fancy-dress ball given by Queen Victoria. The poet was told that Monckton Milnes was going as Chaucer, to which he replied,

[1]
> Is it a reed that's shaken by the wind,
> Or what is it that ye go forth to see?

('Calais, August, 1802.')

'Then I don't see what is left for me, but to go as Monckton Milnes.' These historical facts are relevant here, for they show the judgement of Wordsworth by his contemporaries; the jokes were evidently regarded as exceptional. The irony of Wordsworth is a different thing from facetious wit. It comes out clearly in 'Rob Roy's Grave' in the contrast, the contradiction, between the lawless admiration there explained and the implied or understood respectability of the author. The poet takes the tone of a moralist while he is praising in the most reckless way the votaries of the servants of 'the good old rule', 'the simple plan'. The play of thought between the general advocacy of lawlessness and the two different examples of the ideal lawless hero makes the imaginative argument very far from the hypocritical and hackneyed themes of ordinary moralizing poetry.

One should note, too, what may be called the 'louder' poems of Wordsworth, the poems that sound like war-songs. These are not the highest kind of poetry, for war-songs naturally require the trumpet and drum, and strong emphasis. The sonnet of November 1806, written after Jena,

> Another year!—another deadly blow!
> Another mighty Empire overthrown!

is 'louder' than the rest, and has the true virtue of war-poetry —encouragement. There is nothing in Dryden stronger than this sonnet in the way of fighting poetry, and the motive is as lofty as one finds in any poet making poetry for the sake of his country. The ending of the sonnet,

> danger which they fear
> And honour which they do not understand,

comes, as Wordsworth points out, from Fulke Greville's *Life of Sir Philip Sidney*. One of the differences between the poems of 1800 and 1807 is the greater amount of quotation in the latter volume. Wordsworth had always been fond of quotation, of working in borrowed phrases.

The poems of 1807 show the surrender of Wordsworth's theory of poetic diction, at least of a great part of it. Wordsworth does not really believe that there is no difference between the language of poetry and that of prose, or that the

language of poetry ought to be a selection of the language
common among men. In 1807 he plunges without reserve
into the ocean of poetry, and poetry is now what it had been
for the old poets, and what it really had always been for him,
though he dissembled in his argument. The language of
poetry is anything a poet can make use of, the most magnificent, most uncommon words and phrases if the poet can employ them to a good end; consider, for example, the beauty of

     ... 'with pomp of waters, unwithstood',[1]

and   Armoury of the invincible Knights of old.

The influence of the older poets is shown in the verse also.
Wordsworth had always been attentive to stanza forms, and
there is a good deal of variety in the early books of 1798 and
1800. The 1798 volume, which contains the trivial verse (as
it is sometimes considered) of 'The Idiot Boy', contains also
the lyrical blank verse of 'Tintern Abbey'; one calls it 'lyrical'
because that is Wordsworth's own account of it.[2] He does
not venture to call the poem an Ode, but he thinks of it as
such, and its 'impassioned music' brings it near the sublimest
heights of English lyrical poetry. But while there is this
variety in the earliest book of 1798, there is a good deal more
in 1807, and the variety is there very clearly the result of
artistic study, of meditation on the older poets, and the choice
of modes suggested by them or directly given by them.

Wordsworth had used the Spenserian stanza in 1798, in
'The Female Vagrant'. Now in 1807 he uses some stanzas of
the Spenserian school. 'Resolution and Independence' is in
the stanza used by Milton for some of his early poems, for
'On the Death of a Fair Infant', and, much better, for the
proem of 'On the Morning of Christ's Nativity'. It is a most
beautiful stanza, composed of the old rhyme royal with an
alexandrine, instead of a simple ten-syllable line at the end.
The 'Ode to Duty', which is one of the best proofs to be
found of the continuity of tradition in English poetry, of the

---

[1] Borrowed from Samuel Daniel's *Civil Wars*, ii. st. 7.

[2] See note to the 1800 edition: 'I have not ventured to call this Poem an Ode;
but it was written with a hope that in the transitions and the impassioned music
of the versification would be found the principal requisites of that species of
composition.'

value of example, and yet of what one may call freedom from compulsion in following a pattern, is in the stanza of Gray's 'Hymn to Adversity'; and this itself is in a stanza formed on the principles of the Spenserian school, on the principles Milton followed in his stanzas. It is Spenserian because it ends with an alexandrine, and so belongs to that tradition of the regular long-drawn-out cadence of the twelve-syllable line. Wordsworth follows Gray's stanza exactly. More than that, he copies, repeats the poetical mood of Gray, the temper and emotion of the 'Hymn to Adversity'. And yet all this copying and following leaves the 'Ode to Duty' one of the most original poems in the language, as it is one of the noblest.

The 'Ode to Duty' is one of the poems in which the mythology of Wordsworth comes rather near to the old convention of mythology without being 'conventional'. The personification of abstract qualities is one of the commonest devices— used by every schoolboy, one might say. But, in spite of that dull tradition, of all the misuse of allegory, the goddess in Wordsworth's poem is as real as the goddess in Collins's 'Ode to Evening',[1] as truly imaginative, and therefore as worshipful. At the end of the 'Ode' there is a likeness to one of the old Greek half-mythological, half-philosophical ideas, a likeness which brings out the full dignity of Wordsworth's imagination. Duty, 'stern Daughter of the Voice of God' (a phrase which has been often challenged by those who did not know it had been used before by Milton)[2] is first thought of as a lawgiver to men, giving laws of life, action, and conduct to mortals. But the goddess is more to Wordsworth than that; she is the life of the whole universe. Heraclitus of Ephesus said that if the sun were to wander from his path, the Erinnys, the executors of justice, would punish the wrong-doer and drive him back again.[3] That is the thought at the end of the poem of Wordsworth: moral law is also physical law.

---

[1] Cf. p. 230 below.

[2]
> God so commanded, and left that Command
> Sole Daughter of his voice; the rest, we live
> Law to our selves, our Reason is our Law.
>
> (*Paradise Lost*, ix. 652-4.)

[3] ἥλιος γὰρ οὐχ ὑπερβήσεται [τὰ] μέτρα· εἰ δὲ μή, Ἐρινύες μιν Δίκης ἐπίκουροι ἐξευρήσουσιν. Diels, *Die Fragmente der Vorsokratiker*, frag. 94.

Thou dost preserve the stars from wrong;
And the most ancient heavens, through Thee, are fresh and strong.

The book of 1807 ends with the poem called by Wordsworth simply 'Ode', 'There was a time when meadow, grove,
and stream. . . .' It may be debated whether the 'Ode to Duty'
or this 'Ode' is the greater. There is no doubt that they are
together among the highest, most sublime things, in English
poetry. Instead of discussing which is the greater, it is more
convenient simply to note the difference in form that makes
a difference of quality in the poetry. The 'Ode to Duty' is in
regular stanzas; the other 'Ode' is a Pindaric in the rough
English sense of the term, being in irregular verse, in no
recurring stanza, not like Gray's 'Bard' or 'The Progress of
Poesy', but Pindaric in the seventeenth-century sense, like
'Alexander's Feast', and the 'Ode in Memory of Mrs. Anne
Killigrew'. Note one difference between the 'Ode on the
Intimations of Immortality' and the irregular mode of verse
authorized by Milton in 'Lycidas' and the poems 'On Time'
and 'At a Solemn Music'. The base is the same in all the
poems: all are founded on the old Italian convention, which
has nature for its source, the relation between the ten-syllable
and six-syllable line (in Italian eleven and seven, for in Italian
there is the regular additional unaccented syllable), the harmony of which Dante explained in his Latin essay on Italian
poetry,[1] and which never betrays the hearts of those that have
loved it. The principle has been proved and approved by
Spenser, Milton, Wordsworth, Keats, and all the lyrical
poets of the nobler, more ambitious sort, who have attempted
the lofty Ode. But in Wordsworth's 'Ode' the relations are
not observed so strictly as by Milton. There is much greater
variety of the lengths of verse, and changes of measure, the
iambic not being strictly kept throughout. This change of
measure is found in the seventeenth-century Pindarics, and
Wordsworth no doubt was influenced by them.

∾

Nowhere else than in *The Prelude* is there to be found such

---

[1] *De vulgari eloquentia*, II. v. Cf. Ker, *Form and Style in Poetry*, pp. 332 ff., and
The Art of Poetry, p. 17.

a record of continuous and triumphant passion making a way for itself, under its own laws, through the stages of boyhood and youth to the middle age in which the poetical faculty attained its full powers. The beauty of Wordsworth's autobiography is that nothing in it comes from mere theory or doctrine; the theory and the doctrine reveal themselves as the product of natural forces. More than anything he dislikes and pities the premature intelligence encouraged by educational reformers; precocious learning and reflectiveness in children he thinks pitiable. The story of his childhood and boyhood is an enthusiastic description of all kinds of adventure. His knowledge of Nature was gained in climbing among the crags, setting snares for woodcock, rowing, skating, every possible kind of free exercise and movement. The slow mooning person which Wordsworth seemed to be in later life is hardly to be found in *The Prelude*, at any rate before the period of depression which followed his return from France. The brisk reviewers who made fun of his slowness did not know how fiery a youth had preceded the contemplative temper of *The Excursion*.

Wordsworth claims for himself a mission to interpret Nature. He found himself 'a dedicated spirit' (early one morning on his way home from a dancing party);[1] he was more definitely and intensely conscious of his vocation than any poet, more even than Milton. For Milton's ambition had always something of the school in it, something formal and abstract; he was to compete with the old masters of heroic verse, to win the prize for Epic or Tragedy. Wordsworth took his start from reality; he had something to say—what had been specially revealed to him in the accidents of his life. His poetical task was to find expression for this acquired knowledge, this always increasing knowledge of his. Milton with equal confidence in his mission was less certain about his themes. But this is saying little; for Wordsworth's security in the value of his own experience goes beyond all possibility of comparison and calculation; it is something absolute.

It is not easy to determine or explain what Wordsworth meant by Nature; or, rather, it is easy to explain prosaically

[1] *Prelude*, iv. 309 ff.

in such a way as to leave the result unprofitable. It may be turned from poetry into metaphysics; it is so translated, sometimes, by Wordsworth himself. But the source of Wordsworth's theory is poetical, not distinctly philosophical, though it touches often on philosophy. Where it is most philosophical it is a belief in Imagination (on one occasion called 'the imaginative Will')[1] as a power of interpreting the world; not altering reality nor remoulding the elements of the world, but reading it truly. It is this faculty that gets beyond ordinary partial, trivial, disconnected perceptions, and finds the solemn movement of experience. By Imagination Wordsworth attains something like a mystical vision of the whole world as a living thing, every fragment of the world alive with the life of the whole. But this is hardly what is distinctive of his poetry, for such visions have come to prose philosophers. And a formal theory of this sort is not protected against base uses; it may become, as Blake says of general ideas, the refuge of the scoundrel and the hypocrite.[2] Wordsworth the poet is to be judged by his poetry, and not by the ideas that may be abstracted from it.

Wordsworth separates himself, explicitly, from the eighteenth-century pursuit of the beauties of Nature—pampering the eye with meagre novelties,[3] &c. The picturesque as studied and explained, for example, by William Gilpin had some attraction for Wordsworth (his early poetry shows this); and part of his business was to notice and recollect aspects of scenery hitherto unused in art. But this kind of observation, never without interest for Wordsworth, was a subordinate part of his work. Closeness to reality—'his eye upon his object'[4]—was consistently his aim; but his study of Nature involved more than the notice of facts; Nature was more than the object of the senses. Full of 'danger or desire',[5]

---

[1] *The Excursion*, iv. 1128. [2] Cf. p. 233 below.
[3] *The Prelude*, xii. 117.
[4] 'That [Dryden's] cannot be the language of imagination must have necessarily followed from this, that there is not a single image from Nature in the whole body of his works; and in his translation from Virgil, whenever Virgil can be fairly said to have his *eye* upon his object, Dryden always spoils the passage.' From a letter to Scott, 7 November 1805. *The Early Letters of William and Dorothy Wordsworth* (1787–1805), ed. E. de Selincourt (Oxford, 1935), p. 541.
[5] *The Prelude*, i. 472.

Nature could only be rendered poetically by an enthusiastic imagination. 'The picturesque' might be taken coolly and estimated technically in the terms used by Henry Tylney and his sister in *Northanger Abbey* discussing the landscape around Bath[1]—'fore-grounds, distances and second distances—side-screens and perspectives', and so on—but Wordsworth's point of view is generally different. His didactic exposition of Nature no doubt often seemed to be much the same thing as had been customary for a generation or two before him with students of the picturesque, but his imagination and his theory of imagination were original and his own. Even in the more didactic of his writings, and even apart from his poetical work altogether, as in the tract on the Convention of Cintra, he declares himself for passionate imagination as a nobler guide than dispassionate understanding. 'A creature of a "fiery heart" ',[2] his poetry seemed to him to derive its virtue from something more than observation; the prophetic vision was idle, was nothing at all, without the prophetic ecstasy.

His theory of poetical diction, like his study of Nature, has some superficial likeness to things already current in literature. Pope himself has been vouched for evidence against the common gradus methods of versification.[3] Churchill and Cowper had dissented from the traditional rhetoric, and Johnson had contrasted Truth and Nature with the 'sleepy bards' and their 'mechanick echoes'.[4] In a revolutionary age there was nothing peculiar in the advocacy of simple speech as against ornate terms. Wordsworth, however, had a meaning of his own in the doctrine of poetical language expounded in his Preface of 1800 and his Essay of 1815. His argument included at least two distinct positions. First, a commonplace and generally plausible objection to 'poetic diction', in so far as that was merely a conventional vocabulary, to be learned like grammar by practitioners of verse, and applied as a sort of ornamental plaster to any subject.

[1] Cf. p. 118 below.

[2]   'O Nightingale! thou surely art
                   A creature of a "fiery heart" . . .'
                                 (Poems of the Imagination.)

[3] See p. 92 above.   [4] See p. 67 above.

So far, the spirit of the time was with him. But Wordsworth
had also a theory of his own which went somewhat further
than the correction of false rhetoric, and not only discouraged
any loftiness of style in verse but emphatically recommended
the use of colloquial language. In this there was something,
as Coleridge remarked, of bravado, and in some of the *Lyrical
Ballads* he had to force himself to write down to his theory.
But there was more in his theory than a revolutionary level-
ling of diction; more than a polemic faith in the equality of
words. He had, no doubt, a strong democratic belief in the
vanity of class distinctions among words; and this, like other
democratic equalities, sometimes ended in a preference for
the lower and a proscription of the nobler orders. But besides
this injustice, which sprang from a preconceived and wilful
Sansculottism, he had some genuine artistic and poetical
reasons for his doctrine. He wished to get rid of all inter-
ference between the poetical object and the mind; the theme
as conceived by the poet must tell itself in its own way. The
true poetic conception must find its own language, and that
language must be such as to convey, not particular fragmentary beauties, but the whole conception as a unity. The
poetical ground and the best justification of Wordsworth's
theory is that intense devotion to the subject in hand which
could not endure any frittering down of the single artistic
idea into separate details; the phrasing must be kept low in
order that the conception, the emotional and imaginative
theme complete and self-sufficient, might have its own way.

The fallacies of Wordsworth's prefaces were examined
and detected in Coleridge's *Biographia Literaria*. Wordsworth's own practice was easily shown to be inconsistent,
even in the volumes of 1798 and 1800. In the interval
between 1800 and the poems of 1807, which include the two
great Odes and the Sonnets, Wordsworth had been brought
into a more conformable temper by his study of the Elizabethans, Sidney, Daniel, Drayton, and of Milton; and his
poetical dress became less austere—not refusing even the
loan of jewels from the old masters. But this implicit with-
drawal of his more violent thesis did not affect his main
position, except to strengthen it: the point, namely, that the

poetical idea, or view, or whatever it may be called, the poetical comprehension of the theme, must determine the expression of it to the minutest point of detail. There was nothing
new in this, but few poets have lived in this artistic faith with
such constancy as Wordsworth. If there is light in the body
of his poetry, it is because his eye is single. And the sincerity
of his poetical insight (which he called imagination) is the
same as its passionate motive.

The demonstration of this is the whole scope and upshot
of *The Prelude*. There is the breadth of the world between
this fervent sincerity and the tame collector of scenery, the
disparager of the glories of verse that by many of his contemporaries was mistaken for Wordsworth the poet. Wordsworth's policy has some resemblance to what is commonly
called realism, in its inclusion of subjects beneath the conventional dignity of art. But realism, as that is commonly
understood, works in a dispassionate temper, making intelligent notes and observations, without affection. This was not
Wordsworth's way. He does not fix upon common or mean
things with a cool determination to make them interesting,
to force them into the mould of his poetry. This is what he
often seemed to be doing, and this provoked the fastidious
readers. They thought that they were being held by the un-
courtly poet and compelled to look at disgusting objects:
duffle cloaks, wash tubs, polygamic potters, and so forth,
according to the familiar catalogue which was repeated in
various tones of resentment or ridicule by the adverse and
protesting critics. But the motive of Wordsworth (apart from
some extravagances) was not the prosaic revolutionary prejudice for common things as such, against the noble or the
magnificent. On the contrary, the loftiness of his poetic
thought, the fire of his poetic zeal, transcend anything in his
contemporaries.

Sir Walter Scott

IT is almost impossible to avoid making some comparison between Chaucer and Scott: they have the same virtues—charity, tolerance, sincerity, honesty—and similar faults, faults which in them are as amiable as their virtues: the same recklessness in composition, the same preference of speed, freedom, and the impulse of the moment, to all 'counsels of perfection'. They have the same humorous self-depreciation, so irritating to many earnest persons. The solemn lamentation of Carlyle[1] might have been addressed to Chaucer with no less justice—and no more—than to Scott.

The great defect in the art of Scott is not that charged by Stevenson, namely his carelessness in thinking out and presenting scenes as they come. Stevenson quotes a passage from *Guy Mannering* where he makes out that Scott discovers what is wanted as he goes on and adds as he goes on, instead of going back and reshaping in the right way.[2] But this haste in composition does not really matter; it is carried off by the speed and liveliness of the story. In the passage noted by Stevenson there is life all through; it is a momentous passage in the story, and the little irregularities in presentation do not spoil the effect. The faults are noted only if you stand at the wrong distance.

But the real defect of Scott lies in the frequent sudden

[1] 'Literature *has* other aims than that of harmlessly amusing indolent languid men: or if Literature have them not, then Literature is a very poor affair; and something else must have them, and must accomplish them, with thanks or without thanks; the thankful or thankless world were not long a world otherwise! Under this head there is little to be sought or found in the Waverley Novels. Not profitable for doctrine, for reproof, for edification, for building up or elevating, in any shape! The sick heart will find no healing here, the darkly-struggling heart no guidance: the Heroic that is in all men no divine awakening voice. We say, therefore, that they do not found themselves on deep interests, but on comparatively trivial ones; not on the perennial, perhaps not even on the lasting. In fact, much of the interest of these Novels results from what may be called contrasts of costume. The phraseology, fashion of arms, of dress and life, belonging to one age, is brought suddenly with singular vividness before the eyes of another.' Carlyle, 'Sir Walter Scott' (1838), reprinted in *Critical and Miscellaneous Essays* (7 vols., 1888), vi. 70.

[2] 'A Gossip on Romance' (1882), reprinted in *Memories and Portraits*.

shifting from true imagination to mere literary artifice. He is sometimes theatrical, or, as J. L. Adolphus very truly puts it, 'not properly dramatic but melodramatic'[1] (an early use of the term 'melodramatic' in our modern sense). There is not always in Scott's work the unity or continuity that you find in Jane Austen, the certainty of every part corresponding to other parts and helping the single effect, the unity of impression. There is something of Mrs. Radcliffe in the Waverley Novels, an occasional reliance on the mechanical stock devices.

As in the plays of Shakespeare, the Waverley Novels sometimes have too quick an ending, sometimes too slow a sequel after the real story is over. *The Heart of Midlothian* goes on after the real story is finished, and the end of *Old Mortality*, though in a less degree, is artistically weak after the exile of Henry Morton. Scott may be compared with Dickens in that he has made one compact novel. *The Talisman*, like *A Tale of Two Cities*, is a romance where the plot is carefully knit up, where the plot is the main thing, where the other excellencies of the story-teller do not come out in the same way as in the less carefully constructed stories.

With regard to Scott's gift of story-telling, people apply to him his own phrase of Mr. Jonathan Oldbuck in *The Antiquary*[2]—'he wad wile the bird aff the tree wi' the tales he tells about folk lang syne'. It is a mistake to take this as the whole story. Scott has the gift of story-telling, but not independently of the eternal principles, of the beginning, middle and end, though he varied, as did Shakespeare, in his respect for those principles. The Waverley Novels are not to be considered simply as spun yarns meant to 'wile the bird

[1] 'As the beauty of these tales is often enhanced by their admirable dramatic effect, so too they occasionally lose in elegance and simplicity by an over-ambitious seeking after what are technically called coups-de-théatre. There are some, I will not say many passages of both writers, in which either the transactions themselves are so remote from common nature, or the coincidences of time, place, situation of parties, and other accidents, are contrived with such apparent study, and so much previous sacrifice of probability, that the scene when fully opened appears not properly dramatic, but melo-dramatic.' J. L. Adolphus, *Letters to Richard Heber, Esq. containing Critical Remarks on the Series of Novels beginning with Waverley, and an Attempt to ascertain their Author* (1821), p. 156.

[2] Chapter ii.

aff the tree'. There is a great difference of art among them, and in the best the kind of plot is peculiarly well adapted for the sort of adventure, the sort of humour, of drama, which Scott could manage. Take, for example, *Waverley*. The story makes use of all Scott knew about the '45, both from books and from talk, particularly from the converse of an old friend, Stewart of Invernahyle, who had been out with Charles Edward, so that the story has the interest of the history of the time as experienced by people who were in it. But this is not enough. The hero, Edward Waverley, is dramatically placed so that he is between two attractions, two loyalties, and in very great difficulties between the two motives, the two attractions. Scott gets very near to the tension of tragedy, but never quite uses it. The position of Waverley in his wanderings is a very cruel one, one in which the human being is exposed to a great deal of pain and danger. He is wandering in a way where his own misjudgement contributes something to his troubles, but where much more is due to chance—and chance is another name for the complicating, conflicting opposition of two loyalties. The opposition is like that of Shakespeare's Wars of the Roses, or of the Montagues and Capulets in *Romeo and Juliet*—a great unknown, incalculable, inscrutable force, which might well be used by a tragic poet as similar forces are used in the *Cid* of Corneille. Scott, however, keeps to the narrative romance, and the duty of the narrative romance is not to concentrate as tragedy does on the souls of the personages, but to keep things more diffuse, more comfortable, to give the promise of a happy ending.

There is almost exactly the same position in *Old Mortality*, where the tension is even greater than in *Waverley*. Henry Morton is between two forces also, between loyalty to the king and sympathy with the religion of his countrymen, or, rather, with as much of their religion as meant independence. He is led into the strife by being unjustly accused of sheltering the murderer of Archbishop Sharp, for, though he had helped Balfour, he had not known of the murder. He is sentenced to death by Claverhouse, and within five minutes of his sentence his life is spared. Then, after the battle of Drumclog, he becomes leader of the Covenanters, and has to attack the castle of Tillietudlem where Edith Bellenden is living. Here is all the strain required in heroic drama, and in addition the suspicion against him in the minds of the true Covenanters. After the battle of Bothwell Brig he is again in danger of execution, this time at the hands of the fanatics, Ephraim Macbriar and Habakkuk Mucklewrath, and again the rescue is only just in time.

But Scott, in spite of all this, never turns the screw so as to come out as a tragic poet would, or as a romantic dramatist like Victor Hugo. The story is kept at its true narrative pitch, but never goes beyond it. There is the shadowing of tragedy all through *Old Mortality*, but never the tragic inference. This is the right way of narrative, and it is that sort of tragic shadow, which never turns to tragedy, which makes the narrative unity, the beauty and effect, of *Waverley* and *Old Mortality*.

The peculiar character of Scott's romance, then, is that it *is* romance and not tragedy, and at the same time a record of seemingly ordinary life. It requires generally the strange conditions of romantic setting, which are necessary in romance, though not everything, as the mechanical followers of Scott seem to think. In romance, as distinct from the stronger kind of story which may be called epic or (if in dramatic form) tragedy, the characters need not have much value. The characters in the Waverley Novels are certainly much more definite than the knights in the books of chivalry, but Waverley, Francis Osbaldistone, and the rest are rather focuses of the story than of essential importance as characters. In this comparatively unimportant character-interest Scott differs from Jane Austen.

Romance is distinguished from the deeper forms of the imagination in its refusal to make things definite, to bring things to the highest pitch of definiteness and individuality. Romance is diffuse and vague when compared with the intensity of the drama. Scott's prose romances have the wandering, more comfortable, easy-going breadth of interest in many people and places found in the romance of real life.

The Waverley Novels differ from the rhyming tales in taking in a great many things excluded from the poetic form;

for example, the 'humours'. Few things are more effective in Scott than the way in which the low-comedy characters are made to play into the romantic scheme—for example, the way in which Andrew Fairservice plays into the story of Francis Osbaldistone and Miss Vernon. Of all the passages in Scott's novels there are none more representative than those on Francis Osbaldistone in Glasgow in *Rob Roy*. Everything is there. It is a crisis in the story, where the vague dangers threaten Francis Osbaldistone more and more, till suddenly a great deal of the mystery is cleared up by the revelation in prison of Mr. Campbell as Rob Roy. All the setting of the scene is as true to nature as the author can make it, with nothing exaggerated or uncontrolled. The speeches of Andrew Fairservice are a sort of comic relief, a spice of comedy after the tragic intensity, more or less after the fashion of the old drama when the clown comes in. The whole is cleverly composed—all the different personages being of different values, and all the different modes of conversation playing together artistically.

Scott shows great skill in managing different 'humours' of the same kind. Think of the idiomatic language of Bailie Nicol Jarvie and Andrew Fairservice, two speakers having much in common, and yet distinct, and, again, the extraordinary way in which the fanaticism of the Covenanters in *Old Mortality* is varied according to the personages. Ephraim Macbriar and Habakkuk Mucklewrath and the rest are all enthusiastic users of the Old Testament language and have all been educated in the same way of speaking in denunciation, yet the nature of each individual speaker is brought out in every case. All the prophecies, too, come into the story and form part of the adventures; they are not mere rhetoric, and are not dragged in simply as an exhibition of the different types of humanity, as Ben Jonson drags in his Puritan humours.

The romantic change in the eighteenth century, the increasing vogue of things that seem in a way to anticipate Scott, came much more from architecture, from castles and cathedrals, than from books. This is true of the greatest of modern romantic authors, true even of Scott, who is, of course, a student of old languages. Scott's romance is informed much more by the places, the castles, and churches of his native land than by anything really literary. This fact comes out in many people older than Scott. The Wartons (Thomas the younger and Joseph), for example, were great admirers of old architecture, particularly Winchester Cathedral and Windsor Castle; and the poetry of Chatterton had its origin in every sense in the church of St. Mary Redcliffe, Bristol.

The use of background in Mrs. Radcliffe's novels should be noted. It is not worked in the same way as in Scott, but for the reading public it must have had much the same effect. Scott generally, though not always, had real knowledge of the scenes he was rendering. Mrs. Radcliffe quite boldly worked up a world of her own, in which very little besides the names corresponds with the map. In *The Mysteries of Udolpho* Emily and her father live on the banks of the River Garonne in the sixteenth century with an extensive view of the Pyrénées to the south.[1] When leaving the Pyrénées they seem to travel on a carriage-road along the line of the mountains, more or less.[2] But this does not really matter to the reading public in a work of fiction. The fashion of romantic scenery spread from Mrs. Radcliffe's works and not first of

[1] 'On the pleasant banks of the Garonne, in the province of Gascony, stood, in the year 1584, the chateau of Monsieur St. Aubert. From its windows were seen the pastoral landscapes of Guienne and Gascony stretching along the river, gay with luxuriant woods and vines, and plantations of olives. To the south, the view was bounded by the majestic Pyrénées, whose summits, veiled in clouds, or exhibiting awful forms, seen, and lost again, as the partial vapours rolled along, were sometimes barren, and gleamed through the blue tinge of air, and sometimes frowned with forests of gloomy pine, that swept downward to their base. These tremendous precipices were contrasted by the soft green of the pastures and woods that hung upon their skirts; among whose flocks, and herds, and simple cottages, the eye, after having scaled the cliffs above, delighted to repose.' (Chapter i.)

[2] 'St. Aubert, instead of taking the more direct road, that ran along the feet of the Pyrénées to Languedoc, chose one that, winding over the heights, afforded more extensive views, and greater variety of romantic scenery. . . . Emily could not restrain her transport as she looked over the pine forests of the mountains upon the vast plains, that, enriched with woods, towns, blushing vines, and plantations of almonds, palms, and olives, stretched along, till their various colours melted in distance into one harmonious hue, that seemed to unite earth with heaven. Through the whole of this glorious scene the majestic Garonne wandered; descending from its source, among the Pyrénées, and winding its blue waves towards the Bay of Biscay.' (Chapter iii.)

all from the Waverley Novels. Scott differed from the other romantic novelists of his time by his knowledge and imagination in the use of background and rendering of actual country scenes. He was not the first to introduce background into novel writing.

Jane Austen

A HUNDRED years ago[1] there were a number of young people in England engaged in writing works of fiction and sentiment. Some of those who, in the year 1797, were at work on their new inventions have had a remarkable amount of success, as things go, at least in the way of fame and honour. Miss Austen finished writing *Pride and Prejudice* in August 1797 at Steventon in Hampshire, and in November of the same year began to write the letters in which the history of *Sense and Sensibility* was told in its first draft. About the same time Landor at Swansea was finishing *Gebir* (published 1798); Wordsworth and Coleridge were walking to Lynmouth and talking about the Ancient Mariner and other Lyrical Ballads in that same month of November in which *Sense and Sensibility* was begun. It was a good year for young adventurers.

Miss Austen's work and her fortunes are in striking contrast to those of her famous contemporaries. She had apparently no difficulty and no uncertainty about the subjects and the methods best adapted to her powers. There is nothing in her life corresponding to Wordsworth's failure in tragedy, or to the confusions and distractions of metaphysics and politics in the life of Coleridge. She had never, like Wordsworth, been tempted to interfere in the direction and management of the French Revolution. She laid very little stress upon her duties as a novelist and was as little inclined to literary vanity as Scott himself; but she never was ignorant of her powers, and she never, like Scott, required to be prompted and guided by accident into the right kind of composition. Her literary life is remote from the anxieties and jealousies of competition, from the tumults of the great world and its great contests 'where that immortal garland is to be run for, not without dust and heat'; but not only does her life escape the disagreeable accidents of literary rivalries and ambitions, it is also free from the more dangerous impediments that may rise up and spoil the artist's design just when he is most secure from external annoyances—the impediments and disappointments

[1] This lecture was written before 1900.

of the mind that is not certain in its aim and not in full command of its instruments. No writer is more at ease, more at home in the business of composition. She is never distressed by misgivings about the good of it all, because she has no vanity, but simply goes on with the work she has begun; the work is set up, and because it has been begun that is reason enough for finishing it. She never presses the work or works against time; there is no hurry. Most fortunate of authors! Blessed with faculties that seem to be exempt from all the common human inaccuracies and incongruities, faculties that help and preserve one another instead of wearing one another out, she has nothing to do but to follow her own genius; there is nothing to perplex or delay her. Of course, like other workers, she has things to reconsider; the ease of her manner does not mean that she took no pains: there is the revision of *Sense and Sensibility*, the last chapters of *Persuasion*. The adversary rises at once and asks whether work of this sort can really be so very valuable: 'What's come to perfection perishes', says the adversary; the 'great Campanile is still to finish.'[1]

It is true, no doubt, that perfection implies limitation, and that (as Browning says) it is very often less interesting than imperfect work straining after impossibilities. Perfection, however, is not so common as to be altogether dull; and, besides, it was not we who said Miss Austen's novels were perfect; we only said that they were made in a singularly happy manner, and that the process of making them was only possible in virtue of a very rare combination of qualities.

The Novel has in the last hundred years been almost as exciting a subject for critics and philosophers as the Epic Poem and the Tragedy used to be in the good old times. And, as in the case of the older problems, not merely the critics who have nothing else to do, but also the authors themselves have taken in hand to discuss the ideals of construction and representation, and have fretted themselves in controversy about the proper methods and aims of the art of fiction. After all these years, however, after all the various experiments of the laborious or the daring novelists of the century,

[1] Browning, 'Old Pictures in Florence', xvii.

what if it should prove on examination that the most successful solution was found before Scott, Thackeray, and Dickens,
before Hugo and Balzac, before Flaubert and Turgenev, by
a young lady who made no more of her vocation than if it had
been sewing or knitting?

There is no name for the dominant quality in Miss Austen's work, except perhaps intelligence. It is not *wit* in the
ordinary limited sense of the word; *wits* in the wider sense is
nearer it. It is the philosophic faculty, not as that is commonly
imagined, but as it is described by Plato—the faculty of taking both a comprehensive and a discriminating view of every
subject.[1] It is this that makes her stories so vivid, because it
is this that keeps her from sacrificing the general life of the
story to any one character. It is closely related to the dramatic
faculty, but it has a wider range. It is that which does justice
to all the characters and to each part of the story; which
recognizes all the different ways in which the same things
appear to different people. It is something more than the
ordinary faculty of neat construction, of handiness in shaping
a piece of work. The perfection of Miss Austen's novels is
not mere harmony or proportion or correctness—not the old
pseudo-classic perfection of adherence to the rules. On the
contrary, it is such a vivid understanding of the fabric of life
that the representation of this fabric is itself kept moving and
changing like life itself. 'The same set of events appearing
differently to different people' is a formula that might be used
to describe her stories.

The great beauty of Miss Austen's work is that she gives
along with the separate characters and their humours something corresponding to what in larger histories is called the
'spirit of the age'; an atmosphere enveloping the scene and
the figures, indefinable, impersonal; a general movement of
life. It is this that gives largeness and freedom to her stories.
Of course, the life is restricted. In a letter to one of her nieces
who was writing a story under Miss Austen's supervision she
says, 'You are now collecting your People delightfully, getting them exactly into such a spot as is the delight of my life;
—3 or 4 Families in a Country Village is the very thing to

[1] *Phaedrus, 265d–266b.*

work on.'[1] This of course is a limitation in one way, as one of her first reviewers pointed out in the *Quarterly* of October 1815;[2] but, as the same reviewer, who was also the author of *Waverley*, goes on to remark, this kind of novel is not easy. 'The portrait must have spirit and character, as well as resemblance; and being deprived of all that which, according to Bayes, "goes to elevate and surprise", it must make amends by displaying depth of knowledge and dexterity of execution.'

Miss Austen does not allow the restriction of view to be a hindrance or a degradation; it is 'the delight of her life'. If she made things easy in one way, by limiting her range, she did not shirk the greatest difficulty of all. She allowed herself very little in her subject except the humours, illusions, misunderstandings of very ordinary people. What she writes is Comedy, and the difficulty of Comedy is that the characters have nothing to support them or get them through their parts except their own several qualities. Every comedy is 'Every Man in his Humour', and if his humour is not made interesting there is nothing else that can save it; nothing will help if the characters are not rightly drawn. In other kinds of fiction there are resources which may make up for the want of dramatic sincerity and accuracy; various kinds of rhetoric, philosophical reflections, prophecy, romance, the beauties of nature; but in comedy all these are impertinent. The limitation of view is not idleness or tameness; as Scott says, 'In adventuring upon this task, the author makes obvious sacrifices, and encounters peculiar difficulty.' It is not for the sake of ease, but in order to attempt the hardest kind of portraiture that the range of the action is limited to 'three or four families in a country village'.

Robert Louis Stevenson in his essay on the romances of Victor Hugo in *Familiar Studies of Men and Books* has described the great revolution made by Scott and the difference between Scott and Fielding. The novelist, he says, 'can show his readers, behind and around the personages that for the moment occupy the foreground of his story, the continual suggestion of the landscape; the turn of the weather that will

---

[1] *Letters*, ed. R. W. Chapman (Oxford, 1952), p. 100.
[2] Reprinted in *Famous Reviews*, ed. R. B. Johnson (1914).

turn with it men's lives and fortunes, dimly foreshadowed on
the horizon; the fatality of distant events, stream of national
tendency, the salient framework of causation. . . . This
touches the difference between Fielding and Scott. In the
work of the latter, true to his character of a modern and a
romantic, we become suddenly conscious of the background.'

Miss Austen belongs on the whole to the older school in
which the background was not too much in the foreground,
was seen not too distinctly. She was asked to write another
kind of novel: Mr. Clarke, the Prince Regent's librarian,
afterwards Chaplain to Prince Leopold, suggested in 1816
that 'any historical romance, illustrative of the august House
of Cobourg, would just now be very interesting'. To which
Miss Austen answered that she was 'fully sensible that an
historical romance, founded on the House of Saxe Cobourg,
might be much more to the purpose of profit or popularity
than such pictures of domestic life in country villages as I
deal in';[1] and she drew out a 'Plan of a Novel, according to
hints from various quarters'.[2]

In her novels it will not be found that Miss Austen makes
much use of scenery; what there is—for example, the lawn and
the wilderness at Sotherton, Mr. Rushworth's place—is
necessary for the action, and is described generally as it
appears to the persons in the story, not as it might appear
to a romantic artist.

> Their road was through a pleasant country; and Fanny, whose rides
> had never been extensive, was soon beyond her knowledge, and was
> very happy in observing all that was new, and admiring all that was
> pretty . . . in observing the appearance of the country, the bearings of
> the roads, the difference of soil, the state of the harvest, the cottages,
> the cattle, the children, she found entertainment that could only have
> been heightened by having Edmund to speak to of what she felt.[3]

In *Northanger Abbey* the beauties of nature are made to play
into the comedy, not in a romantic or poetical manner, but

---

[1] *Letters*, ed. cit., pp. 451, 452.
[2] Published in the *Memoir* (1870). *The Works of Jane Austen*, ed. R. W. Chapman,
vi (Minor Works) (Oxford, 1954), pp. 428–30.
[3] *Mansfield Park*, chapter viii.

with reference to that taste for the picturesque which was one of the fashions of a hundred years ago:

But Catherine did not know her own advantages—did not know that a good-looking girl, with an affectionate heart and a very ignorant mind, cannot fail of attracting a clever young man, unless circumstances are particularly untoward. In the present instance, she confessed and lamented her want of knowledge; declared that she would give anything in the world to be able to draw; and a lecture on the picturesque immediately followed, in which his instructions were so clear that she soon began to see beauty in every thing admired by him, and her attention was so earnest, that he became perfectly satisfied of her having a great deal of natural taste. He talked of fore-grounds, distances, and second distances—side-screens and perspectives—lights and shades;—and Catherine was so hopeful a scholar, that when they gained the top of Beechen Cliff, she voluntarily rejected the whole city of Bath, as unworthy to make part of a landscape.[1]

The beauties of literature are treated in the same ironical way, when the sentimental Captain Benwick is allowed to talk poetry:

For, though shy, he did not seem reserved; it had rather the appearance of feelings glad to burst their usual restraints; and having talked of poetry, the richness of the present age, and gone through a brief comparison of opinion as to the first-rate poets, trying to ascertain whether *Marmion* or *The Lady of the Lake* were to be preferred, and how ranked the *Giaour* and *The Bride of Abydos*; and moreover, how the *Giaour* was to be pronounced. . . .[2]

Miss Austen knew quite well the value of the background —in its own place—and it was not because she ignored the poetical efficacy of the weather that she made so little imaginative use of it. It comes in without any emphasis in such passages as the following from *Persuasion*:

An hour's complete leisure for such reflections as these, on a dark November day, a small thick rain almost blotting out the very few objects ever to be discerned from the windows, was enough to make the sound of Lady Russell's carriage exceedingly welcome; and yet, though desirous to be gone, she could not quit the mansion-house, or look an adieu to the cottage, with its black, dripping, and comfortless

---

[1] *Northanger Abbey*, chapter xiv.   [2] *Persuasion*, chapter xi.

veranda, or even notice through the misty glasses the last humble tenements of the village, without a saddened heart.[1]

Or this, perhaps one of the best-sounding passages in her writings, from *Emma*, when Emma is finding out all her errors of judgement, and suffering for them:

The evening of this day was very long, and melancholy, at Hartfield. The weather added what it could of gloom. A cold stormy rain set in, and nothing of July appeared but in the trees and shrubs, which the wind was despoiling, and the length of the day, which only made such cruel sights the longer visible.[2]

The great danger in comedy is that the characters shall present the appearance of a number of separate fixed ideas, each talking its own vanity and not listening to any of the others. Some artists appear to have committed themselves, in resignation or in malice, to this kind of composition. Their stage is filled by separate atomic indestructible crazes, and nothing that any of them says has any effect on the nature of the rest. The author of *Engaged*—how long is it since that great work was last acted?[3]—and the author of *Hedda Gabler* have occasionally diverted themselves with this kind of drama.

Miss Austen does not shirk the difficulties. On the contrary, if there is anything that can be discovered as a formula or common device for her conversations, it is this, which is an essential part of all comedy, that the characters have their own views and that they go on talking their own views whether they are appreciated or not—every man in his humour.

So extremely like Maple Grove! And it is not merely the house— the grounds, I assure you, as far as I could observe, are strikingly like. The laurels at Maple Grove are in the same profusion as here, and stand very much in the same way—just across the lawn; and I had a glimpse of a fine large tree, with a bench round it, which put me so exactly in mind![4]

---

[1] Chapter xiii (= vol. iv, chapter i).
[2] *Emma*, chapter xlviii (= vol. iii, chapter xii).
[3] W. S. Gilbert's *Engaged. An entirely Original Farcical Comedy* was first performed in 1877.
[4] *Emma*, chapter xxxii (= vol. ii, chapter xiv).

That is life, but it is too cruel, too hard or too comic if it is represented entirely in this way as a jostling of ridiculous atoms. One way out of the difficulty is to bring in the background—to set off Joseph Poorgrass and his kinsmen against the sky of the downs of Wessex. There is more than this sort of scheme, of course, in Hardy's books, but it counts for a good deal. This was excluded from Miss Austen's method. Nor was it permitted to bring in the weightier moral problems or the larger romantic interests such as those in which Dogberry and Andrew Fairservice are involved. Miss Austen was committed to a kind of story that never rose very far above, that opened no view beyond, the scenes in which Mrs. Bennet and Mrs. Norris, Mr. Collins and Mrs. Elton might appear at any moment. The nobler personages still belong to comedy, and they too, Elizabeth Bennet and Emma and the rest, have all their vanities and illusions, and there is no way out of the difficulty by any extraneous means such as were at the disposal of Scott; no way except by the proper limited means of the narrative itself. It is the distinction of Miss Austen that her stories, with all their multitude of 'humours and observations', never look like a collection of oddities, never fall into that disconnected style in which the movement of life is lost and dispersed among the crowd of independent figures. How it is done, I will not try to discover. But if one is asked what it is that has given these novels their rank in English literature, a plausible answer will be that Miss Austen is one of the very few authors who have given without any metaphysical aid, without any means except ordinary plain narrative and conversation, a lively idea of the action of life as a whole, of the effect of Time carrying on human fortunes and working them out through successive illusions and corrections of illusions. The problem is the problem of all fiction; it is not often that one finds so much variety of characters together with such comprehension of the general movement of life.

John Keats

ALASTOR and *Endymion* are both poems about the life of a poet. The difference between them is shortly this, that *Alastor* keeps to the history of the poet's aspirations, worked out in the story of his travels, while *Endymion* plunges into other matter, not keeping simply to the life of the hero or pilgrim. *Endymion* purposes not only to make a poem of the poetic life or the quest for beauty, but to revive the mythology of Greece, to take subjects from Greek mythology and bring them into English poetry, as Keats says in the Preface. 'I hope I have not in too late a day touched the beautiful mythology of Greece, and dulled its brightness: for I wish to try once more, before I bid it farewell.' When he speaks of 'touching the mythology of Greece' he is thinking not only of the fable of Endymion but of the other themes he has worked into the poem—Glaucus, Adonis, Alpheus and Arethusa, and the rest.

The view of the ancient world given at the beginning of *Endymion* is a sort of generalized version of what one may gather from a great deal of ancient poetry and from a great deal of history about the fashions of Greek religion. The interest of it is the interest of the 'Ode on a Grecian Urn'. In that poem Keats has separated, extracted the quintessence of, what he had already imagined in *Endymion*. The vision is of a simple antique world—the idea of a fresh, reasonable life under what one may call the conditions of early religion and purified by poetic abstraction. The same sort of idea is to be found occasionally in Horace's odes about the country rituals of the villages of the Sabine Hills, and in Herrick's transferences from Horace to the English landscape.

In Keats's 'Ode to Maia', written in the May of 1818, just after *Endymion*, there is again the idea of the beauty of the antique world, unencumbered with any definite mythology, without any history of god or goddess or hero. The 'Ode to Maia' opens with the phrase 'Mother of Hermes', but it is not of the Mother of Hermes that Keats is thinking, but of the quiet life and the little clan, the same sort of world as appears again in the 'Ode on a Grecian Urn'. There is a likeness in this imaginary world to the 'golden age' of ancient and pastoral poetry. But Keats escapes from the conventions of pastoral poetry, and is never touched by them any more than is Shakespeare when he speaks of 'fleeting the time care-lessly, as they did in the golden world'[1] or 'the old age'. Through the help of the Elizabethans and his own instinct Keats learned to think of the imaginative primitive world of the old poetry without convention, without the insipid beauties which come in the pastorals of Pope.

In the Hymn to Pan in *Endymion* Keats has taken the old idea of Pan and a few of the particulars—the pursuit of Syrinx, for example—and made an occasion for a lyric sum-mary of the ancient world, a picture of the ancient days from what he knew of English country life, giving the elements of English country life the simple, ancient, imaginative ritual of religion, so simple that nothing is done to impair the reality of the picture. And, further, the extraordinary com-plex idea of Pan in Greek mythology, the idea of Pan as the author of 'panic terror', as a god of the mystery of lonely places, is brought in without harming the simplicity of the poem. Pan also has a half-allegorical meaning as the universe, the meaning that makes the name familiar in the usage of Christian poets, for example, Spenser. That idea of Pan is of great importance to Keats, but he does not work it out in the same way as Shelley does the kindred idea in *Prometheus Un-bound*. Keats, although he shows how he is moved by the spiritual conception of Pan, does not so employ it in his poem as to break the impression of the simple ancient world which is the main poetic object of the Hymn to Pan.

With Wordsworth there is often a strain of reflection which is unpoetical or not of necessity poetic, whereas with Keats the form of thought is necessarily poetical. His thought is poetical in such a way that you cannot separate the prose meaning from the imaginative expression. One may say this is true of all true poetry, but if one compares the poetry of Keats with that of Shelley one easily sees the difference be-

[1] *As You Like It*, I. i. 124.

tween the poet wholly poetical and the poet who has other forms of thought, who is not limited to the poetic or imaginative form. In Shelley philosophical ideas run through the poetry; and he himself, as shown in the Preface to *Prometheus Unbound*, thought it possible to detach his ideas from poetic shape, and aimed indeed at philosophical expression. Both *Endymion* and *Prometheus Unbound* are allegorical. But in *Prometheus Unbound* one can see that the ideas could be expressed in a different way: Shelley tells us in the Preface that the time may come when he will give these ideas philosophical utterance. With Keats the blending of the two is so perfect that one may read *Endymion* without detecting the allegory. The poet has put his abstract theory of poetic life and his ambition into the romantic poetry of the story in such a way that one follows the story and never thinks of the meaning as a separable thing. The abstract meaning is incarnate in the story; or, to apply the famous phrase of Donne, its body thinks;[1] its body and soul are inseparable.

The Hymn to Pan in *Endymion* is not in strict stanza. It is brought in rather as a heightening of the narrative verse, with variations in the use of short lines but without strict pattern, like a lake made by the spreading of a river, where one is hardly able to say whether it is river or lake. The coming of definite form is indicated by the short six-syllable lines, which are the support of the ten-syllable line in the solemn ode in English.[2] Keats has in his mind this form of ode, which he begins to use distinctly in the fragment of the 'Ode to Maia'.

The verse of *Endymion* is the free heroic couplet, not under the rule of Waller. This is one of the types of Elizabethan couplet which Keats learned, no doubt, from Drayton, Chapman, and Browne. One must not take those names or any term like 'Elizabethan couplet' as denoting any one particular form of heroic couplet. Elizabethan poets use all varieties, from couplets as strict as the couplets of Waller and Pope to couplets as loose, as run-on, as those in *Endymion*. When one says that Keats imitated the Elizabethans in his couplets, one means that he imitated some among many types of that form

[1] Cf. Donne, *Of the Progresse of the Soule* (*The Second Anniversary*), 246.
[2] Cf. p. 100 above.

of verse used by the Elizabethan poets. One must not think either that the verse of *Endymion* is alike all through. The beauty of it is that it is not compelled to be licentious, to run on over the rhyme-word. It also has command of the solemn, dignified effect given by the sense concluded in the couplet, by the pause at the end of the line.

Endymion offended old-fashioned readers not only by letting the sense run on over the couplet, but also by the varieties of stress within the line. Keats occasionally uses that curious discordant double rhyme fairly common down to the end of the sixteenth century, and used sometimes by Shakespeare. Consider, for example, the couplet

> Of grass, a wailful gnat, a bee bustling
> Down in the blue-bells, or a wren light rustling . . .[1]

In the first line one has first to suppose an inverted stress in the last foot—'bústling' instead of 'bustlíng'. But it is more than simple inversion that is used here. If the rhyme were simple we should find a corresponding 'sing' or 'ring', but the rhyme is 'bústling', 'rústling', and the line ending 'rústling' has eleven syllables while the line ending in 'bústling' has only ten. This is the irregular, ill-fitting rhyme noted in poets from the time of Wyatt to the end of the sixteenth century, but difficult to find after that. Near that place there is another licence which was certainly intended, for Keats mentions it to his publisher in a letter[2] about punctuation:

> Bránch down sweeping from a tall ash-top.[3]

This is the nine-syllable line, wanting the first short syllable and therefore beginning on the strong stress, so frequently found in Chaucer.

Keats's tour in Scotland comes at a critical time in his life, after *Endymion*. It is sometimes neglected by biographers and commentators, but it has a meaning known to Keats himself

---

[1] *Endymion*, i. 450–1.
[2] To John Taylor, 27 February 1818; *The Letters of John Keats,* ed. M. B. Forman (Oxford, 1935), p. 109.
[3] *Endymion*, i. 335.

and a purpose which Keats well describes in a letter to Haydon:

I purpose within a Month to put my knapsack at my back and make a pedestrian tour through the North of England, and part of Scotland—to make a sort of Prologue to the Life I intend to pursue—that is to write, to study and to see all Europe at the lowest expence. I will clamber through the Clouds and exist. I will get such an accumulation of stupendous recollections that as I walk through the suburbs of London I may not see them—I will stand upon Mount Blanc and remember this coming Summer when I intend to straddle Ben Lomond.[1]

One ought not, of course, to treat the pedestrian tour too seriously; Keats and his friend had the ordinary proper, simple, holiday motives, the same sort of motive as took Wordsworth on his walking tour through the Continent in his Cambridge days. But in the letters written from different places by Keats on his journey one can see how much his mind is alive, and how his imagination and reason are working on the things he sees. He was probably led north by Wordsworth. He went to Rydal and saw Wordsworth's house, but, unfortunately, Wordsworth was not at home.[2] Also, for every tourist there was the old picturesque attraction of Scotland, the places where the scenery was renowned, and, in addition, the new romantic associations from the work of Scott, which probably had some influence in turning Keats and Brown through Galloway—Meg Merrilies, for instance, is remembered by Keats.

The interest of the journey lies greatly in the things Keats notices. Compare his searching thoughts about the life of Burns with the humorous, romantic interest in scenery which comes out best in what he says of the tourist steamboat business at the upper end of Loch Lomond:

Steam Boats on Loch Lomond and Barouches on its sides take a little from the Pleasure of such romantic chaps as Brown and I. The Banks of the Clyde are extremely beautiful—the north End of Loch Lomond grand in excess—the entrance at the lower end to the narrow part from a little distance is precious good—the Evening was beautiful, nothing could surpass our fortune in the weather—yet was I worldly

[1] *Letters*, ed. cit., p. 128.   [2] Ibid., p. 158.

enough to wish for a fleet of chivalry Barges with Trumpets and Banners just to die away before me into that blue place among the mountains . . . the Water was a fine Blue silverd and the Mountains a dark purple, the Sun setting aslant behind them—meantime the head of Ben Lomond was covered with a rich Pink Cloud.[1]

He notices before this what Burns never mentions, almost one may say never 'saw', although they were before him all his early life in Ayrshire—the mountains of Arran.[2] This admiration of Keats brings out clearly the difference of mind between the two poets, and the extraordinary limitation, in one way, of Burns's range.

Keats's journey is a pilgrim's progress, and it is probable that he thought of it in that way himself and enjoyed it the more for that reason. It was not merely an exploration of landscape, but a journey to see the world, and Keats found what he went out to see, including the 'reed shaken with the wind'. The tour brings out the energy of Keats's life, and the difference between his following of beauty and the languishing, idle love of beauty ascribed to him by those who did not understand.

From *Endymion* Keats went on quickly. In May 1818 he had written the fragment of the 'Ode to Maia', showing that he had learned the art of the ode. Next came the poems published in the volume of 1820, containing all the best poetry of Keats: 'Lamia', 'Isabella', 'The Eve of St. Agnes', 'Hyperion', and the Odes. The four narrative poems of the 1820 volume are very different in their narrative element and scheme. Between 'Isabella' and 'Lamia' there is not so much difference as between these two and the other two or each of the other two. It is not much good to attempt to distinguish between 'Isabella' and 'Lamia'; both are straightforward tales in verse, stories in which the points were fixed before the poet took them up. Both are paraphrases, the one from Boccaccio, the other from Greek story.

'The Eve of St. Agnes' is different in kind. It is narrative

---

[1] To Tom Keats, 17–21 July 1818 (*Letters*, ed. cit., p. 185).
[2] 'Besides all the Beauty, there were the Mountains of Arran Isle, black and huge over the Sea. . . .' To J. H. Reynolds, 11–13 July 1818 (ibid., p. 176). Cf. Ker, *Collected Essays*, i. 136.

in form and would be taken at once as a story, but the story is not the determining principle as it is in 'Isabella' and 'Lamia'. It is a theme rather than a narrative fable, the theme of the true lover carrying off his bride from among his enemies. That old romantic theme is taken by the poet and treated in a new way, in a way that combines an immense amount of detail, immense riches of ornament and amplifications, with that vagueness, mystery and romantic charm brought out best of all in the last stanza:

> And they are gone: ay, ages long ago
> These lovers fled away into the storm.

Instead of the narrative plot such as you have in 'Isabella' and 'Lamia', where the different characters and events and adventures go through a considerable space of time, here there is the moment chosen—extending the word 'moment' to include the whole of the time of the story—and the poetic meaning of the course of time is brought out to the subordination of the adventurous part.

'Hyperion' is different from all these and from all the other poems of Keats. It may be regarded as a poem that properly follows *Endymion*, according to the promise of the Preface of *Endymion*, taking up again 'the beautiful mythology of Greece'. It is similar also to *Endymion* in the use of mythology for conveying the author's own wishes and aspirations. The difference in the story of *Endymion* and of 'Hyperion' is distinctly this, that *Endymion* with all its variety is the story of one adventurer, while in 'Hyperion' the interest is distributed. 'Hyperion' is much more dramatic; each of the characters has his own value, and one cannot say that any one dominates unfairly the course of the story.

The story of 'Hyperion' is taken from nearly the same place in Greek story as Shelley's *Prometheus Unbound* and Aeschylus' *Prometheus Bound*. Here one comes back to the old wonder, which really returns at every reading of the *Prometheus Bound*, at the extraordinary depth of that poem, at the capacity of the poem for agreeing with modern ideas. *Prometheus Bound* contradicts many of the things generally told about the Greeks; it is full of the idea of progress, and it is the idea of progress which is the meaning of 'Hyperion', which makes its narrative and dramatic interest. There could not be a better choice—except the choice Shelley was making at the same time of *Prometheus Unbound*—for a modern poem on a Greek mythological subject. For the lines of the Greek story are such that they do not need any twisting, any sophistication, to make them fit for any modern idealism the author chooses to put into them. They are such that the whole of life, as it may be interpreted in any age, can be explained sincerely, though abstractedly and generally, through the story.

The drama of 'Hyperion' is the drama of two ages—'the old order changeth, yielding place to new'. It is a story of the triumph of time, not as that theme is often treated by the older poets, by the Anglo-Saxon poet of 'The Ruin' and 'The Wanderer' or by Spenser in the cantos on Mutability in *The Faerie Queene*, but as replacing old things by better things, as bringing new life. In all this there is something very different from the ordinary opinion about Keats, a serious thought and dignity, quite other than the soft luxurious beauty which was all that even some of his admirers allowed to him. The letters of Keats bring out what many of his readers failed to find in his poetry, what, however, may be found in his poetry long before, his concern with the sorrows of the human race, with 'the burthen of the mystery' of the world. The philosophical speculations of Keats are not to be passed over as mere words, as mere showy argument. This comes out clearly in one of his journal-letters to his brother and sister-in-law, where he speaks of 'soul-making', of the minds of men as coming from God, as intelligences with the power of perceiving, but with no character till they have been through the world.

The common cognomen of this world among the misguided and superstitious is 'a vale of tears' from which we are to be redeemed by a certain arbitrary interposition of God and taken to Heaven—What a little circumscribed straightened notion! Call the world if you Please 'The vale of Soul-making'. Then you will find out the use of the world (I am speaking now in the highest terms for human nature admitting it to be immortal which I will here take for granted for the purpose of showing a thought which has struck me concerning it) I say '*Soul making*' Soul as distinguished from an Intelligence—There may be intelligences or sparks of the divinity in millions—but they are not Souls till they acquire identities, till each one is personally itself. Intelligences are atoms of perception—they know and they see and they are pure, in short they are God—How then are Souls to be made? How then are these sparks which are God to have identity given them—so as ever to possess a bliss peculiar to each one's individual existence? How, but by the medium of a world like this? . . . Do you not see how necessary a World of Pains and troubles is to school an Intelligence and make it a Soul?[1]

This theory of Keats is thoroughly in agreement with the story of 'Hyperion', for the story of 'Hyperion' is the conflict or debate between two orders of soul, between characters shaped in one way, according to one fashion, and characters of a newer sort who are going forward and making discoveries, and are ready to displace the old order.

Robert Bridges said that in 'Hyperion' the story was strangling itself.[2] This is not quite right. He thinks the poem was dropped because the story had lost itself; but the story in one sense has really been told: the fragment gives the conflict between the ancient gods and the Olympians. The difficulty was this: not that Keats had lost the thread of the argument, but that the course of the argument led him into problems for which he had not then the proper resources. The story requires that the Olympians should approve themselves, show themselves more glorious than the old gods, but Keats had given so much dignity to the old gods and so much beauty to the earlier part of the poem that he had nothing to spare for Apollo and the Olympians. He must have felt the danger of an anti-climax, that people, if he had finished the poem and not proved the Olympians' case, might say the old order was the better.

The speech of Oceanus in the second book gives the meaning of the poem. Oceanus, the prophet of the old gods, sees into the future and tries to teach his fellows:

[1] *Letters*, ed. cit., pp. 335–6.
[2] Robert Bridges, *John Keats, A Critical Essay* (1895), reprinted as an introduction to *Poems of John Keats*, ed. G. Thorn-Drury ('The Muses' Library', 1896), vol. i, and in *Collected Essays, Papers, &c.*, vol. iv (Oxford, 1933), pp. 106–8.

We fall by course of Nature's law, not force
Of thunder, or of Jove. . . .
. . . On our heels a fresh perfection treads,
A power more strong in beauty, born of us
And fated to excel us. . . .
            . . . Say, doth the dull soil
Quarrel with the proud forests it hath fed,
And feedeth still, more comely than itself?
Can it deny the chiefdom of green groves?
Or shall the tree be envious of the dove
Because it cooeth, and hath snowy wings
To wander wherewithal and find its joys?
We are such forest-trees, and our fair boughs
Have bred forth, not pale solitary doves,
But eagles golden-feather'd, who do tower
Above us in their beauty, and must reign
In right thereof; for 'tis the eternal law
That first in beauty should be first in might:
Yea, by that law, another race may drive
Our conquerors to mourn as we do now.[1]

The speech is not the finest passage in 'Hyperion', but it best
brings out the abstract meaning of the fable. Oceanus refers
to the old Greek theogony, the old strange barbaric history
of the early gods, in which the idea of progress is implicit, the
successive generations becoming more and more human,
more and more reasonable.

Among the beauties of 'Hyperion' the similes are to be
noted. It is strange how the epic simile seems to come exactly
in the right place in blank verse narrative poems in English
—over and over again, in 'Hyperion', in 'Sohrab and Rus-
tum', in *Idylls of the King*. Not that similes are limited to that
form—the first epic similes in English, and some of the best,
occur in Chaucer's rhymes. But there is something in the
blank verse form in English which allows similes their proper
place. In 'Hyperion' you may find similes that exemplify perfectly the theories of Wordsworth and Coleridge about fancy
and imagination. The best of all the examples, perhaps, is the
comparison of the old gods in their discomfiture and their

[1] 'Hyperion', ii. 181-2, 212-14, 217-31. Cf. Ker's essay on Keats in *Collected Essays*, i. 233.

silence to the motionless stones of Druid circles like Stonehenge:

> But for the main, here found they covert drear,
> Scarce images of life, one here, one there,
> Lay vast and edgeways; like a dismal cirque
> Of Druid stones, upon a forlorn moor,
> When the chill rain begins at shut of eve,
> In dull November, and their chancel vault,
> The Heaven itself, is blinded throughout night.
>
> (ii. 32–38)

This has the qualities in it noted for the epic simile by
Wordsworth—the simile not only illustrating what it starts
from, but being itself qualified and illustrated reciprocally by
what it illustrates.[1] This proves how right Wordsworth is,
and what is the value of the epic simile as an instrument of
imagination. Here the poet is drawing from Nature, not in
the conventional sense of seeking for the picturesque, but
from life and experience in all its forms. Here the recollection
of Stonehenge is qualified by the picture of the great fallen
gods, and in such a way that it is not a mere conceit to think
of the standing and fallen stones as giants sleeping or giants
defeated; there are universal and real qualities in both pictures, the same blending of power and strength and life-
lessness, the same dignity of great creatures that cannot
move, cannot do anything. That imaginative power, as distinct
from the vividness of conceits, may be found all through the
similes of the poem.

Browning's *Sordello* may be compared in plan with Keats's
Endymion and 'Hyperion' together, and the comparison needs
to take in the new version of the latter poem. The likeness is
this: *Sordello* is the story of the life of a poet, and the first part
of it is strongly influenced both by Shelley and Keats—in its
form undoubtedly. In the first part of *Sordello*, in the descriptions of the young poet, his aspirations, his failure, his discontent, there is a great likeness to *Endymion* and not less to
the letters of Keats, the actual feelings of Keats as experienced
and expressed in the letters. The story of *Sordello* changes
halfway through—Sordello changes his plans, his ideals. He

[1] Preface to *Poems* (1815).

has been self-centred in the first part; in the second part he learns some things new to him about the human race, and he devotes himself to the service of mankind. This second part of *Sordello* corresponds to 'Hyperion', or perhaps it is better to say to the actual life of Keats while he is engaged upon 'Hyperion'. The life of Keats changes something in the way the life of Sordello changes. Keats was never so vain as Sordello is represented in the first part of the story, and was never called upon for action as Sordello is in his later life. Keats had not to discover his fellow creatures as Sordello had. But as Keats went on he learned more about the human race, till in many places he uses the same sort of moralizing language as Shelley does in the Preface to *Prometheus Unbound*.

'Hyperion' is the story, not of the life of the poet, but of the life of the world, the history of the world given in a kind of mythological abstract—poets are abstractors of quintessence, as Rabelais says.[1] 'Hyperion' is the story of collision between different ideals, not the conflict of right and wrong, but the conflict of different ideas about right. 'Hyperion' as published first is superior in many ways to the revised version; but 'The Fall of Hyperion' reveals much of the mind of Keats which is not so declared in the first version, and particularly his notions of the relative values of different kinds of life, of the man of action on the one hand and the poet on the other, and of the life of the poet, the dreamer, as far inferior to the life of the hero.

One can make out another motive of Keats in rewriting 'Hyperion'. One reason, as said before, was that he found he could not properly express the Olympians, having given so much poetic imagination to the older gods. The other was his discontent with the epic form. The epic style would not allow him to say all he wanted. He says that in order to bring out what he means he must have a form of poetry capable of deep meaning. The objective form of the narrative or epic does not encourage the poet to express his own opinions. The epic is too simple for the complex opinions he had in mind, so he goes back to the method allowing reflection; he writes a

---

[1] On the title-page of *La vie tres horrificque du grand Gargantua pere de Pantagruel* (1542) the author describes himself as 'Abstracteur de Quinte Essence'.

reflective version. One of the chief persons in 'Hyperion' is Mnemosyne, goddess of memory, who is the mother of the Muses and who comes from the old mythology. For Keats she is the goddess of the mind of the world, the prophetic and reflective soul of the great universe. In the revised version Keats calls her Moneta, a Latin name which he took to be the equivalent of Mnemosyne. She takes the place of Dame Philosophy in Boethius and of Virgil in Dante, explaining the vision to the dreamer, and showing that the man of action is preferable to the visionary.[1]

It does not follow that because the poet enlarges his philosophy he will write better poetry; it does not follow that because there is more thought in 'Hyperion' it is therefore better than *Endymion*, or that because there is deeper thought in the revised version of 'Hyperion' the earlier is not so good. Philosophical poetry if it goes wrong may lead to such tedious stuff as Coleridge and Wordsworth occasionally write, to passages so well described by Matthew Arnold, to passages recited by orators at social science congresses.[2] One must not take it as proved that Keats's poetry grew stronger as it grew more philosophical, but the passages in 'Hyperion' and many of the letters prove that Keats's mind was active in a way different from that supposed by his false admirers, who saw in him only a soft luxurious beauty.

The return to reflection in 'The Fall of Hyperion', after Keats had launched himself freely into narrative poetry, into stories where he himself does not appear, may seem to show an end of his poetic strength as a builder in poetic fabrics that can stand on their own merits, apart from any personal interest in the author. One cannot be sure how Keats's mind and poetic imagination were shaping. Some readers may find something

---

[1] i. 147 ff.

[2] 'One can hear them being quoted at a Social Science Congress; one can call up the whole scene. A great room in one of our dismal provincial towns; dusty air and jaded afternoon daylight; benches full of men with bald heads and women in spectacles; an orator lifting up his face from a manuscript written within and without to declaim these lines of Wordsworth ['O for the coming of that glorious time' . . . &c.]; and in the soul of any poor child of nature who may have wandered in thither, an unutterable sense of lamentation, and mourning, and woe!' (Preface to *The Poems of Wordsworth*, chosen and edited by Matthew Arnold (1879); reprinted in *Essays in Criticism*, Second Series.)

unhealthy in the second 'Hyperion', something of the fever in which he was living in the last months of his life; but then the Odes must be remembered, the Odes which are Keats's greatest work, beyond the narrative poems in poetic beauty, and in all of which there is reflection into which the whole mind of the poet is undoubtedly merged. The Odes are philosophical poetry which is poetry and not philosophy, poetry which is much concerned with the nature of poetry itself and which has therefore a subject like that of *Endymion*, but poetry which does not concern itself with the life of the individual poet, which does not make too much of Keats himself, which throws the meaning of aspirations and so on into a lasting form. Hence, when one reads the 'Nightingale' or the 'Grecian Urn', one gets the expression of the poetic mind of Keats, of all his thought, without any of the distracting, false, romantic, personal interest which one finds when the poet is merely talking about poetry and not creating it.

The problem in the 'Nightingale' and the 'Grecian Urn' is the same (the idea is also the same as in Shelley's 'Skylark'). In these two Odes the mind of Keats is dealing with the contrast between the momentary glimpses and the eternal life of art, of poetry or of the other art shown in the 'Grecian Urn'.

There is a certain amount of symbolic interpretation in the 'Nightingale'. The song of the bird is taken as a sort of symbol of poetry. One does injustice to the poem in speaking of it so, but some such rough analysis is necessary to explain the argument. The poetic interpretation of the song of the nightingale is the poetic interpretation of all poetry:

> Thou wast not born for death, immortal bird.

The song is taken by Keats as poetic music untouched by time, one which takes the mind away from itself and from the accidents of time into a world where the accidents of time have no power. Poetic beauty is unalterable beauty; and so the song of the nightingale brings the poet's mind into communion with ancient things as if they were present, and with fairy, imaginative things as if they were what we call 'real'. The song takes the mind into a more 'real' world, where past is present and remote is close at hand. In this, as thus expressed, there may appear to be something of conceit, something of hypocrisy; that is because the meaning of poetry is difficult to translate into prose, and because when translated into prose it seems to have little meaning.

In the 'Ode on a Grecian Urn' there is the same sort of idea, and with a little more of the appearance of conceit. Critics may make objections to this ode, asking if it is not mere meaningless fancy when Keats sees life in the figures on the urn, when he addresses them as if they were alive. Is this to be compared with the fancies of Hans Andersen when he puts life into the furniture of a room, bringing to life the Dresden shepherdess and chimney-sweep on the mantelpiece? This is the weakness in the argument of the poem, that it leaves one in doubt as to its meaning. But the doubt is wrong. The life that Keats sees in the figures on the urn is seen through them, and what he quickens is not the mere figures as seen, but the old life they represent. What is represented in sculpture Keats re-represents in poetry, re-representing that old age he had brought out in the beginning of *Endymion*, in the passage containing the Hymn to Pan, the life of simple dignity, the life again of that little clan imagined in the 'Ode to Maia'. And so the mind of Keats, when it seems in danger of false fantasy, is true to that simple poetical vision, that idea of life which is something like the old pastoral, but without the pastoral conventions.

Further, one must remember the form of the Odes, some of the noblest things done in the solemn stanza. The best poetic work of Keats proves the value of the old tradition, and his use of the old tradition proves the strength of his reason and the soundness of his poetical and critical judgement. The author, so very naturally blamed at first for excesses, irregularity, and rebellion, accomplishes poems which are under the best rules and traditions of poetry and in a classical tradition which, though not quite the same thing as eighteenth-century classicism, had been recognized in the eighteenth century by some of the best poets, notably by Gray.

Anthony Trollope

ANTHONY TROLLOPE usually wrote for three hours in the morning early, and timed himself to write 250 words every quarter of an hour.[1] He also wrote in railway trains. These historical facts are fairly well known, and in consequence the imaginative work of Trollope is lightly valued and often neglected. It is taken as mechanical hackwork; what was so easily and regularly turned out is supposed to be of corresponding small value. Obviously there is a *petitio principii* here; it is assumed that the value varies inversely as the velocity. Further, Trollope never took to himself any great credit as a literary man; he does not seem to have thought much of literary fame; he was not ambitious, he was not jealous; he did not want to differ from the kindly race of men who played whist in clubs between five and seven in the afternoon. His own opinion about himself and his writings is worth some consideration from those who are curious about the lives and methods of artists. The books themselves are worth reading, whatever the author may have thought about them; I have a long acquaintance with many of them, and undiminished readiness for more, and I am still left wondering at the modesty of Anthony Trollope and his apparently low estimate of his own achievements in fiction. He had much to be proud of and good excuses for boasting, if his temper had led him that way. But in truth he was too proud and secure to boast; his even, balanced soul knew what it required from the world and what it was prepared to give, and so his business was carried on without any overdraft at the bankers.

It is always interesting to find out what artists think about their work, and Trollope has told a good deal about his aims and processes; much more than the common facts about his rate of words to the minute. He wrote a book on Thackeray for the 'English Men of Letters' series in 1879, and there he explains very clearly a far from easy standard of imaginative

---

[1] *An Autobiography*, chapter xv (ed. F. Page, 'The Oxford Trollope', Oxford University Press (1950), pp. 271–2).

work. Fluency in writing is all very well. Trollope has so much of that talent by nature that he undervalues it. But he is not misled by his own fortunate, ready-running style to think that everything will do which comes on the spur of the moment, or that the pen may be trusted to write by itself. 'Whether I guide the pen or the pen me' is a problem that occurs at times to all of us. Dr. Johnson's advice to poets to sit down doggedly[1] (which is the same as that given to Mr. Crawley in *The Last Chronicle of Barset*—'it's dogged as does it')[2]—this advice, to poets or prosers, is really confidence in the magic of the pen, which is not to be despised. The way to write is to write. But the magic of the pen will not do everything, not even for geniuses like Scott and Thackeray. They may think of glorious things as they write, but they must have done some thinking before they sit down; and Trollope is uncompromising, remarkably austere, in his rule for novelists. The loose construction of *Vanity Fair* and *Pendennis* he will not pass without censure; he distinguishes *Barry Lyndon* and *Henry Esmond* as showing more intellectual care than the rest, and *Henry Esmond* as the one book in which there is 'no touch of idleness'. Whether Trollope was right or wrong about Thackeray is not my concern; I wish to note what the ready writer of a thousand words an hour thought necessary before the hour began.

When we were young we used to be told, in our house at home, that 'elbow-grease' was the one essential necessary to getting a tough piece of work well done. If a mahogany table was to be made to shine, it was elbow-grease that the operation needed. Fore-thought is the elbow-grease which a novelist,—or poet, or dramatist,—requires. It is not only his plot that has to be turned and re-turned in his mind, not his plot chiefly, but he has to make himself sure of his situations, of his characters, of his effects, so that when the time comes for hitting the nail he may know where to hit it on the head,—so that he may himself understand the passion, the calmness, the virtues, the vices, the rewards

[1] 'Somebody talked of happy moments for composition; and how a man can write at one time, and not at another.—"Nay, (said Dr Johnson) a man may write at any time, if he will set himself *doggedly* to it."' Boswell, *The Journal of a Tour to the Hebrides*, 16 August 1773. (Boswell's *Life*, &c., ed. Birkbeck Hill, rev. Powell, v. 40).

[2] Chapter lxi.

and punishments which he means to explain to others,—so that his proportions shall be correct, and he be saved from the absurdity of devoting two-thirds of his book to the beginning, or two-thirds to the completion of his task. It is from want of this special labour, more frequently than from intellectual deficiency, that the tellers of stories fail so often to hit their nails on the head. To think of a story is much harder work than to write it. The author can sit down with the pen in his hand for a given time, and produce a certain number of words. That is comparatively easy, and if he have a conscience in regard to his task, work will be done regularly. But to think it over as you lie in bed, or walk about, or sit cosily over your fire, to turn it all in your thoughts, and make the things fit,—that requires elbow-grease of the mind.[1]

In Trollope's strict requirement of preliminary hard work from the novelist there is evidently nothing pedantic or hypo-critical; it is his rule and theory for himself in his own prac-tice; he is neither conceited nor ashamed of it; to him it is the merest common sense. We know that his rule was not acknowledged by Scott or Thackeray. Thackeray in one of the *Roundabout Papers* ('De Finibus') has described his own easy-going want of method in contrast to the definite scheme as used by his favourite Alexandre Dumas.

Alexandre Dumas describes himself, when inventing the plan of a work, as lying silent on his back for two whole days on the deck of a yacht in a Mediterranean port. At the end of the two days he arose and called for dinner. In those two days he had built his plot. He had moulded a mighty clay, to be cast presently in perennial brass. The chapters, the characters, the incidents, the combinations were all ar-ranged in the artist's brain ere he set a pen to paper. My Pegasus won't fly, so as to let me survey the field below me. He has no wings, he is blind of one eye certainly; he is restive, stubborn, slow; crops a hedge when he ought to be galloping, or gallops when he ought to be quiet. He never will show off when I want him. Sometimes he goes at a pace which surprises me. Sometimes, when I most wish him to make the running, the brute turns restive, and I am obliged to let him take his own time. I wonder do other novel-writers experience this fatalism? They *must* go a certain way, in spite of themselves. I have been sur-prised at the observations made by some of my characters. It seems as if an occult Power was moving the pen. The personage does or says something, and I ask, how the dickens did he come to think of that?

[1] *Thackeray* ('English Men of Letters' series), pp. 122–3, 124.

But what is here to the point is that Trollope, who has told us of his easy writing, tells us also of premeditation and careful planning; so that if any of his stories seem to be loose, rambling, ill constructed, we may be sure that the author has fallen short of his ideal method. A critic who has recently done good service in writing a preface to a new edition of *The Barsetshire Novels*[1] makes a contrast between Trollope and Flaubert, speaking as though Trollope had no literary principle or aim. Trollope on Thackeray has escaped his notice. Trollope did not trust to mere luck, and he thought not so poorly of his own writings as he sometimes in his *Autobiography* may appear to have done. If Trollope was not a great artist, he knew what the art of fiction demanded. I do not think that he failed, and I hope to give reasons for this opinion.

But first I should like to notice some other opinions of Trollope on the subject. One of them is specially interesting, because the subject of it—realism in fiction—has been discussed and debated so extensively and comprehensively by such eminent persons that it will probably figure in future histories of literature in the same way as the Dramatic Unities in former ages. I quote again from Trollope on Thackeray. I am strongly inclined to quote the whole chapter on 'Thackeray's style and manner of work', so full of plain good sense is it, resembling Aristotle in his literary judgements and discriminations. This is what Trollope says about Realism:

A novel in style should be easy, lucid, and of course grammatical. The same may be said of any book; but that which is intended to re-create should be easily understood,—for which purpose lucid narration is an essential. In matter it should be moral and amusing. In manner it may be realistic, or sublime, or ludicrous;—or it may be all these if the author can combine them. As to Thackeray's performance in style and matter I will say something further on. His manner was mainly realistic, and I will therefore speak first of that mode of expression which was peculiarly his own.

Realism in style has not all the ease which seems to belong to it. It is the object of the author who affects it so to communicate with his reader that all his words shall seem to be natural to the occasion.

---

[1] *The Barsetshire Novels*, ed. F. Harrison, 8 vols. 1906, &c.

We do not think the language of Dogberry natural, when he tells neighbour Seacole that 'to write and read comes by nature.' That is ludicrous. Nor is the language of Hamlet natural when he shows to his mother the portrait of his father;

> See what a grace was seated on this brow;
> Hyperion's curls; the front of Jove himself;
> An eye like Mars, to threaten and command.

That is sublime. Constance is natural when she turns away from the Cardinal, declaring that

> He talks to me that never had a son.

In one respect both the sublime and ludicrous are easier than the realistic. They are not required to be true. A man with an imagination and culture may feign either of them without knowing the ways of men. To be realistic you must know accurately that which you describe. How often do we find in novels that the author makes an attempt at realism and falls into a bathos of absurdity, because he cannot use appropriate language? 'No human being ever spoke like that,' we say to ourselves,—while we should not question the naturalness of the production, either in the grand or the ridiculous.

And yet in very truth the realistic must not be true,—but just so far removed from truth as to suit the erroneous idea of truth which the reader may be supposed to entertain.[1]

Is not the whole essence of the thing in that? Does it not explode the stupid realists? Realism is not mechanical imitation; it is inventive and imaginative; in fact, it is idealism. Trollope was clear in his own mind as to the scope and range, the limitations and the exigencies of the art of fiction. He knew that its business was an allusion to real life in which realities were not to be treated with superstitious respect. He knew also that the novel must itself be alive. And the result was, though now it is neglected, that Trollope's best novels compete with Jane Austen's in giving a sense of the movement of life, keeping the right relations and proportions between different characters and their surroundings, through changes of time, so that the reader finds himself moving along with a number of people who are all changing in different ways as their several lives are determined on the scene of the world.

[1] *Thackeray*, pp. 184–5.

Trollope reckoned himself a moralist, and he had no scruple in repeating the old commonplace about mingling amusement with instruction. He does not pretend to be indifferent about good and evil, nor yet to have any peculiar standard of conduct; ordinary sane common sense is good enough for him. But his moral judgements are not those of ordinary common sense, nor of the moral philosopher. He is more discriminating than the jury of common sense and less abstract than the philosopher, and so, for all his common sense there may be something paradoxical in his morality. There generally is, in comedy, and comedy is what the great novelists are mostly engaged in. An example of the difference between the moralist and the comic poet has lately been recalled to notice in Émile Faguet's book on Rousseau and Molière.[1] It is clear enough that Molière was thinking in one way about life and conduct, Rousseau in another. Rousseau, it seems, was aggrieved because Molière promised him a misanthrope and presented Alceste instead; that is, Rousseau wanted the abstract quality, the high-minded detestation of human vices, and he was discontented when he found Molière's misanthrope often behaving like an ordinary man. Alceste breaks out and loses his temper. 'This', says Rousseau, 'is not what we came to your theatre to see; your misanthrope is not one perfect misanthropic crystal; on the contrary he is changeable and his behaviour not consistently directed according to the principle of misanthropy.' The author of comedy, the novelist, if he is a careful man, might do well to take note of this danger; for even if it should not be really dangerous, he can always keep the philosopher filed for reference and get something out of him in one way or another.

In *Barchester Towers* Trollope makes another note about his theory of novel writing. The chief thread of the story is the life of Eleanor Bold (daughter of Mr. Harding, the Warden) between her widowhood and her marriage with Dr. Arabin, the new Dean of Barchester. This is all part of the ecclesiastical history. The Bishop and Mrs. Proudie, Archdeacon Grantly and his wife (Mrs. Bold's elder sister),

[1] *Rousseau contre Molière*, Paris, 1912.

the remarkable family of Dr. Stanhope, Mr. Slope the Bishop's chaplain—these are the other chief personages. Mrs. Bold is courted by Bertie Stanhope and by Mr. Slope, who are both in different ways absurd; and it looks as if the story were going to inflict some anxiety on the reader. Is Mrs. Bold to be given to either of these unsatisfactory wooers? But no! the author comes forward to explain that she is not, and that he has no wish to harrow our feelings in that way. His heroine is too good for either of them, and he does not intend us ever to think otherwise. Then he explains his general opinion about his work, viz. that the reader, the spectator, should be in the confidence of the author; the people on his stage have to play out their comedy of errors, but the audience must not be confused or in doubt which Antipholus or Dromio is which. Of course, this confidence does not mean that the spectator knows all the story beforehand. It means that what is going on is comedy; that the mistakes and misjudgements on the stage are understood as such, and interesting and amusing as such to the lookers-on. Hence it follows that, as in comedy, so in the novels of Anthony Trollope, there is no great stress or strain. Life and the conduct which is three parts of life, or possibly more, must not be taken too seriously.

This does not mean that the novelist or the comic poet does his work without any use of what are commonly reckoned tragic motives. It is certainly not true of Trollope, any more than of Miss Austen, what is sometimes said in depreciation of them—that all their matter is insipid, ordinary, conventional life, at best the small interests and humours of un-heroic people. (Trollope does not seem to have cared for Jane Austen; he calls her conventional. It is a pity, but it can't be helped.) Trollope's stories of ordinary life are not wanting in the sensational elements; some of them are 'full of novelty and crime'. Phineas Finn has to stand his trial for the murder of Mr. Bonteen in the Curzon Street passage, which was really the work of Mr. Emilius, Lady Eustace's eloquent Asiatic second husband. Do not those names imply enough detective business? There is much more than detective business, of course, in *The Eustace Diamonds* and in *Phineas Redux*; but to say that Trollope is wanting in incident is a proposition which can be plainly refuted without any cavilling as to what is meant by incident. But cavilling (if that be the proper word) is unavoidable if one is not only to silence but to convert the objector. Surely at this time of day one may be allowed to reckon as 'incident' in a story whatever comes to affect the minds and lives of the personages. Is it incident when Johnny Eames saves Lord de Guest from the bull or knocks Mr. Adolphus Crosbie into Smith's bookstall at Paddington Station?[1] Most certainly and agreeably. It is also incident when Crosbie's first letters to Lily Dale are delivered at the small house at Allington, and equally when the letters cease, and much more when Lily Dale's letter comes to Crosbie at Courcy Castle just after he has engaged himself to Lady Alexandrina. 'He would have given all that he had in the world three times told, if he could have blotted out that visit to Courcy Castle from the past facts of his existence.'[2] Trollope's work is comedy, the comic epic in prose. He is a prose author, not a poet. Yet he is not to be reckoned among the prose authors who are that and nothing else. He was a lover of poetry (as a reading man he threw Dr. Johnson out of the window once,[3] in disgust at his treatment of 'Lycidas'), and though his business was prose one can see that he kept away from the tragic heights through a right understanding of his limitations and his proper scope, not through any want of sense or sensibility. He tells, in a plain easy-going way, of many things that might be matter for tragedy—adversities, sorrows, trials. Is he superficial? Certainly he is, with regard to such passionate things as are represented in *Wuthering Heights* or *The Ordeal of Richard Feverel* or *The Woodlanders*. But he always lets you know that the tragic motives are at work when to ignore them would falsify his record. The charges brought against Scott by Carlyle[4] may be brought against Trollope—with equal justice.

The best of Trollope's novels, it is pretty generally agreed,

---

[1] *The Small House at Allington*, chapters xxi and xxxiv.
[2] Chapter xxiv.
[3] *An Autobiography*, chapter iii ('The Oxford Trollope', p. 53).
[4] See p. 106 above.

is *The Last Chronicle of Barset*. In this there is more than usual of a continuous anxiety throughout. It begins with the accusation of theft against the Reverend Josiah Crawley, perpetual curate of Hogglestock. He had cashed a cheque for £20 which did not belong to him, and for his possession of which he could not account; and it is only at the end of the book that the matter is happily cleared up. The reader is not allowed to have any doubts as to Mr. Crawley's innocence, but he has to follow the stages of the long ordeal. It is the most serious thing Trollope wrote, and there are two heroic characters in it, Mr. Crawley and his wife, not to speak of Grace Crawley his daughter. His wife is of the finer temper and better judgement; Mr. Crawley full of pride, selfwill, bitterness, contempt, and anger, unmistakably true and courageous—all that was wanted for a tragic figure, if the author had been so inclined. The author's intention is different: he is a prose author and not a tragic poet; the pain of Mr. Crawley is left to be understood by the reader just as he chooses to take it; it is not brought to bear upon the reader's mind with the concentration of tragedy. The story is not simply Mr. Crawley Agonistes; it has a broad field and many other interests. Among these there is one which shows how well Trollope knew his own powers. *The Last Chronicle of Barset* tells the end of the story of the Warden. Old Mr. Harding has to suffer some cruelty, not comparable to the distress of Mr. Crawley, but still bad enough for an old weak man. Trollope has no particular delight in misery, but he understands what it means, and he also understands the limits of the novel (which is comedy) in dealing with miserable things. The story of Mr. Harding (in *The Warden* and *The Last Chronicle*) is a beautiful thing in itself if you follow it apart from the other stories; and, if there were any need to cavil about incident, one might maintain that this, too, is an adventurous story.

Trollope in his remarks on *Henry Esmond* is unexpectedly classical and exacting;[1] he is unjust, it may be, to *Vanity Fair*

---

[1] *Vanity Fair, Pendennis,* and *The Newcomes* 'are comparatively idle books. His only work, as far as I can judge them, in which there is no touch of idleness, is *Esmond*. . . . All his full-fledged novels, except *Esmond*, contain rather strings of

and *Pendennis*, and to Thackeray's conception of the unities of story-telling. His own books are most of them rather complicated. Many of them show great skill in managing a number of different interests and plots, and keeping them all together. Some of them are failures in this respect. There is a comic underplot in *Can you Forgive Her?* which might be taken out with no trouble and great advantage. It looks like the old style of farce; and Trollope in his *Autobiography* says that he worked it in from an early experiment of his in drama.[1] It is seldom, however, that there is so little meaning in Trollope's secondary characters or their stories. No English novelist has done anything to equal his Chronicles of Barset, and what may be called the later political series with all its branches, in keeping up through thousands of pages the image of a coherent world to which we return again and again—the world of Barchester, Bishop, Dean, Archdeacon, prebendaries, parsons, curates, of the county of Barset to which Freeman gave his approval on historical and philological grounds,[2] the Duke of Omnium and Plantagenet Palliser, the Greshams, Thornes, De Courcys, and then the London, and that extraordinary comic version of politics in which hardly any political motive is recognized except the glory and profit of being in and the discomfort of being out —more truly comic and more coherent even than the politics of *Coningsby* or *Sybil*. Nothing in Trollope except the fox-hunting scenes is better written than the politics of *Phineas Redux*: the disestablishment of the Church proposed by the leader of the Conservative party, the perplexity of the Liberals and particularly the speech of Mr. Daubeny the Conservative Prime Minister after his defeat in the House of Commons.[3] As an author of political comedy Trollope had two advantages over Disraeli. He was disinterested and kept his

incidents and memoirs of individuals, than a completed story. But *Esmond* is a whole from beginning to end, with its tale well told, its purpose developed, its moral brought home,—and its nail hit well on the head and driven in' (*Thackeray*, pp. 123–4).

[1] Chapter x ('The Oxford Trollope', p. 180).

[2] E. A. Freeman, 'Anthony Trollope' in *Macmillan's Magazine* xlvii (1882), p. 239.

[3] Chapter xxxix.

politics purely superficial and imaginary; that is one thing. In the second place he had Disraeli himself to draw from and has caught exactly, as far as it suited his purpose, the attitude and gesture of that hero confronting his great antagonist in the House.

Thinking of Barsetshire, I do not forget Mrs. Oliphant[1] and Carlingford, and I am not competent to choose between Salem Chapel and Barchester Cathedral. But Trollope's scene is immensely larger. It is like Balzac's in extent; but I will not attempt a comparison, except in one respect. Wherever else Trollope may fall short—in dialogue, that is, in pure and proper comedy, he can do what the great Frenchman refuses. He makes people talk like life. He is a dramatist, and Balzac is not.

[1] Author of nearly one hundred novels, including several with the general title, *Chronicles of Carlingford*.

II. CRITICAL PAPERS

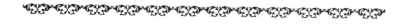

On Criticism: A View in 1889

'NOTHING if not critical' is a phrase that does not seem to have retained quite so many evil associations as one might have expected, considering who its author was. At any rate many people seem to be content to accept for themselves and their friends this description of the character of Iago as it appeared to Iago himself. 'Nothing if not critical' has been transplanted from its context, and, like the hard-worked 'touch of Nature', is made to do duty in very respectable quarters without any recollection of its equivocal origin. 'Nothing if not critical', like many isolated texts, can be made to take many different interpretations, and fits in with many pre-conceived opinions. It suggests the character of the strict, scientific, impartial judge whose mind is a dry light, who names accurately the objects of his study, keeps a sort of ledger of authors, with strict debit and credit accounts under every heading. The phrase suggests also one of the common-est popular opinions about criticism, an opinion which itself deserves to be criticized; the opinion that power of criticism is inconsistent with power of original production. 'Nothing if not critical' is the proposition; the corollary to it is, 'the critics are the fellows who have failed in literature and art'.[1] That a number of people are critics who are fit for nothing else—that all critics would be artists if they could—is a preju-dice that may be traced in many different ages and seems to summarize the revolt of much enduring humanity against a provoking tyranny. Humanity may have to admit that its works might be better, but it takes out its satisfaction in delivering home truths at its correctors, its critics.

[1] Cf. *Lothair*, chapter 35.

The superior critical person is known and despised and pitied by the very children, who know all about him from Hans Andersen. 'It is only a little story', says the story-teller, 'but it never has an end, as long as the world lasts.'[1] The youngest of five brothers became a critic, as the only real way of being something. 'I will criticize what you do', he says to his brothers; 'there is always something crazy in every piece of work; that will I pick out and talk about, and that is something.' The critic, you will remember, was treated somewhat disrespectfully when he died and tried to get an entrance at the gate of Heaven. He was allowed another chance, for the sake of his elder brother, an honest brickmaker; but the angel at the gate told him that he might not come in till he had done something. 'I could have said that much better', thought the critic to himself, when the angel had done speaking, but he did not say it out loud; and that was always something.

This popular opinion, or prejudice, about the futility of critics and criticism is developed sometimes into a rather imposing piece of philosophical theory. Criticism is regarded as a sort of parasitic plant, coming after and growing over the good old stock of poetry, of original literary production generally. There are many instances in favour of this theory. There is the literature of criticism and analysis and over-refinement that flourished in Alexandria at the courts of the Ptolemies. That is contrasted with the spontaneous imagination, the creative genius, of the great Athenian time. The diffuse and trifling academic disputations, the laborious and learned researches of the seventeenth and eighteenth centuries in Italy came to supplant the poetic and artistic originality of the sixteenth. Pope and Boileau follow Shakespeare and Corneille. Reflection increases as the imagination is relaxed.

A theory of this sort was formulated, in regard to philosophical criticism especially, by Hegel, who saw that Greek philosophy flourished best just after the real power of Greece had begun to decline. According to this view, Plato and Aristotle were the executors for Greece, coming into the empty house when the master had passed away, and going

[1] *Noget* ('Something').

about with solemn faces making an inventory of his personal property and a balance-sheet of his affairs. Philosophy comes after the lively and vigorous adventures of a great age and gives an account of it all. Hegel, an entertaining writer in his way, has a parable for us here, and says that *the owl of Minerva does not begin to fly abroad till the twilight shadows are falling*. Philosophy is the owl.[1]

Hegel is thinking of strict philosophy, regarded as a scientific criticism of beliefs and morals, institutions and constitutions, a scientific criticism of science itself. He is not thinking of criticism in its ordinary sense of literary criticism. But his theory is plainly connected with the popular idea of the separating line to be drawn between original workers and critics. It illustrates that view in a striking way, and it may easily be applied to the history of literature. Those who talk of the decadence shown in an age of critics, those who talk of literary decline and of the degeneration of productivity into criticism, have the same kind of view of the progress and the succession of historical periods as Hegel had. There are times of great activity in which men rise above their average, do great things, and throw themselves away heroically; discover and conquer empires, and go in quest of the Fountain of Youth; build great monuments, and crowd the stage with a myriad of imaginary figures, the creations of their strenuous and unwearied intellects. Then the change comes, the glow and enthusiasms pass away, the adventurers are disillusioned, and those who live to grow old grow fat and respectable. A sober and reasonable, an unproductive and critical set of people hold the ground, with more or less title to esteem. But Walpole and Pope do not take people captive, neither can they provoke such fury, as Cromwell and Milton can: 'The second temple was not like the first.'[2] There is a great deal in this view which can hardly be confuted. Over and over again in history one finds the sequence. There is a difference between

---

[1] Wenn die Philosophie ihr Grau in Grau malt, dann ist eine Gestalt des Lebens alt geworden, und mit Grau in Grau lässt sie sich nicht verjüngen, sondern nur erkennen; die Eule der Minerva beginnt erst mit der einbrechenden Dämmerung ihren Flug. *Philosophie des Rechts*, Vorrede, *ad fin.* (*Werke* (Berlin, 1854), viii. 20).

[2] Dryden, 'To my Dear Friend Mr. Congreve, On his Comedy, call'd, The Double-Dealer'.

Athenian and Alexandrian literature, between the age of
Shakespeare and the age of Pope. There are times of great
origination, followed by times of eclecticism, discussion,
criticism. Some generations are occupied with their own
inventions, other are inquisitive rather than inventive, and
show a boundless curiosity about everything that is not their
own business. The fathers pile up great works and their sons
arrange them.

This, however, is not the whole truth, and it will be found
that criticism has another function besides that of executor to
a dead genius. If executor to the dead, it is also guardian to
the heir. In different ages and in many ways criticism has
preceded great successes in literature, has shown the way to
the poets, the makers. Careful and elaborate literary criticism
is not very old in modern literature. But though reviewing is
new, the critical and analytic mind has been in existence for
some time; and it may be said with some plausibility that no
great things have been accomplished in literature in any century, since the dark ages, that have not been heralded to some
extent by a revival of criticism, by some renewed display of
that curiosity about old or foreign things, which we sometimes take, too rashly, for an indication of senility and decline.

Dante assigned the date 1300 for his journey through the
three realms of Hell, Purgatory, and Paradise. The century
which was thus closed by a great imaginative work was one
marked by an extraordinary amount of curious research into
old and foreign documents, and the *Divine Comedy* is decorated from beginning to end with the treasures picked up by
laborious students. The learning of the thirteenth century
was not critical as the learning of Bentley or Munro was
critical. It was not exercised on the same problems. But it had
all the qualities that distinguish critical from imaginative
minds; it analysed and refined; it was infinitely keen. Nothing
could be more unlike the work of the free poetic imagination
than the work of Albertus Magnus or Thomas Aquinas; and
if any philosophy is parasitic and derivative it is their philosophy, which never could have existed but for the enterprise
of the explorers and translators who got hold of the Arabic
versions of Aristotle's Greek, and turned them into Latin.

All this heavy load, the product of an erudite and over-subtle age, is taken up and melted into the mould of the great poem —the greatest of all human achievements, perhaps, in sustained imagination. And not only in its matter is Dante's poem indebted to reflection and research and learning. Dante has left us an example of his own critical studies preliminary to the labour of artistic creation. Preliminary criticism was so far from being unnecessary that he had even to choose first of all what language he should write in, the Italian language having as yet hardly a literary existence. Discussions on language are supposed to be a very proper employment for learned academies with not much to do. Yet the *Accademia della Crusca*, if reproached for the futility of its labours, might point to the treatise *De Vulgari Eloquentia*; the great poet himself had written an essay on the Italian language.

The life of Dante is peculiarly illustrative of the function that may belong to scholarship and reflection in the career of an artist. In his life there are two poetical stages, one at the beginning, one at the end; and they are separated by a period in which apparently he wrote little poetry but devoted himself to study, to scientific and philosophical inquiries. He was as unsparing in the work of mere scholarship, making notes and abstracts and disquisitions, as in his proper poetical work when he resumed it later.

We know the way the schoolmen were treated in the sixteenth century by men of letters proud of their Greek, and philosophers who were planning the conquest of Nature. We have been taught to distinguish the Baconian bees of inductive and practical science from the Scotist and Thomist spiders spinning refined and airy tissues out of their own inner consciousness. The age of the great schoolmen and their works, of those 'vermiculate questions', as Bacon called them,[1] of those 'questionists and all the barbarous nation of schoolmen', as Ascham called them,[2] was certainly over-refined and over-subtle. 'Nothing if not analytical' one is inclined to say. But one of the questionists was Dante.

[1] *The Advancement of Learning*, I. iv. 5.
[2] *The Scholemaster*, book ii; *The English Works of Roger Ascham*, ed. W. Aldis Wright (Cambridge, 1904), p. 282.

Petrarch came in the next generation, and in a new world. It is easy enough to point out the faults of the *Canzoniere*, the *Sonetti e Canzoni in Vita e in Morte di Madonna Laura*; it has been done often enough. Not even those who are blind to its great beauties can refuse to admit the historical fact of its widespread influence. Who can reckon up the number of the amorists, the sonneteers, the eloquent lovers who are either *tenants-in-chief* of Petrarch, or the vassals of his vassals. Those who wish to realize the power of his literary genius, the success of his poetical innovations, may be advised to inquire what importance belongs to Ronsard and Spenser in their respective countries, and what opinion was entertained of Petrarch by the French and the English poet. Yet Petrarch's sonnets form a smaller part of his life than his scholarship and his criticism. One of his chief interests was critical; to understand and to enable others to understand the beauty of the classical literature of Rome was one of his ideals. The work had to be done by criticism, by explanation of the difference between good and bad in literature. All criticism has a negative side to it, getting rid of all false conceptions, all mists and vapours that colour or distort the vision. Petrarch did this sort of service, and was one of the first men to teach the duty and the necessity of dispassionate observation. With his critical euphrasy he purged the eyes of scholars,[1] and restored the glory of Rome untravestied by any superstitious or superfluous decoration.

Petrarch, it has been said, is 'the first of the moderns'. In that epithet there is a suggestion of the psychological and analytical malady supposed by some to distinguish the modern world from the supposed healthiness and unconcern of ancient Greece. Petrarch has affinities with Rousseau; he is interested in the soul; and his own soul is restless and dissatisfied. But the suspicion of over-sensibility in Petrarch does not diminish in any way the praise due to him for two things: for sane criticism and exposition of classical literature, and for his great poetic mastery of style.

[1]   to nobler sights
  Michael from *Adams* eyes the Filme remov'd
  Which that false Fruit that promis'd clearer sight
  Had bred; then purg'd with Euphrasie and Rue
  The visual Nerve, for he had much to see.   (*Paradise Lost*, xi. 411.)

In Europe generally the age of the humanists, the critics and translators, is followed by the age of the great artists. But this is not the whole truth. The truth is that in many cases the first great critics were the first to show not only precept but example to the artists that followed. After Petrarch and Boccaccio, at once students of the ancient schools and masters of the modern, there comes such a representative man as Politian, in a time when the work of criticism was much more exact and more exacting than in Petrarch's time, and when there was perhaps less encouragement to original composition, at any rate in the vulgar tongue. Yet Politian the student and critic is among the eminent Italian poets, not only a discoverer and a systematizer, but an inventor. If the distinction between the age of the humanists and the age of the artists is pretty clearly marked in Italy, it is hardly less so in England. Of course, both of the periods fall much later in England; one has to allow for difference of meridian in literature as well as in more practical affairs. In England the age of the humanists lasts down to about the middle of the reign of Queen Elizabeth. The chief intellectual interest in England after the accession of Henry VII was (apart from religious controversy) concerned with education, with the formation of character, in which process learning was held to have an important place. Colet, Erasmus, More, Elyot, Ascham—these are representative intellects of the first half of the sixteenth century. And the first work, brilliant and successful in its own day, which ushered in a new and more varied sort of literature, was *Euphues: The Anatomy of Wit*, a book that treated the humanist problems in a captivating style. The style of *Euphues* would hardly have commended itself to Ascham, the severe critic of all romantic extravagances. But, for all that, *Euphues* depends upon Ascham and derives from him. And *Euphues* is a harbinger of the great host of poets. Spenser's *Shepheardes Calender* appeared in the following year. There had been an anticipation of some great new literature to come. 'An over-faint quietness' seemed to 'strew the house for poets', as Sidney said.[1]

Spenser himself, and Sidney, were much given to criticism,

[1] Cf. p. 13 n. above.

and lived in a critical set. Not that their criticism is of a
very valuable order; it was chiefly engaged in trying to
impose the classical metres—hexameters, iambic trimeters,
sapphics, and so on—on the long-suffering English tongue.
Both Sidney and Spenser, fortunately both for their critical
and their poetical reputation, soon gave up this ill-omened
project of theirs. What is interesting is that both of them—
in their different degrees and ranges pioneers and *conquista-
dores* of poetic territory—should have had so minute an
education in criticism.

Shakespeare, one is reminded, had 'small Latin and less
Greek'; but that is not to say that he had none. We may
appeal to a critic not generally kind to Shakespeare, one of
his French critics, La Harpe, who says that 'Shakespeare,
rude as he was, was not entirely destitute of book learning'.[1]
One is glad to agree with this impartial gentleman. There
went something more than mere chance to the creation of
Shakespeare's plays. They could never have existed but for
a vast amount of labour, for the most part critical, under-
taken by a number of writers of Shakespeare's own generation and the generation preceding. Though this critical activity found but little expression in formal critical essays or
reviews, we can trace the gradual adoption by the playwrights
of literary inventions that were the result of critical study.
We can recognize the great distinction between the scholarly
dramatists who wrote bookish plays, and the heedless vigorous popular drama that had no literary scruples at all. We
can trace the gradual occupation of the popular theatres by
writers who took what they could from the school of the
bookish dramatists and turned it to their own uses. Marlowe,
the real first founder of the Elizabethan drama, was the inventor of dramatic blank verse. That is to say he took the
metrical scheme that had been tried before him by learned
and scholarly poets, and showed how it should be used. The
blank verse of English drama, the blank verse of Milton, are

[1] 'Shakespeare lui-même, tout grossier qu'il était, n'était pas sans lecture et sans
connaissance.' (Jean-François de La Harpe, *Cours de littérature* (Paris, 1799), quoted
by Victor Hugo in his *William Shakespeare* (1864), II. i. 1), and included by Flaubert in his 'dossier de la bêtise humaine' (*Lettres de Gustave Flaubert à George
Sand, précédées d'une étude par Guy de Maupassant* (Paris, 1884), p. xxxii).

due to the poet of *Dr. Faustus*. But it should not be forgotten that the metre, though not the music, of blank verse was used in England first by poets who were also critics—by the Earl of Surrey, who systematically imitated the Italians, and by Sackville, the great representative in England of the Italian school of drama, that tried to follow the classics, and drew out classical rules of composition. 'Shakespeare, rude as he was, was not entirely destitute of book-learning'; and he is more indebted to the critical researches and experiments of his forerunners than the popular theory of Shakespeare's unpremeditated and extempore way of writing would be at all inclined to allow.

In the lives of the great poets of the time of the French Revolution, and later, criticism is mixed up with original work in the most extraordinary way. No neat theory of the incompatibility of criticism and original work can be made to square with what we know of the life of Wordsworth and Coleridge in the Quantocks, or of the stormy years in which Victor Hugo fought the orthodox playgoers and made bonfires of their classical apparatus.

With those poets criticism is no longer anything implicit, unconscious. Criticism, by the end of the eighteenth century, had come to be, if not a science, at any rate a complex body of opinion; if not a code, at any rate an immense series of Law Reports. Critics had set up for themselves, and formed a great military power that had to be reckoned with. We have to reckon with it now. Criticism, elaborate detailed criticism of new books and old books, of all the literatures under the sun, exerts an influence in modern civilization that may be compared with the influence of the pulpit. At every turn we are met with opinions, not on books merely, but on matters of practical life and morality, that have their origin in literary criticism. A man reads a review of a lady's novel in the *Spectator*, and when he meets his friend begins straightway to hint that he has some new ideas about a new religion. When people fall to talking about general or abstract or serious subjects, the odds are considerable that some magazine article is at the bottom of it. No one can appreciate the popular thought, the current views, without taking into account the power of the critics to form and spread beliefs and disbeliefs.

Yet criticism as an independent and comprehensive department of literature is not of very old standing. In the history of its growth we may notice a pretty clear division between two periods.

In the seventeenth and eighteenth centuries criticism was to a great extent *a priori* and dogmatic. The French set the fashion. A number of strict rules were established, by which literary composition was to be directed and appraised. The critics were inquisitors and persecuted any heretic who showed want of respect for their orthodoxy. Dick Minim the critic, in Johnson's essays,[1] began by learning to talk of the unities, and the catastrophes of plays. Those were the catchwords. The literary air was full of such meteoric dust, shed from the classical system.

The catchwords nowadays are different, and there is no orthodoxy any more. Critics are no longer *a priori* and abstract, no longer acknowledge the authority of Aristotle or Longinus. Criticism now follows the prevailing fashion. If it is scientific, it resembles natural history rather than exact science; it uses historical and comparative methods, when it uses any methods at all.

The old sort of criticism is well represented by 'A Receipt to make an Epic Poem' included in the great work of Martinus Scriblerus, *Of the Art of Sinking in Poetry*.[2] The critics had drawn up a number of strict formulas, to be observed by all authors. An epic poem must be worked out on their pattern. They had a name for the supernatural agencies that were admissible in an epic. The gods and goddesses that appear in the *Iliad* and *Aeneid* were classed by the orthodox critics as *machinery*. On this subject Martinus Scriblerus is not more instructive than M. Bossu. 'The next question is, where and on what occasions, machines may be used? It is certain Homer and Virgil make use of them everywhere and scarce suffer any action to be performed without them. . . . The Gods are the causes of the action, they form the intrigue, and they bring about the solution. . . .' And, in conclusion, 'Thus the machinery crowns

---

[1] *The Idler*, Nos. lx and lxi.
[2] Chapter xv; first published in *The Guardian*, No. lxxviii, in 1713.

the whole work, and renders it at once marvellous, probable, and moral.'[1]

Here is Martinus Scriblerus his instructions on the same subject.

For the Machines

Take of deities, male and female, as many as you can use; separate them into two equal parts, and keep Jupiter in the middle. Let Juno put him in a ferment, and Venus mollify him. Remember on all occasions to make use of volatile Mercury. If you have need of devils, draw them out of Milton's Paradise, and extract your spirits from Tasso. The use of these machines is evident; for since no Epick Poem can possibly subsist without them, the wisest way is to reserve them for your greatest necessities; when you cannot extricate your hero by any human means, or yourself by your own wit, seek relief from Heaven, and the Gods will do your business very readily. This is according to the direct prescription of Horace in his Art of Poetry.

> Nec Deus intersit, nisi dignus vindice nodus
> Inciderit.

That is to say, *A poet should never call upon the gods for their assistance but when he is in great perplexity.*

And so on—for the Descriptions (Tempest, Battle, Burning Town)—for the Moral and all the rest of it, Martinus gives his rules. The biographer of Scriblerus, we may be sure, had his eye not only on the epic poems of the day but also on the systematic theory they followed. He was acquainted with Bossu the critic as well as with Blackmore the rhapsodist.

The Intrigue, the Catastrophe, the Unities were by no means empty names in those days. People fought about them as they had fought about the freedom of the will and the doctrine of sufficient grace. Dr. Johnson counted the Unities as straw and stubble in his preface to his edition of Shakespeare, but even that leviathan of criticism seems to have had some misgivings afterwards about his treatment of them.[2]

---

[1] From the summary of Bossu's treatise (as 'A General View of the Epic Poem, and of the Iliad and Odyssey') prefixed by Pope to his translation of the *Odyssey* (1725); cf. p. 255 below.

[2] Ker probably had in mind the words with which Johnson concluded his discussion of the Unities: 'I am almost frighted at my own temerity; and when I estimate the fame and the strength of those that maintain the contrary opinion, am ready to sink down in reverential silence. . . .'

Voltaire, when he speaks of the Unities, has religious reverence in his voice. Poetical Justice was another of the idols; and plays and poems were judged by their morals. Dr. Johnson did not like the moral of *King Lear*. He thought that Tate improved the play by saving the life of Cordelia. This moralizing sort of criticism survives curiously in the notes of Gifford to his editions of the dramatists, as the love of Poetical Justice does in the hissing and hooting with which the gallery receives the villain of a melodrama.

Probably no one wishes to see the old sort of criticism revived. The new sort is at any rate, whether sounder or not, infinitely more interesting. Criticism has now become a province of history. The growth of history in the nineteenth century is hardly less remarkable than the growth of physical science itself—with which history is not entirely unconnected. In a certain university in the island of Britain there is a Chair of Natural and Civil History (I suppose there was a reason once for this union, as for that other strange one of Probate, Divorce, and Admiralty) and, I believe, a professor of those two oddly united subjects.[1] There is one theme which he might take, if he desired to 'combine his information'. The author of *The Origin of Species* represents much more than mere natural history, and his general view of the world is anticipated or shared by many historians, many poets and romancers. By their methods of observation, by their regard for the minutest particulars bearing on their study, by their sense of the vastness of the world, and the power of time to work changes, history and criticism share the same intellectual character with studies in widely different subject matters.

Taine is representative of the power and the range of criticism in our days. He, too, has his theories, but they are not like those of Martinus Scriblerus. His criticism is not a reading of the riot-act, a denunciation of pains and penalties against the transgressors of the law. Criticism, for him, is an

---

[1] The university was St. Andrews. A chair of Civil History was instituted there in 1747, and proved a complete sinecure. By an ordinance of 1862 the Professor of Civil History became the Professor of Natural History as well, and continued so until 1897, when the Commissioners ordained that the chair should henceforth be known as the chair of Natural History.

attempt to construct an account of the past, to trace the growth of ideas and literary fashions, to find, as far as possible, the conditions of intellectual progress. Everything is pressed into the service. To interpret a book, he asks for the life of the author, for the history of the age he lived in. There is no end to his curiosity. He would like to see the house and furniture and dress of the author he is studying; to know his dinner hour, and whether he drank wine or beer or water. The English climate interprets English literature. Each English writer sums up in himself and his books certain subtle effects of the *environnement* in which the English nation lives, and shows some peculiar variety of the general hereditary racial type of Englishmen. One is familiar with this sort of method in the brilliant impromptu essay on Celtic Literature by Matthew Arnold. Arnold, a man of genius, with the intuitive and divining faculty of genius, found analogies in Shakespeare and Milton to the beauties of Celtic poetry and romance; and for his convincing and enlightening interpretation of poetry we cannot be grateful enough. He is not content with interpretation of poetry, however. 'The Celtic note' in Shakespeare, 'the Celtic aërialness and magic', are considered in connexion with a hypothesis in the field of natural history, a theory of the Celtic element in the English race. Part of the ancestry of the English race is Celtic, and this explains the Celtic natural magic in *A Midsummer-Night's Dream* and *The Merchant of Venice*. 'Let us go to those who say it is vain to look for Celtic elements in any Englishman, and let us ask them, first, if they seize what we mean by the power of natural magic in Celtic poetry; secondly, if English poetry does not eminently exhibit this power; and, thirdly, where they suppose English poetry got it from?'[1]

The time may come when this employment of natural history to explain the growth of poetry may seem as idle as Dick Minim's vocabulary of unities and catastrophes. Where did Shakespeare get his 'natural magic'? Where does the music come from? There are different ways of trying to solve that problem, and some of them are unsuccessful.

Perhaps we may even go the length of saying that it is

[1] *On the Study of Celtic Literature* (1867), vi; Everyman's Library edn., pp. 127–8.

probable this mode of criticism will also pass away; that the climate and the scenery and the ancestry and all the rest of it will be neglected by the criticism of the future; that even the general tendencies and characteristics, which play such a part in modern criticism, may come to have a reduced importance. To know and appreciate the natural magic of Shakespeare is a more proper occupation for the critic and the student, than the inquiry whether it is to be called Greek or Celtic or Teutonic. There are signs of a return of criticism from its wide historical divagations, to an insistence upon principles of art—not arbitrary, dogmatic, positive rules, like those of the unities, and the machineries, but principles founded upon the historical discoveries of critics like Sainte-Beuve and Taine, and inspired by a high ideal of literary perfection. Flaubert wrote to George Sand in 1869:

Vous me parlez de la critique dans votre dernière lettre, en me disant qu'elle disparaîtra prochainement. Je crois, au contraire, qu'elle est tout au plus à son aurore. On a pris le contrepied de la précédente, mais rien de plus. Du temps de La Harpe on était grammairien, du temps de Sainte-Beuve et de Taine on est historien. Quand sera-t-on artiste, rien qu'artiste, mais bien artiste? Où connaissez-vous une critique qui s'inquiète de l'œuvre en *soi*, d'une façon intense? On analyse très finement le milieu où elle s'est produite et les causes qui l'ont amenée; mais la poétique *insciente?* d'où elle résulte? sa composition, son style? le point de vue de l'auteur?[1]

Yet that is in the future, if it is at all; *we* belong to the generation of the historians. It is only paying a just debt, if we take an audit and find out how much we owe to them.

We sometimes forget what an infinite widening of the horizon came when the unities and the machineries were sold up and cleared out of the way; when, not much more than a hundred years ago, *the Past* disclosed itself, and there was borne in upon the wits of living man the rumours and the turmoil of those who had lived before them; when the long-past life of Greece and of the Middle Ages came like the wind of the spirit upon Goethe, and he communed with them like Odysseus in the land of the dead, speaking to the shadows across the trench. We have forgotten that it was ever miracu-

[1] *Lettres de Gustave Flaubert à George Sand* (Paris, 1884), p. 81.

lous, this disappearance of the barrier that kept past history unintelligible, undiscovered. Indeed there are fewer things in the past more difficult to realize than the utter want of curiosity about past ages that prevailed in the eighteenth century. Then, Taine has written, 'they imagined the men of every stock and every age as more or less alike: the Greek and the barbarian, the Hindoo, the man of the Renaissance and the man of the eighteenth century, all cast in the same mould, and that an abstraction, which did duty for the whole human race'.[1] It was a dull grey abstract view of history they had, with neither colour nor perspective; it haunts one sometimes in reading the political theories and the moral essays of Johnson or Rousseau. The change came through criticism, through an increased fineness of perception. It began to be surmised that a good deal of humanity escaped the philosophical meshes. The critics gradually passed over from the universal—their Catastrophes and Machineries—to the particular, to studies of the peculiar value of individual writers. Differences, not agreement, came to be emphasized and made much of. There was some loss of logical precision, but who regretted *that*, in the quickening of the senses? To have a neat theory of the denouement of a piece, to stickle for Poetical Justice, might be honourable and virtuous. But it was better still to gain, without logic, the freedom of a wanderer among old literatures, to have correspondents and hosts in every century. One's set theories did not prosper; but there was life and exhilaration in it.

It is true that the results gained by the new schools of criticism differed very greatly in value. The curiosity of some was empty enough, and returned empty from the widest excursions into Greece and Spain, into *Eddas* and *Vedas*. The vanity of discovery gained on them, and brought its own penalty by making them irritable, discontented, fidgety, unable to enjoy their present study for thinking of the next stage to which they were to proceed. But the defects of the Schlegels and others do not detract from the great works of Goethe, Scott, or Hugo, the three great writers of three different countries, three successive generations, who, raised

[1] *Histoire de la littérature anglaise* (1864–9), i, p. xii.

far above the multitude of critics, directed them in their studies of antique and foreign literatures and made them see the wide prospects open to them. All modern criticism, in spite of dissensions and disagreements, acknowledges one guiding principle at least, one rule: to distinguish things different.

The *Iliad* is not of the same genus as the *Aeneid*. That is a commonplace now; it would have been a paradox to Addison. It may serve to mark the great change that has arisen from the strengthening of the historical past of criticism. It is not the historical aspect that should be emphasized, however. The historical theorizings about environments and all the rest might disappear and leave still the essential valuable part of modern criticism. Not to confound things different; to reckon every author as one individual, with his own particular story to tell, his own individual manner, his own value—that is the essence of it. Not to judge abstractedly, but to see concretely, is the end and aim of it. Of course, there are certain writers whom it is impossible to see, who are altogether abstract, in whom there is no residuum, no core, when their involutions of commonplaces and generalities have gone. Still, every writer should be considered as a real person till he proves the contrary. Criticism and literary research, which have added such a brilliant company of forgotten worthies to the old select circle, can afford to make an occasional false step, to waste a little time occasionally. Their enterprise is big enough to cover a few bad debts.

On Culture: A View in 1896;
With a Postscript on the Humanities

Nemo adeo ferus est ut non mitescere possit
Si modo culturae patientem commodet aurem.
(Horace, *Epistles*, i. i. 39–40.)

Culture is a good word, which has had a long history. It is used by Horace very much as we use it now, without any qualifying word, simply as a short title for mental and spiritual discipline. Like other good words it has been badly treated. In this generation it has suffered a good deal of injustice, especially since it was recommended by Matthew Arnold as a cure for Anarchy. One of the results of his argument was that the good word Culture was immediately turned into a popular catchword among all the hosts of Anarchy, and generally made rather ridiculous. There seems, however, to be no reason to think that the word will go out of use. On the contrary its meanings are being extended in all directions. It is the regular word among anthropologists and antiquarians for the civilization of any form of society, even the most illiterate; you hear of the culture of the Stone Age, of the Bronze Age, and so on. The word, in spite of its hard treatment, has survived as a good common useful word, which may be used (in certain references at any rate) without provoking a faction, fight, or even a sneer.

There can be no doubt that the word has been hardly treated. It has been treated almost as cruelly as the word religion, and in much the same way. Both words have suffered from being carried far away from their original meaning. It is a fallacy, of course, and a familiar one, to say that words are only to be used in their strict etymological sense. The original sense need not be the right one. But very often the original meaning is nearly the best, and that is the case with the words culture and religion. Religion, meaning duty and implying reverence and awe, is degraded to mean a sort of invention that may be picked up, or a kind of sentiment to be proud of. Culture, which implies some process of training and discipline, a definite aim, and the choice of adequate means, often is made to denote the very reverse of all this—the dissipation of the mind, without aim or study or even any strong desire, among ready-made opinions, with a wearisome pretence of interest in 'ideas'.

'The weaker brother', as usual, is responsible for a good deal of the mischief. His opportunities are unfailing, because every increase of knowledge and every new adventure in the regions of the imagination give him a chance to make them ridiculous. There is an ironical sentence of Antoine Rivarol, the observer of the first years of the French Revolution, in one of his sceptical leading articles of 1789, in which he describes how the works of great philosophers are either ignored or misapplied by the majority. He is talking of the influence of philosophers on the courts of the day, and he says that the writings of the philosophers have done no harm in themselves, because the general multitude cannot read them and could not understand them. But the philosophers put it into the heads of ten people to write books which are easy enough to understand. The governing powers will not listen to the greater writers who give them good advice; they give time and opportunity for meaner minds to write the commentary, and the commentary comes home to the masses.[1]

There is some meaning and good sense in this piece of aristocratic wickedness; whether it is right or wrong in that particular instance, it calls attention to the faculty of the human race for taking up things in the wrong way, and for poisoning the diffusion of knowledge. That is what has hap-

[1] 'Il faut pourtant observer que les livres des philosophes n'ont point fait de mal par eux-mêmes, puisque le peuple ne les lit point et ne les entendrait pas; mais il n'est pas moins vrai qu'ils ont nui par tous les livres qu'ils ont fait faire, et que le peuple a fort bien saisis. Autrefois un livre qui ne passait pas l'antichambre n'était pas fort dangereux; et aujourd'hui il n'y a que ceux qui en effet qui ne quittent pas les antichambres qui sont vraiment redoutables. En quoi il faut louer les philosophes qui écrivaient avec élévation pour corriger les gouvernements, et non pour les renverser; pour soulager les peuples, et non pour les soulever: mais les gouvernements ont méprisé la voix des grands écrivains, et ont donné le temps aux petits esprits de commenter les ouvrages du génie, et de les mettre à la portée de la populace.' *Journal politique national*, première série, No. xii (*Œuvres choisies de A. Rivarol*, éd. M. de Lescure (2 tom., Paris, 1880), ii. 88.

pened in many quarters in the degradation of the ideal of Culture. The results of learning are hawked about and used freely by people who have no conception of the spirit of learning, and no part or lot in the ambitions of the scholar.

The most disgusting spectacle in history is the degradation of ideas in and through their very success. 'But one hath seen, and all the blind will see'.[1] The original discoverer, we may suppose, writes down a number of noble sentiments and observations which he has found out for himself, living like a free man and an adventurer outside the dullness and insensibility of custom and routine. Suppose that his visions and his prophecies have some effect; that his awakening call is listened to and taken up by the multitudes, and that they go out to follow him to his mountain of vision. Even though they follow the same track they cannot go in the same spirit; they cannot go as adventurers, they want to take their luggage with them, they hate to be made to live too energetically; and when they come to the specular mount they are not satisfied until they have built a railway up it and a hotel at the top. This is the March of Intellect.

It is useful to have an extreme case to start from, and that is what is provided by Crabbe in his story of 'The Learned Boy', an example of the effect of culture and enlightenment in the wrong place.[2] The learned boy is a weak-minded youth, a farmer's son, who is brought up by his grandmother and made objectionable to his strong-minded father by his general uselessness and his conceited piety. His grandmother remarks of him:

> Once he the names of saints and patriarchs old,
> Judges and kings, and chiefs and prophets, told;
> Then he in winter-nights the Bible took,
> To count how often in the sacred book
> The sacred name appear'd, and could rehearse
> Which were the middle chapter, word, and verse,
> The very letter in the middle placed,
> And so employ'd the hours that others waste.

He is sent to London to be a clerk in an office, and there he

---

[1] Tennyson, 'The Holy Grail'.   [2] Cf. p. 76 above.

'gets culture' and learns to read rationalist books. His fellow
clerk tells him the Bible is all very well in its way:

> 'Nay, nay!' the friend replied,
> 'You need not lay the good old book aside;
> Antique and curious, I myself indeed
> Read it at times, but as a man should read;
> A fine old work it is, and I protest
> I hate to hear it treated as a jest;
> The book has wisdom in it, if you look
> Wisely upon it as another book.'

The Boy comes back with his new opinions and uses them to
enlighten and alarm his grandmother:

> 'I now am wiser—yet agree in this,
> The book has things that are not much amiss;
> It is a fine old work, and I protest
> I hate to hear it treated as a jest:
> The book has wisdom in it, if you look
> Wisely upon it as another book.'

The point of Crabbe's satirical demonstration is that the
Boy's early religion and later culture are equally despicable
and futile. The case is summed up by the father with a
horsewhip:

> 'Vain, worthless, stupid wretch!' the Father cried;
> 'Dost thou presume to teach? art thou a guide?
> Driveller and dog, it gave the mind distress
> To hear thy thoughts in their religious dress;
> Thy pious folly moved my strong disdain,
> Yet I forgave thee for thy want of brain;
> But Job in patience must the man exceed
> Who could endure thee in thy present creed.
> Is it for thee, thou idiot, to pretend
> The wicked cause a helping hand to lend?
> Canst thou a judge in any question be?
> Atheists themselves would scorn a friend like thee.'

It is well to have an extreme instance like this stated by an
historian of moral cases like Crabbe. It is convenient to start
from zero. The unfortunate thing is that there are infinite
gradations, and that the case of the Learned Boy is repeated

in higher, more complicated and more dangerous forms, whenever in the confusion of modern civilization we are tempted to comply with intellectual fashions that are beyond our capacity, or that do not appeal to or satisfy a natural instinctive taste.

No doubt modern culture is suffering still from the heroic example of the great masters of the Revival of Learning, the men who took all knowledge to be their province, whose ambitions were infinite and who never thought much about any limitations of their powers. From Petrarch at the beginning (the first modern man who understood what was meant by culture as the ancients understood it), to universal geniuses like Leonardo and Michael Angelo, and on to Leibniz working with equal industry at metaphysics, mathematics, and the antiquities of the House of Brunswick, with numbers of less original men playing easily about in huge libraries and tossing the heaviest learning about with no apparent effort (like the author of *The Anatomy of Melancholy* and the author of *Hudibras*), there are plenty of dangerous good examples—the worst possible examples for people who begin to study without any natural impulse and only with a serious wish to do the right thing or a frivolous wish to appear to have done the right thing.

Shakespeare in his *Love's Labour's Lost*—one of the most didactic of his plays—has done something to show up the fallacy of the slow serious-minded persons who try to imitate the heroes of learning, not from any heroic impulse but merely to improve their minds. To improve one's mind is the end of culture; but culture has suffered from the imitation of great authors and artists who had different motives more directly rising from the subjects of their study, less self-regarding.

One of the most notable things in modern history is the gradual formulation of a protest in the seventeenth and eighteenth centuries against the omniscient frame of mind that was encouraged by the Revival of Learning and by the 'Renaissance'—whatever that may have been. Milton's ideal of culture is explained in his letter *Of Education* to Mr. Samuel Hartlib. His theory of education is that of the old-fashioned, comprehensive, ambitious scholarship, which aimed at including the whole of knowledge, and which thought of a well-educated man as one who had studied, if not every subject, at least every kind of subject. Milton's theory is the same on the whole as that of Rabelais. One distinctive thing about this old ideal is the scanty attention to the limitations of human life. The studies are piled up without any regard for what is possible in a certain time; to attain such wide and profound knowledge the earthly year, to use Sir Thomas Browne's phrase, would have to be a 'revolution year of Saturn',[1] that is, thirty years long.

In contrast to this uncompromising ideal of knowledge, there is a more economical plan, which comes into favour very clearly at the end of the seventeenth century, and which characterizes the age of Anne as contrasted with the middle of the seventeenth century, the time of Milton.[2] The motive of this plan of study, this ideal of culture, is to keep proportion in the human being. It is one of the humanistic aims to make the best of man, to bring out to the best advantage all the capacities of the human creature. But, while Milton and Rabelais thought of the human being as infinite and unwearied, the humanists of this other school had regard to what is possible, planning the studies in relation to the time allowed and the necessities of human life. So Milton is representative of one school of humanism, the unsparing and uncompromising, and Swift is representative of the other, the humanism that takes into account the possibilities of our attainments, and that takes consequently a rather low estimate of knowledge obtainable.

One is inclined to take the contrast between these two ideals as one between the age of expansion and the age of reflection and caution. This view is not wrong, but it is not right to take the limited, economic sort of culture as a new thing. It was not invented first by way of reaction against the ideal of Milton and the rest. It is one of the humanist modes found quite early in the history of the Revival of Learning. It is found in More's *Utopia*, and constitutes one of the things

---

[1] *Religio Medici*, I, sec. xli.
[2] Cf. Ker, *Collected Essays*, i. 97–99.

in which *Utopia* differs from the great ambitious Renaissance ideal. The theory of life in *Utopia* is one that deals out the day with attention to what is possible in an ordinary day. The Utopians are men who live in the best possible way, and who realize in the best possible way what is in human nature. They all work for their living; none are parasitical; they are in one way equal, being all working-men. And they are all students; none of them works too hard, and all have some leisure for study. It is clear that in life of this sort the exorbitant study we find in Rabelais and Milton is shut out. More in *Utopia* is thinking about time and possibilities, and, as a consequence, the studies of the Utopians are not very extravagant. They are also studies that may be turned to profit, not like those of Browning's Grammarian, where the student never gets any good from his study, never sees to what use his grammar may be put in literature.

It is interesting to see how Browning in different places deals with different ideals like the two contrasted ones of Milton and Swift. Again and again he comes back to the man of infinite ambition, like Marlowe's Faustus, and again and again he states fairly the argument of Bishop Blougram, which is an argument like that of *Utopia* and that of Swift. The Bishop's parable about the voyage and the folly of putting too much into the cabin points the moral that men are foolish if they spend too much time in preparation, too much thought on the furniture for the short voyage of life. The limitation of one's supplies was a common policy recommended by moralists. It is found also in one of Cowley's *Essays*,[1] in *Utopia*, and in many other places.

In the seventeenth century, after the disappearance of the great original generations—the extravagant, ambitious, productive ages—the extravagance and exuberance still remained in many quarters, but without the original energy. Then there came a protest in the name of sound reason. There was a cooling down and a restriction of intellectual life, all for the good of general culture and rather to the disadvantage of original work and enterprise. It is shown

---

[1] 'The Shortness of Life, and Uncertainty of Riches', in *Several Discourses by way of Essays, in Prose and Verse*, ix.

very curiously in the writings of Samuel Butler.[1] The author of *Hudibras* in his tastes and accomplishments belonged to the old school, the school of Rabelais and the enormous omnivorous scholars of the great age, quaint, eccentric, variegated, unlimited. Yet in his prose writings and in the notes that he made for his own private use he shows a distaste for intellectual adventures; he is not hopeful, he discourages zeal and enthusiasm, he has a very moderate opinion of human capacity. He would never have prescribed a hundredth part of the texts that are set by Rabelais in his educational chapter (ii. viii).

After Butler, the great writers in the next age are most of them full of distrust of all things complex and eccentric, of variety apart from order. They saw plenty of variety in contemporary studies; they did not see genius or humanity. This is the temper of Pope and Swift. They disparage modern science, as Butler before them had done. The explanation of their attitude is that they were thinking of culture, not of intellectual adventures. They are the advocates of the majority of reasonable men, and they do not wish to see them taken beyond their depth. Swift felt the grievance much more keenly and painfully than anyone else. His protest against witless science, science that is too good for human nature, is expressed satirically in the voyage to Laputa, and much more finely in the account of Brobdingnag, which is his ideal state. This is Gulliver's account of the learning of that country—Swift's own view of what is essential in the liberal arts:

The learning of this people is very defective, consisting only in morality, history, poetry and mathematics, wherein they must be allowed to excel. But the last of these is wholly applied to what may be useful in life, to the improvement of agriculture and all mechanical arts; so that among us it would be little esteemed. And as to ideas, entities, abstractions and transcendentals, I could never drive the least conception into their heads.[2]

This is the deliberate opinion of a great moral teacher, a rationalist, a teacher of the humanities. It is a long way from

---

[1] Cf. pp. 4–9 above.
[2] 'A Voyage to Brobdingnag', chapter vii.

the enthusiasm and hopefulness of the sixteenth century, though it is really the working out of the earlier humanist theories of education, after a period of disillusionment and with a lower estimate of the average man. In his protest against indiscriminate science Swift was asserting the claim of common humanity to be exempt from unnecessary studies in order to think of the things that are essential to body and soul. Ordinary men are not to wander into Laputa. They must be directed to see clearly what is about them, like sensible wakeful beings. This is Swift's case. A simplifying and clarifying process is to be carried out in the interests of common sense, in order to save the limited human intellect from being overdriven and wasted in unprofitable work. After all, there is something exhilarating in Swift's medicine in the summary way in which he throws the whole unnecessary library and apparatus out of the window, and asks the shivering, half-awakened, 'unaccommodated' man what he really needs to keep his soul alive in such a world as this is. It is bracing; but it is not hopeful. And you see this in Johnson also. From his build you would say he was meant for an East Indiaman, for the long adventurous voyages which were to bring home everything knowable. But Johnson is dispirited and desultory, and except as a lexicographer keeps to the limited range of Swift and Addison. And Johnson in one of the essays in *The Rambler* has a curious note on the separation of studies which might be taken as a caricature of our modern specialists:

Even of those who have dedicated themselves to knowledge, the far greater part have confined their curiosity to a few objects, and have very little inclination to promote any fame, but that which their own studies entitle them to partake. The naturalist has no desire to know the opinions or conjectures of the philologer; the botanist looks upon the astronomer as a being unworthy of his regard; the lawyer scarcely hears the name of a physician without contempt; and he that is growing great and happy by electrifying a bottle, wonders how the world can be engaged by trifling prattle about war or peace.[1]

Wordsworth's theory, a hundred years later, has many things in it like Swift's. He also has a dislike for complexity

[1] *The Rambler*, No. 118, 4 May 1751.

when it is the sort of complexity that entangles a soul in business too difficult for it. But his solution of the problem is almost altogether different from Swift's. I think it may be shown that it is a better solution, and further that, with or without direct relation to Wordsworth's own utterances, it is possibly the best solution arrived at in the nineteenth century, where it may be traced in many diverse ways as a governing idea.

Swift's attitude towards most of the deeper studies is that they are generally impertinent silliness, the vanity of creatures who are as fit for flying as for thinking.[1] The creature is to be saved by temperance, by a strict diet, a limitation of freedom. Wordsworth also saw the vanity of the creature; and he himself has gone through the severest trial and ordeal, in the depths of humiliation, almost of despair, over the break-up of his philosophy and his attempt to find a logical explanation for everything moral. His resource, however, is not a diet like Swift's prescription. It is the difference between the eighteenth and the nineteenth centuries. Swift wanted to reduce the extent of human enterprises. He begins at the outside. Wordsworth leaves the extent as infinite as it was in the great days of the new learning. He has his gibes at certain kinds of science, but these are innocent. Swift could never have imagined Wordsworth's lines on Newton:

> . . . where the statue stood
> Of Newton, with his prism and silent face,
> The marble index of a mind for ever
> Voyaging through strange seas of thought, alone.[2]

It might appear to a reader of Wordsworth as if his antidote for the complicated maladies and confusions of modern culture were a very simple rejection of what is called culture, in favour of the natural life of North-country shepherds and people of that sort. There is some truth in this view, but there

[1] '. . . the bulk of mankind is as well qualified for flying as thinking, and if every man thought it his duty to think freely, and trouble his neighbours with his thoughts (which is an essential part of freethinking) it would make wild work in the world.' *Mr C[olli]ns's Discourse of Free-Thinking, Put into plain English, by way of Abstract, for the Use of the Poor* (1713); *Prose Works,* ed. Temple Scott, iii. 182.
[2] *The Prelude,* iii. 60–63.

is much more in Wordsworth than this. His ideal characters are found among the shepherds of the North country. The character of this kind of life which impressed Wordsworth was its sincerity, its singleness of mind. It was life with the spring, the movement running all through it.

The humiliation out of which Wordsworth had escaped, as he tells us, was a horrible disintegration of his mind and his life, the sickness of the analytical understanding when it sees the universe all 'in disconnection dead and spiritless'.[1] Simplicity, sincerity, unity of life—in these things, whenever he found them, there was rest and refreshing.

He did not mean, of course, to advise his audience to give up their business in town, because 'the world is too much with us', and to take to the pastoral life for a change, like Don Quixote.[2] The simplicity and sincerity of Wordsworth's ideal life exhibited in such a character as Michael does not mean the rejection of the other most varied interests that are recorded in *The Prelude*, in the Sonnets on the political destiny of England, in the pamphlet on the Convention of Cintra, and in a thousand other forms very far beyond the range of Michael or the leech-gatherer. He does not put forward any model of virtue to be copied. The natural instinctive virtue and rectitude which Wordsworth knew and for which he found expression, the right life which for him is part of the same scheme of things as the austerity of the hills and the silence of the eternal spaces, is not anything like the Stoic model of a man or any other pattern advertised by any prose moralist. Like the hills and the day it is an element in his poetry, an imaginative vision. In so far as it is part of his teaching it is like all his teaching: a corrective for the 'disconnection dead and spiritless', which is the aspect of the world to modern culture when culture goes rancid.

Both in the eighteenth century and in the nineteenth the malady of too much culture and mistaken culture has been recognized. The difference between the two centuries is this, that the eighteenth, in a depressed, disheartened way, says with Swift, 'Cut down your expenses ninety per cent. and try to live within your income. Your mind is not much at the

---

[1] *The Excursion*, iv. 962.   [2] II, chapters lxvii, lxxiii.

best, and it will do you no good to think so. Don't be a fool, or at least not more than you can help. Be simple and clear and use all the wits you have on things you have a chance of understanding.' Or again briskly, with Voltaire, 'There is no reason to distress yourselves, good people; keep your minds quite easy. It is true that you can't find out for yourselves anything worth knowing about the Old Testament, or the essence of tragic poetry, or Charles XII of Sweden or the ways of Providence, but only wait and you shall have the universe all explained to you, as easy to follow as the *Arabian Nights*.'

On the other hand, the doctors of the nineteenth century say, 'It is not for us to tell you how far you are to go or how much you are to carry. There are many things to be done and won that have never been done yet, and some of you may have the doing and winning of them. Culture in the spiritual sense as well as the literal sense needs light and air and time. There are a number of substances that are useful in culture, but it is not culture to collect these, though they are useful. There are other substances that are neither fit for the land nor yet for the dunghill. You may have to give up your work when it is half done or less than half. You need not complain about that—"better men fared thus before you". What you can do, is to keep in good training, whatever your strength may be; you can always be ashamed when you are out of training.'

With the nineteenth century there came something like a revival of the ambitions and the productive energy of the sixteenth, and along with that a return of the temptation to play at universality and omniscience. Against that, various modern teachers have set the view of a life simple and energetic and all in one piece; like Wordsworth throughout; like Walt Whitman when he turns away from his favourite tumults of human competition to praise the aplomb of the animals;[1] like Robert Louis Stevenson when he returns again and again to think of the beauty of mere life and movement. These are a few instances out of many that might be taken.

[1] I think I could turn and live with animals, they are so placid and self-contain'd;
I stand and look at them long and long.
They do not sweat and whine about their condition;
They do not lie awake in the dark and weep for their sins;
They do not make me sick discussing their duty to God;

There is nothing in them like the old fallacy of the return to nature, nothing like Coleridge's *pantisocracy*. They are not independent substantial ideals of life, set up in opposition to modern culture. They are controlling and directing ideas—abstractions, if you like, but abstractions or rather extracts of the quintessence of life, the essential spirit of courage, which, to use an inexhaustible phrase of Wordsworth's[1] once more, is 'both law and impulse'.

∾

A POSTSCRIPT ON THE HUMANITIES

No one with any historical sense at all can be disrespectful to the humanists; no modern scholar ought to think of Petrarch without reverence for the memory of his ancestor, that pious founder and benefactor of learning—'Fraunceys Petrark' (as Chaucer describes him),

> whos rethoryke sweete
> Enlumined al Itaille of poetrye.[2]

Petrarch is the first of the moderns—not of modern scholars only, but of all that critical spirit which is expressed by Montaigne in one age, by Goethe in another, and which even more than anything in creative or imaginative art has made the difference between the modern and the medieval world. The letters of Petrarch are little read and his poetry is often hardly judged. But he can be recognized in a single sentence which is enough to make every reading man take his hat off in a salute as he passes by: the sentence where he speaks of his Latin authors, how he has read Virgil, Horace, Boethius, and Cicero till he hardly can tell the difference from the thoughts of his own mind, so deep have the roots been struck into the substance of his being.[3]

The excesses and defects of this study have not escaped

Not one is dissatisfied—not one is demented with the mania of owning things;
Not one kneels to another, nor to his kind that lived thousands of years ago;
Not one is respectable or industrious over the whole earth.

('Song of Myself', sec. 32.)

[1] In 'Three years she grew in sun and shower'.
[2] Prologue of the Clerk of Oxenford, 31.
[3] *Familiarium rerum, lib.* XXII. ii. 12.

notice. They are described by Bacon among the types of erroneous learning.[1] Pure classical scholarship may lead to the worship of pure empty form; and this was the character of the Renaissance generally in different countries, not in literature only but in other arts. Petrarch is one of the authors of Ciceronianism, that is, the imitation of Cicero's grammar and rhetoric with no interest in any matter apart from the exercise of language. In reading Petrarch's letters one cannot help sometimes being reminded of Mr. Shandy's getting comfort as he proceeds in his meditation on his son's death when he discovers what a number of fine things may be said about it. But one ought not to put a slight on Petrarch for his obvious pleasure in Latin sentences of melancholy reflection or consolation; and Mr. Shandy's philosophy is not despicable either. Indeed, there could hardly be found a better example of what is meant by the humanities than this very passage.

Will your Worships give me leave to squeeze in a story between these two pages?

When Tully was bereft of his dear daughter Tullia, at first he laid it to his heart,—he listened to the voice of nature, and modulated his own unto it.—O, my Tullia!—my daughter! my child!—Still, still, still,—it was, O, my Tullia!—my Tullia! Methinks I see my Tullia, I hear my Tullia, I talk with my Tullia.—But as soon as he began to look into the stores of philosophy, and consider how many excellent things might be said upon the occasion,—nobody upon earth can conceive, says the great orator, how happy, how joyful it made me.

My father was as proud of his eloquence as Marcus Tullius Cicero could be, for his life, and, for aught I am convinced of to the contrary, at present, with as much reason: it was, indeed, his strength,—and his weakness too.—His strength, for he was by nature eloquent; and his weakness, for he was hourly a dupe to it; and, provided an occasion in life would but permit him to show his talents, or say either a wise thing, a witty, or a shrewd one—(bating the case of a systematic misfortune) —he had all he wanted.—A blessing which tied up my father's tongue, and a misfortune which set it loose with a good grace, were pretty equal: sometimes, indeed, the misfortune was the better of the two; for instance, where the pleasure of the harangue was as *ten*, and the pain of the misfortune but as *five*,—my father gained half in half; and consequently was as well again off as if it had never befallen him. . . .

[1] *The Advancement of Learning*, I. iv. 2-3.

Philosophy has a fine saying for everything.—For Death, it has an entire set: the misery was they all at once rushed so into my father's head that 'twas difficult to string them together, so as to make anything of a consistent show out of them.—He took them as they came.—

' 'Tis an inevitable chance,—the first statute in Magna Charta;—it is an everlasting act of parliament, my dear brother,—*All must die.*

'If my son could not have died, it had been matter of wonder, not that he is dead.

'Monarchs and princes dance in the same ring with us.

'*To die* is the great debt and tribute due unto nature: tombs and monuments, which should perpetuate our memories, pay it themselves; and the proudest pyramid of them all, which Wealth and Science have erected, has lost its apex, and stands obtruncated in the traveller's horizon.'—(My father found he got great ease, and went on.)—'Kingdoms and provinces, and towns and cities, have they not their periods? and when those principles and powers which at first cemented and put them together have performed their several evolutions, they fall back.' ... 'Brother Shandy', said my uncle Toby, laying down his pipe at the word *evolutions* ... 'Revolutions, I meant', quoth my father. ...

'Where is Troy and Mycenæ, and Thebes and Delos, Persepolis and Agrigentum?' continued my father, taking up his book of post-roads, which he had laid down.—'What is become, brother Toby, of Nineveh and Babylon, of Cyzicum and Mitylenæ? the fairest towns that ever the sun rose upon are now no more; the names only are left; and those (for many of them are wrong spelt) are falling themselves by piece-meal to decay, and in length of time will be forgotten, and involved with everything in a perpetual night. The world itself, brother Toby, must —must come to an end.

'Returning out of Asia, when I sailed from Ægina towards Megara,' (when can this have been? thought my uncle Toby,) 'I began to view the country round about.—Ægina was behind me, Megara was before, Piræus on the right hand, Corinth on the left.—What flourishing towns, now prostrate upon the earth! Alas! alas! said I to myself, that man should disturb his soul for the loss of a child, when so much as this lies awfully buried in his presence!—Remember, said I to myself again, —remember thou art a man.'[1]

One ought not to labour this text too hard, but still it is noticeable that Mr. Shandy's quotation is not from Cicero himself but from Cicero's correspondent Servius Sulpicius—that is, it is what any ordinary Roman gentleman writes to

[1] *Tristram Shandy,* v, chapter iii.

N

his friend.[1] It is part of the *humanitas* of the ancient world which is so modern that, but for familiarity with the names of Cicero and Virgil, we should be often as much put out as Captain Shandy was when his question about the date was answered. The letter of Sulpicius written in 'no year of our Lord' is not distinguishable, as far as its thought and sentiment go, from the character of Mr. Shandy's time; it is exactly in the gentle tone of good society, *les honnêtes gens*— it might come from a funeral oration of one of the great French preachers, from an essay of Sir William Temple, from the author of *Rasselas* and of *The Vanity of Human Wishes*. Captain Shandy's mistake, and the resemblance in style between his brother and Servius Sulpicius, is an example of what is meant by the Humanities, of what was discovered by the Renaissance and revived at the revival of learning; a world of gentle and honourable thought where all are contemporaries. And one of the pioneers whom we may commemorate is Dante's Ulysses who gave the doctrine of the Humanities to his companions as they put out through the straits to the Atlantic: 'Consider the stock from which you are sprung; you were not made to live like the brutes, but to follow Virtue and Knowledge.'

> Considerate la vostra semenza;
> fatti non foste a viver come bruti,
> ma per seguir virtute e conoscenza.[2]

Or, as it is put by the English poet Chapman in his appeal to Henry Prince of Wales:

> Let all men judge; who is it can denie,
> That the rich crowne of ould Humanitie,
> Is still your birth-right? and was ne're let downe
> From Heaven, for rule of Beasts' lives, but your owne?[3]

[1] Cicero, *Epist. ad Fam.* iv. 5.
[2] *Inferno*, xxvi. 118–20.
[3] 'Euthymiae Raptus', 564–7; *The Poems of George Chapman*, ed. Phyllis B. Bartlett (New York, 1941), p. 185.

On Polite Literature

THERE used to be such a thing as polite literature; probably there is still; but the name at any rate does not seem to be much in use.[1] What once was called polite has now become general literature, a fact which may be recommended to the collectors and philosophical interpreters of facts, as, for example, to the author of *Descriptive Sociology*, or the author of *Typical Developments*[2]—if indeed they be not one and the same person.

Both the names are vague enough, and the term polite was a conventional one. Even in the times when it was current, men of polite letters produced a great deal that was polite in very few senses of the word. There is *The Narrative of Dr. Robert Norris, concerning the strange and deplorable frenzy of Mr. John Dennis, an officer of the Custom-house—Written in the year MDCCXIII* by one of the most finished stylists of that great age, who followed it up later by *A Full and True Account of a Horrid and Barbarous Revenge by Poison, on the Body of Mr. Edmund Curll, Bookseller*, with further realistic narratives on the same subject. Modern writers, even of the least fastidious taste, are somewhat gentler to their enemies than Mr. Pope was. Yet there can be no question that Mr. Pope was polite and that M. Zola is not. The standard of literary delicacy, in some things at any rate, was higher in those days than in these; the conditions of authorship were in some respects more exacting. It used to be expected of an author that he should preserve a certain dignity and remoteness in his disquisitions, and even those who adopt a more familiar style, like Addison in one generation and Goldsmith in another, allow it to be felt that though they are ready to talk with any one in any coffee-house they are not disposed to adopt the language or the style of every

---

[1] We are unable to date this lecture, but it probably belongs to the early 1890's.

[2] Herbert Spencer published *Descriptive Sociology; or, Groups of Sociological Facts* compiled and abstracted by D. Duncan, R. Scheppig, and J. Collier (1873–81). We are unable to throw light on 'Typical Developments'.

loafer. They have their own conceptions of their own worth, and the obligations they are under to the genius of literature. Has this old nobility of authorship been kept? That it is not altogether extinct, there are some modern names to exemplify. It is not fair to take the greatest names in poetry; they are out of the competition. But among the authors of 'general' literature there are some who are 'polite'. Hume's *Essays* and Gibbon's *History* are typical instances of the eighteenth-century faculty for writing about serious things without pedantry. But in the gift of investing dry and scholarly stuff with literary dignity and grace they are not more remarkable than Sir Henry Maine's *Ancient Law*. Other works will occur to others; *Culture and Anarchy* perhaps may be suggested. Will anyone challenge the claim of *The Autocrat of the Break-fast-Table*? One might not care to defend all the ingenious gentlemen from Boston, but the *Autocrat* will receive votes.

It is matter for gratitude that in our time there are authors who have retained some of the old spirit, the old high spirit and self-respect that gave dignity of bearing to the prose of Swift and Johnson, Hume and Gibbon. Yet the author of *Typical Developments* can hardly fail to draw his sorrowful conclusion that this dignity is exceptional and that literature has lost some of its graces, as the House of Commons has lost its appreciation of Horace and Virgil. The author aforesaid is welcome to make some comparative sociology out of this. The House of Commons (with all due respect) might be taken as a standard of literary dignity. Where fifty years ago you had as decorations of oratory such venerable trifles as *non tali auxilio*, or *timeo Danaos*, what have you now? 'There's the door, and your name is Walker!' Our comparative author might make something out of this.

Let him beware, however, of working the Democracy argument too persistently, for men are growing aweary of this explanation of all the virtues and all the vices on which we pride ourselves. The decline of polite literature may be due to the growth of Democracy, to the toe of the peasant galling the kibe of the courtier. But woe be to the author who proceeds to expand on this subject. Democracy itself has brought no greater evil (one is perversely inclined to think) than the elucubrations of the doctors about the moral effect of democracy on intellectual tone, on the literary and speculative character of the age.

Democracy, if it chose to interest itself in its own nature and belongings, might make a point by inquiring whether the gentlemen and ladies who read the old *Spectator* were more or less civilized than the moderate and reflective democrats who read the new. Which subscribers got better value for their money is not the question. Really the Democracy theory may be carried too far. Addison is 'politer' than most modern journalists, but he wrote for a mob, like them, though not such a large one. The apologist of Democracy might counter heavily, if he thought it worth while. Let us imagine, if possible, some University Extension lecturer, in some candid moment, explaining to the children of Freedom and the People, in Shoreditch or Stepney, that modern literature is vulgar and degraded, and that they, the people, are responsible for all the change; that *The Spectator* was written by gentlemen for gentlemen, and that its place has now been taken by another newspaper which began on the same lines and has given them up. We know of course that University Extension lecturers do not talk nonsense of that sort, but let the daring fancy be indulged for this occasion. What would become of this free-speaker, this Coriolanus of lecturers, if some pained and scandalized opponent, an old frequenter of the place, were to rise and, out of the memory of some previous session, to repeat fragments of Swift's *Polite Conversation*?[1] Would not Stepney be avenged? Would it not be made evident that in the great age of polite literature the average gentleman and lady were in intellect and manners somewhat unfitted for setting a standard of good taste, and by no means markedly superior in either to those denizens of Stepney who do not come to Extension lectures—among whom the commonplaces of Swift's *Polite Conversation* survive in the currency of every day? Great and reverend and multiform and multifarious is Democracy, but neither Democracy nor Evolution is capable of explaining everything all at once.

It is humbly submitted that more harm has been done by

---

[1] *A Complete Collection of Genteel and Ingenious Conversation . . .* 1738.

science and by poetry than by anything else to the form and style of general literature. And this is said with the greatest apprehension and searching of heart, and foreboding of some nemesis to come, some penalty for rash and foolish blasphemy against the serene and most high Muses. But it is said, and the vain speech must take care of itself; the speaker will do all he can to show that he means no want of reverence to their divinities, desiring only to convey that in an indirect way and *per accidens*, as it were, science and poetry have blasted, or withered by their excessive tropical splendour, the old familiar comely Dutch garden with its peacock yews, in which Cowley and Sir William Temple set the stately fashion to the followers of polite letters.

Science has ways of its own. It is too majestic to be generally elegant. Books of Science are very often ugly. They have a trick of scattering symbols over their pages. Our philosophers, who ought to know better, have caught this ugly trick. Locke, Berkeley, and Hume had more self-respect than to patch themselves with algebra—like Mr. W. S. Jevons and Mr. F. H. Bradley and others. Modern psychologists again will consort with medical students and bring away nasty things out of the dissecting rooms. The older generation had many friends in the faculty of medicine, but they were treated like men of the world; there was no prurient curiosity about the *arcana* of the profession. There were certain famous cases, of course, which were matter of common talk in good society. 'Mr. Cheselden has given us a very curious story of a boy, who had been born blind, and continued so until he was thirteen or fourteen years old; he was then couched for a cataract, by which operation he received his sight', and so on. Mr. Cheselden and his famous case might be appealed to by any philosophers, without impropriety; the philosopher of those days had no desire to go vivisecting on his own account.

The quotation just given about Cheselden's case comes out of a treatise which shows better than some others the magnitude of the change: Burke's *Philosophical Inquiry into the Origin of our Ideas of the Sublime and Beautiful*.[1] To some

[1] IV. xv.

extent that is a scientific work. It is a systematic discussion of aesthetic problems—with quite enough of scientific formalism, one is inclined to think. The Parts and Sections, and all the grouping of the various topics are regular and symmetrical, not random or discursive. There is no flippancy in it. Yet it is impossible to regard the essay as mere philosophy, as other than a work of literature: a book with a style, and that an impressive one. A hundred years later comes another book on aesthetic matters also systematic, and minutely subdivided, and solemn: Alexander Bain's 'Emotional Qualities of Style' (Part II of *English Composition and Rhetoric* (1887)). In this meritorious work the evil effects of science are painfully obvious. Burke's argument is scientific and carefully arranged, but it is at the same time continuous; there is an oratorical progression in it as well as a scientific precision. Bain is a museum. One passes from one case, one pigeon hole to another, and observes the specimen arranged and ticketed by the keeper. Here you have 'Beneficent Strength' and here you have 'Malignity' (a great amount of space is allotted to Malignity); here you have 'Gregariousness—Patriotism'; here 'the Hilarious and the Healthy' (at least they are indicated in the preface), and here 'the special conditions of Erotic feeling', and 'the various means of guarding against Extravagance and the Maudlin'. All this is set out in the most bewildering and disgusting variety of type that the most vitiated taste of a biologist could ask for. Instead of the natural transitions of Burke, and the apparently spontaneous examples from Homer or Milton, everything here is in a wooden scientific framework. And yet the scientific result is not really more than in Burke. Burke had a real theory which he wanted to prove. He wanted to prove that the Beautiful was relaxation, and the Sublime contraction, and he set to work vehemently and proved all this to his own satisfaction. With Dr. Bain, the classification, the naming, the scientific apparatus, seem almost to be an end in themselves. It is not meant that the book is not an interesting and a valuable one. But it may be argued with some confidence that it is inferior in style to Burke's essay, and that it is the iron rule of science that has spoilt the style.

No work can stand high as literature that allows itself to jumble up large type and small type on the same page. The Germans do it, but we know what the Germans are. M. Renan, in one of the most accomplished recent pieces of polite literature, has told us his opinion:

Une science pédantesque en sa solitude, une littérature sans gaieté, une politique maussade, une haute société sans éclat, une noblesse sans esprit, des gentilshommes sans politesse, de grands capitaines sans mots sonores, ne détrôneront pas, je crois de sitôt, le souvenir de cette vieille société francaise, si brillante, si polie, si jalouse de plaire.

There could not be a better example of the old fine manner, or a better description of the new bad one.

But Poetry is to blame, no less than Science, for loss of tone in general literature. M. Renan himself is sometimes an example of this. He does not always write this plain, contemptuous, militant French; sometimes he loses his self-possession, and permits himself some escapades of poetry. Now, it requires great skill to be imaginative or metaphorical or sentimental in prose. Since poetry became poetical again some eighty or ninety years since, prose has not been quite so sure of its balance. Prose practising short flights of poetry from one rafter to another is very far from politeness. All emphasis, all forcing of the tone, is alien to polite literature. Great literature may be wrought by the masters of eloquent, metaphorical, imaginative prose; but not polite literature. 'Polite' is not the name for it. 'Polite' is not the name for Mr. Carlyle or Mr. Ruskin, at any rate in the strict literary sense of the word; neither is it good for Canon Farrar or Ouida. Prose writers who are not content to write plain prose may do great things in their self-chosen, self-made art. Still, one bears something of a grudge against them for the bad example they set. They spoil the market for sober people; and they set all the boys and girls imitating their wild ventures. An eminent Irish scholar with a mind of his own complained humorously not long ago that it had now become possible to pluck a man in an examination for comparing the wrong author to an Alpine crevasse. And an Oxford moderator came to support this theory with some fragments from his own experience of undergraduate sallies in literary criticism. Among the real authentic compositions done in the Schools of Oxford of recent years are the following opinions:

'Homer speaks as a Voice from the Darkness.'

'Thucydides is like the tolling of a great bell.'

'Euripides resembles the lesser rumblings of the thunder.'
This fashion may change, the fashion of cramming simple English prose with daring metaphor. It may come to be recognized that there is no good reason, because the poet goes a-roving, for ordinary mortals to put ivy leaves round their walking sticks and brandish the same. And if ordinary mortals take to shouting *Evoe!* and *Io Bacche!* in Grub Street and Paternoster Row, there ought to be a literary police to restrain them. It is too bad that, for instance, Mr. John Addington Symonds cannot tell us about the progress of the English drama without making us listen to rhythmical prose, and blank verse printed as prose, about 'the bride-elect of Shakespeare's genius', and a number of other finely imagined creatures. The whole passage is worth considering.

What a future lay before this country lass—the bride-elect of Shakspere's genius! For her there was preparing empire over the whole world of man:—over the height and breadth and depth of heaven and earth and hell; over facts of nature and fables of romance; over histories of nations and of households; over heroes of past and present times, *and airy beings of all poets' brains!* Hers were Greene's meadows, watered by an English stream. Hers, Heywood's moss-grown manor-houses. *Peele's goddess-haunted lawns were hers, and hers | the palace-bordered, paved ways of Verona.* Hers was the darkness of the grave, the charnel-house of Webster. She walked the air-built loggie of Lyly's dreams, and paced the clouds of Jonson's Masques. She donned that ponderous sock, and trod the measures of Volpone. She mouthed the mighty line of Marlowe. Chapman's massy periods and Marston's pointed sentences were hers by heart. *She went abroad through primrose paths with Fletcher*, and learned Shirley's lambent wit. She wandered amid dark dry places of the outcast soul with Ford ... &c.[1]

Now that sort of thing is either too good or too bad for

[1] J. A. Symonds, *Shakspere's Predecessors in the English Drama* (1884), 1900 edition, p. 210.

ordinary prose, and in either case it is corrupting and licentious. It is bad form, like a masquer or a reveller going home by daylight. Good prose is not written in this way. Good prose may be imaginative, may be lofty and dignified; it does not flutter into poetry like this. There may be more poetry, better appreciated, in these days than when literature was more polite. That is no excuse for the awkward decoration favoured by a number of modern writers, and apparently by some of the youth in our academies. That the modern heavily decorated prose is all bad literature no one of any sense will affirm. The old polite literature is not always stimulating. *Rasselas* is not as attractive as *Sartor Resartus*. But *Rasselas* and the *Lives of the Poets* and other works of the old time have a value of their own—apart from their matter— in the pitch of their style. They are content to forgo such literary advantages as may be got from a sudden change of key. The author is himself throughout and speaks with his own voice. He would keep the tragic and the comic mask, with their speaking trumpets, for their own proper stage, and is not tempted to carry them about with him into ordinary conversation.

On Progress in Poetry (1895)

P R O G R E S S is a word that has some disagreeable associations.
The meaning of it in political matters is not always quite
clear, and its application in the history of art or literature is
still more hazardous. 'The Progress of Poesy' in Gray's ode is
represented as leaving Greece and Italy behind for the sake of
England. Historically it is true, as a matter of fact, that English poetry is later than Greek. It is possible that some
English poetry may be better than some Greek poetry. Yet
it is natural to find that the idea of progress as applied to
literature is misleading and perplexing. Even in ethics and
politics, where the idea of progress is more familiar, it is not
always acceptable. The idea of progress is rather cruel to
those whose lives are spent in the earlier stages of the
journey. Where are all those that died in the wilderness? If
you believe too strongly and exclusively in progress you will
come to be unjust to your ancestors. Even in politics and
ethics the idea of progress is essentially imperfect and partial.
In all life there is progress to something else, but also in all
life each single period has its own laws, its own proper
virtues; and it is illiberal and unintelligent to pass a con-
demnation on any age for wanting the virtues of its successor.
There is no condition of mind more fatuous than that of the
trumpeters of the march of intellect; those who pity the poor
ancients for their ignorance of the things that every schoolboy knows.

But if 'progress' is a questionable and incomplete idea
even in the field where it certainly has some right of do-
minion, that is, in the field of political and social life, its
validity is much less in the provinces of art. Progress in
politics is a progress that deletes the old for the sake of the
new; whereas in the progress of poetry the old order does
not change to give place to the new. The old order, if it ever
was of any good at all, need be none the worse on account of
that which follows it. A revolution in politics can never be
wholly undone. Nothing is ever restored in politics. A

revolution is a twist which cannot be untwisted. Restoration in politics is only one revolution the more. In politics a man may think himself back to a previous stage of history, but he cannot get the rest of the world to agree with him in his dream.

With poetry it is not quite the same. The specific quality of all works of art is that they are detached from the operation of natural causes, except in so far as moth and rust and other accidents may interfere with the material substance of which they are composed. So long as a work of art is extant it belongs to no particular time at all. The conditions and circumstances of its production are historical and belong to a time of which only a faint and illusory image can be projected by the most cunning historian. The work itself, however, is present. The Progress of Poesy is a progress which does not touch or affect the completed poem. Historically the genius of literature may pass from one nation to another, from Greece to Italy, from Italy to England. But this is not like the political progress in which one stage is the refutation of the one before it, and the iron, the clay, the brass, the silver, and the gold of the monarchies of the world are 'broken to pieces together and become like the chaff of the summer threshingfloors'.[1] The images made by the artists are not subject to these dangers. They are there for you to look at. If you happen to be a dissentient from your own age in matters of taste you have recourse at once, at a wish, to the world where all your wrongs are righted. The Jacobite exile may comfort himself in his daydream by imagining the funerals of the Hanoverian dynasty. The discontented student of poetry has a more satisfactory refuge. His dream is a reality. He may let the world go on its own progressive way, while he loiters with his own friends in any bypath meadow he chooses. The progress of the world does not touch his library, and *his* friends are none the worse on account of the world's neglect of them.

The histories of literature and the philosophical theories of artistic development may possibly have done something to disseminate wrong opinions about the progress of poetry.

[1] Daniel, ii. 35.

A man may have a consistent and plausible theory of the history of literature and of successive schools of art, and still be somewhat uncertain in his own mind as to the absolute value of poetry. To speak plainly, it is generally in those respects where poetry is least poetical that it trenches on the domain of history.

What is meant by saying that a poet is representative of his age? This must imply that there are many average things in him and his work which he shares with his contemporaries. These things are the object of the literary and philosophical historian. He shows you how the poet is compounded out of simples. Necessarily in doing so he has to deal with many things that are irrelevant to poetry. Necessarily also the quintessence of the poet evades him; for that is always individual and therefore ineffable and inexhaustible.

About Milton, for instance, there are many valuable and undeniable things to be said by an historian of literature. The poetry of Milton has its place in an historical series. It is the poetry of an autumnal period in literature; it is the perfection of a school beyond which nothing is to be gained without dissolution and a new beginning. It is full of the commonplaces of the earlier and later days of the classical revival, of the mythology of Dante and Chaucer, the poetics of Scaliger. And then there is Puritanism, and Republicanism, and Divorce, and Smectymnuus. It is an historical fact that *Paradise Lost* is an experiment in competition for the prize of epic poetry, according to the rules laid down by scholars and scholarly poets. *Paradise Lost* has a great deal in common with some of the worst poems that ever were written: namely, with the futile modern attempts at epic poetry, the experiments of modern poets furnished with all the most correct and authoritative critical principles of the schools. Milton, like all the bad epic poets, believed in the academic and critical theory of the epic, and tried to write up to it; and there you have *Paradise Lost* considered as an historical fact, as a moment in an historical series. It represents a bygone fashion of literature, like the epics of Trissino and Chapelain, like Wilkie's *Epigoniad*.

The history of literature has for part of its subject, at any rate, the development and succession of literary modes, of the commonplaces that cannot be said to belong to this or that author, the critical ideas that are shared by Dryden with Settle or Tate, by Scott and Coleridge with the Editor of the *Tales of Wonder*. Part of the function of the literary historian is to write the history of ideas and of fashions of thought that are not literature but only the general conditions of literature, and conditions that may be shared equally by good literature and bad. The individual genius of the poet who makes something of his own, something original and wonderful, under these general conditions—the genius that being individual is therefore incalculable and inexhaustible—this escapes through the meshes of the philosophical historian. The philosopher may discuss and describe the fashions of the Globe Theatre and the Elizabethan Drama, or of the reflective-didactic-satiric poetry in couplets, but he cannot predict or deduce the play of *Henry V* or the satire of *Absalom and Achitophel*. And works such as these are always something more than the sum of all their conditions. Great poems are miraculous; like everything which is individual, they are transgressions of scientific laws, and irreducible to formulas.

This does not mean that the study of literary history is vain and unprofitable. On the contrary, it is of the greatest interest to discover those portions of his work in which the great artist conforms to the fashion of his time. It is hardly possible to appreciate rightly his greatness and singularity except by a process of discrimination which shall detect the common alloy, the common tricks of handling, in his work. All poetry is determined more or less, to begin with, by certain critical ideas or conceptions. These are always inadequate in the case of the great artists, or, at best, they are general rules which leave the hardest part of the work to the intuition and the impulse of the moment. The work, however, cannot be understood without some comprehension of the author's critical formulas, the critical grammar and rhetoric of his day. It is by no means easy, and the difficulty of the work is enough to make it respectable.

No form of study is more beset by fallacies and 'idolisms' than the history of literature. The *Memoirs of Scriblerus* have collected some of these, but the record is incomplete, and the forms of error are prolific and given to rapid variation. Some of the modern idols have come to be recognized and so have lost their influence. It may be, for example, that the Celtic element in our composition, whereby one was able to deduce Shakespeare from a Welsh ancestry, with some help from the environment and natural scenery of Warwickshire, is no longer an idol of today. Probably the *History of English Literature* by M. Taine has come to lose a good deal of its gloss and appearance of liveliness. To derive the English genius from the English mutton was at one time thought to be an enlightening piece of philosophy.

Here and there one still may meet with some strange and antiquated machinery, some examples of perverted logic in the demonstration of literary theories. The other day an eminent German scholar tried to refute the common opinion about the birthplace of Cynewulf.[1] He conducts his historical proof in the following way. The choice lies between Northumbria and Mercia. Now *let it be granted* that poetry flourishes better in a quiet than in a turbulent society; it follows that Cynewulf belonged to Mercia and not to Northumbria. Proof: there were more kings of Northumbria than of Mercia in Cynewulf's time, and a quick change of kings implies political misfortune and insecurity. Is not this making things too simple? Again there are occasions in which the inquirer in his appetite for philosophical analogies, for the common pervasive idea in the literature of an age, for proofs of influence and literary filiation, has permitted himself to make too much of his evidence. An instance may be taken from the study of Chaucer. It has been shown that when Chaucer wrote *The House of Fame* he had been reading Dante: *The House of Fame* is like a dream of which the various incongruous elements have been contributed by the *Divine Comedy*. It is of interest to discover and make a record of these points of contact. The books that Chaucer read and the parts of them that remained with him in the workshop of his mind are well worth consideration by people who have time to spend upon Chaucer. But it is one thing to find the

[1] Richard Wülcker, 'Cynewulfs Heimat' in *Anglia*, xvii (1895), 106–9.

literary references in a poem, it is another thing to understand it. That there are references to Dante in Chaucer's *House of Fame*, that there are reminiscences and reflections, cannot be denied and ought to be observed. But this discovery cannot pass for an explanation of Chaucer's poem. Considered in itself, in its temper, its purport, in its rhetoric, *The House of Fame* is altogether different from the *Divine Comedy*, altogether the opposite of Dante's poetry: a casual careless piece of improvisation, a 'Roundabout' paper in which the careful and laborious artist let his hand run free, gave free scope to all his natural tastes for digression, for popular science, for common medieval tricks of composition. To forget the spirit of humour and whim in this irresponsible dream of Chaucer's, and to turn it into a solemn parody of the *Divine Comedy*, is merely to allow oneself to be paid in the wrong currency, in something wholly inconvertible and unprofitable.

The comparison of incommensurables is one of the easiest fallacies, if a man will only give his mind to it. A German scholar[1] has compared the second part of 'Christabel' to Keats's 'The Eve of St. Agnes', and discovers that the setting and the mood of the two poems are very much alike. Of course you will remember that in the one poem there is a witch, the Lady Geraldine, and in the other a lover, Porphyro; conversely in the first, there is no lover, and in the second no witch. The critic notes the difference and explains that in 'The Eve of St. Agnes' *the part of Geraldine is taken by the lover*.

These are small things and trivial humours. There are other conceptions more daring and more magnificent: large generalizations professing to be scientific, and imposing by their weight and solemnity, such as this statement by Brunetière:

Nous étudierons . . . *comment un Genre se transforme en un autre*; et, pour cela, j'essayerai de vous montrer comment, dans l'histoire de notre littérature, sous l'action de quelles influences du dedans ou du dehors, l'éloquence de la chaire, telle que l'a connue le XVIIe siècle, est

---

[1] Alois Brandl, *Samuel Taylor Coleridge und die englische Romantik* (1886), p. 227.

devenue de nos jours la poésie lyrique de Lamartine, d'Hugo, de Vigny, de Musset.[1]

The pulpit eloquence—the eloquence of the funeral orations—has become the lyrical poetry of Lamartine and Victor Hugo. The energy of the funeral orations has undergone a transformation; possibly the energy of the poets of this century may be disengaged again from the forms they gave it, and may reappear as sermons. It would be interesting to follow the process, and lectures might rise in popular estimation if this or anything of this sort were their ante-natal history. But perhaps a sermon would be a sermon still.

> And it receives a different name
> Because they are not quite the same.

Some things in the history of literature, some of the principles, categories, methods employed in the study, would seem to be ambiguous and hazardous. Yet when all is said, the study is still possible. If it is not and cannot be a complete exposition of the nature of poetry or of any single poem (for these are alike inexhaustible), the history of literature is still of some value. Whatever effect it may have on criticism, it is at any rate one of the most interesting kinds of history, and there is no want of sport in it.

The history of forms of literature will carry one far, though it stops short of the miracle of individual genius. There are, for instance, the analogies of history in different nations and periods—the sequence of epic, lyric, and dramatic poetry which is found in different ages and different tongues and appears to fall under some constant rule, some general law of the progress of society, if one could only discover it. Even if one cannot discover the law it is something to recognize the succession of those types; to see the early French heroic poetry trying unconsciously to be Homer, and giving place, as the Greek epic gave place, to schools of courtly and elaborate lyric. The progress and the influence of poetic schools are capable of exposition by a positive method, under a dry light, without the aid of any expensive theory of transformation of energy. The dependence

---

[1] Ferdinand Brunetière, *L'Évolution des genres dans l'histoire de la littérature* (Paris, 3rd ed. 1898), p. 13.

of early Italian poetry on the poetry of Provence, the influence of Italian poetry on English, French, and Spanish, these things are capable of explanation and verification in detail.

The history of the common forms of verse is one of the most fruitful and one of the most amusing of all the departments of this inquiry. To find the rhythms of *Poems and Ballads* in verse of the thirteenth century, to find Dante noting the relation of the ten-syllable to the six-syllable line, which is observed in 'Lycidas' and in 'The Scholar Gipsy', to find in all modern poetry everywhere the echoes of old times, these are things more lively than the concoction of solemn formulas of evolution.

There is a mystery and an excitement in the study of literary progress. It is the study of a kind of impersonal life, which is also a spiritual life. There are difficulties in it which are insoluble, but it is possible to see where the difficulties lie, and to appreciate in some way the multiplicity, the exuberance, of the life that is displayed in the growth of common literary forms. While over all there is the mystery of individual genius, which takes its own way with the common forms.

In Spain and in England, at the same time but independently, and without communication, there grew up forms of drama with many kindred faults and excellencies. It is possible to compare these; it is possible more or less to account for them, to point to this or that foreign influence common to both, this or that native similarity or difference of conditions or temperament. When all is said it may amount to very little; but it may be something to call the attention or stimulate the curiosity of people who are fortunate enough to have leisure. What is altogether and absolutely inexplicable and glorious, is that in England there was Shakespeare and in Spain Cervantes: Shakespeare, who took the common form of the drama, learned all he could about it from Marlowe and everyone else who had anything to teach him, and worked his own will with the common form; Cervantes, who made nothing (so they tell me) of the drama, the popular form of literature in his day, and wrote his great book in a different kind altogether, making the life of *Don Quixote* in his own way—an exceptional, unfashionable book, of a kind invented by the author, and itself the only example of the kind in its day. These are the incalculable humours, these are the divine contingencies, of the progress of literature.

On Comedy

THERE is a fragment on Comedy ascribed to Aristotle, in which there is a kind of parody of his definition of Tragedy.[1] Tragedy, by means of pity and terror, works the purification of these emotions in the spectator. Comedy (in this curious document) works by means of pleasure and laughter, effecting their purification as Tragedy does with pity and fear. What Aristotle meant by his κάθαρσις is a question for a philosopher; it is pleasantly treated by one of the best of modern wits, Jules Lemaître, in his little tract on Aristotle and Corneille.[2] It does not matter for the present purpose. Without discussing it, we may accept the definition of Comedy as at any rate a góod and intelligible description. The effect of it is indeed a purification of pleasure and laughter; and so to think of it is itself a pleasure.

Perhaps one should apologize for abstract discussions of this sort, for they are too apt to be dim glimpses into the obvious. Abstract talk about the principles of the drama was long a favourite business with idle people—amateur and confident critics like Dr. Johnson's Dick Minim, or like Polonius with his formulas of classification, tragical-comical-historical-pastoral, his references to Seneca and Plautus, his weighing of classical against romantic, scene individable, or poem unlimited, the law of writ and the liberty—just such talk as might have been heard at the Mermaid or the Devil Tavern in Shakespeare's time or at Wills's or The Grecian a hundred years later. But Dr. Johnson himself was interested in the same matters as Dick Minim. And Hamlet is a critic as well as Polonius; which means of course, that Shakespeare was a critic too; he had meditated on the same things as Polonius —the law of writ and the liberty. Many dunces have dis-

---

[1] κωμωιδία ἐστὶ μίμησις πράξεως γελοίου καὶ ἀμοίρου μεγέθους τελείου, χωρὶς ἑκάστου τῶν μορίων ἐν τοῖς εἴδεσι, δρώντων καὶ ⟨οὐ⟩ δι' ἀπαγγελίας, δι' ἡδονῆς καὶ γέλωτος περαίνουσα τὴν τῶν τοιούτων παθημάτων κάθαρσιν· ἔχει δὲ μητέρα τὸν γέλωτα· γίνεται δὲ ὁ γέλως. *Tractatus Coislinianus*, 3 (*Comicorum Graecorum Fragmenta*, ed. G. Kaibel (Berlin, 1899), p. 50).

[2] *Corneille et la poétique d'Aristote* (1888).

cussed the principles of the drama. But the subject has also been treated by intelligent people: Aristotle, Hazlitt, and Charles Lamb; and it has not been left altogether to spectators; the workmen themselves have often come forward to discuss and explain their problems and methods: Ben Jonson, Corneille, Dryden, Alexandre Dumas. There is a fascination, often both for mere critic and for critic-author, in the theory of the perfect work, the dream of a poem or a play which shall be everything in form that everyone has desired. In Milton, in Corneille and Dryden, in Fielding and Flaubert and Stevenson, how strong is the influence of the unbodied spirit!—the epic poem, the heroic play, the novel, in its quiddity before it has condescended on any definite plot or personage.

It may be convenient if I say beforehand what I wish to prove, 'just to show that there is no deception'. I think that Charles Lamb was right in his doctrine of the artificial comedy; that Macaulay[1] was right, too, in the details of his opposition to Lamb; which means that Wycherley and Congreve were not altogether the best examples on which Lamb might have founded his argument.

From Lamb's essay on Comedy, taken along with his discussion of the acting of Shakespeare's tragedies, one gathers that comedy ought to be tried and judged by the stage effect. Hazlitt and Lamb agree about the artifice of comedy—the imaginary world with laws of its own, a counterpart of reality but not a true or adequate reflection. We all remember how Lamb's position was challenged by Macaulay, and probably most of us think Macaulay had the better of it in that debate. If you are interested at all in the question and look into it carefully, you may perhaps conclude that what Macaulay has done is to capture several redoubts, leaving his opponent still undefeated at the centre. What really happened I think is this. Lamb had a vision, an ideal which has appeared at different times to many others—a vision of comedy, the perfect drama, pure spirit and air, the quintessence of human

---

[1] In his review of Leigh Hunt's edition of Wycherley, Congreve, Vanbrugh, and Farquhar (1840) in the *Edinburgh Review* (1841); reprinted in his *Critical and Historical Essays*.

vanity in its utmost grace. He found this, as Hazlitt also did, in Congreve's Millamant, and from his worship of this lady he elaborated his philosophy of the comic ideal world and its paradoxical law. Here is Hazlitt's description of her:

> Millamant is the perfect model of the accomplished fine lady:
>
>> Come, then, the colours and the ground prepare,
>> Dip in the rainbow, trick her off in air;
>> Choose a firm cloud, before it falls, and in it
>> Catch ere she change, the Cynthia of a minute.
>
> She is the ideal heroine of the comedy of high life, who arrives at the height of indifference to every thing from the height of satisfaction; to whom pleasure is as familiar as the air she draws; elegance worn as a part of her dress; wit the habitual language which she hears and speaks; love, a matter of course; and who has nothing to hope or to fear, her own caprice being the only law to herself, and rule to those about her. . . . Her charms are so irresistible, that her conquests give her neither surprise nor concern. 'Beauty the lover's gift?' she exclaims, in answer to Mirabell—'Dear me, what is a lover that it can give? Why one makes lovers as fast as one pleases, and they live as long as one pleases, and they die as soon as one pleases; and then if one pleases, one makes more.' . . . She is good-natured and generous, with all her temptations to the contrary; and her behaviour to Mirabell reconciles us to her treatment of Witwoud and Petulant, and of her country admirer, Sir Wilful.
>
> Congreve has described all this in his character of Millamant, but he has done no more; and if he had, he would have done wrong. . . . Millamant is nothing but a fine lady; and all her airs and affectation would be blown away with the first breath of misfortune. Enviable in drawing-rooms, adorable at her toilette, fashion, like a witch, has thrown its spell around her; but if that spell were broken, her power of fascination would be gone. For that reason, I think the character better adapted for the stage [than Rosalind or Perdita]: it is more artificial, more theatrical, more meretricious. I would rather have seen Mrs. Abington's Millamant, than any Rosalind that ever appeared on the stage.[1]

Where Lamb went wrong, I repeat, was not in his philosophy of comedy but in some of the examples on which he founded it. The Restoration Drama is hardly good enough for his theory. It is really too brutal to be, ideally, what Lamb

[1] *Lectures on the English Comic Writers*, iv.

saw in his vision. But that his vision is right, I do believe most firmly. I have seen, I think, and probably many of us have seen, exactly what Lamb describes in the acting of *The School for Scandal*—the game of comedy spoilt by actors and actresses playing for themselves, and turning the vanity of Sheridan into serious Domestic Drama, with implications of the real world, of passion and the cruel ordeals of life quite irrelevant and distractive and destructive. *The School for Scandal* is spoilt when it is played with any insistence on problems, when its satirical reflection of life is deepened to touch the quick.

Lamb's description of Malvolio in the essay 'On Some of the Old Actors' should be compared with his theory of the artificial Restoration Comedy. In dealing with Malvolio Lamb has no scruple about the difference between the stage world and reality. Malvolio is for him a real character, and he thinks of him as he would of a man of his own acquaintance. The immorality or non-morality of the artificial comedy of which Lamb speaks, and which in a way he defends, is a morality belonging to a certain kind of art and is necessary for a certain kind of artistic effect. That is why everything he says about *The School for Scandal* is borne out by successive attempts to produce it on the modern stage; contradictions, an incongruous mixture of moralities, appear. The morality of the artificial comedy is right for the illusion, for the special harmony; it does not go direct for life as Shakespeare's comedy usually does. It aims, whether consciously or not, at making a kind of subtle, shadowy reflection of life, where the *relations* between people are the same as in real life, but where the *meaning* is different. Artificial comedy is in a realm of literature like that of pastoral art in poetry or in drama or in painting; the elements of landscape seem the same as in the real world, but much reality is excluded as incongruous and inconvenient and disturbing. Whereas in the comprehensive drama of Shakespeare anything may happen, any sort of character may appear without spoiling the illusion, the artificial comedy is kept to one sort of society and a limited range of ideas. Lamb's argument is not meant as a paradox; he is thinking of the subject, and his motive is to save a peculiar, and to him pleasant, kind of art from destruction through misunderstanding.

Yet, on thinking over the disquisitions of Lamb and the others on artificial comedy, one is prompted sometimes to put the favourite kind of question of Wordsworth's friend, the Commissioner of Stamps (whom Lamb treated so uncivilly with, 'Sir, will you allow me to look at your phrenological development?'),[1] namely, 'Don't you think Shakespeare a great genius?'; which is really not an unreasonable question, and not impertinent in relation to comedy and to Lamb's essay, 'On the Artificial Comedy of the Last Century'. Might not Lamb have done better and saved some of his outworks from Macaulay, if he had thought more of Shakespeare and less of Wycherley? Is it not in *Love's Labour's Lost*, in *A Midsummer-Night's Dream*, in *Twelfth Night*, that we get the true aerial comedy, the perfect game?

Meredith's Essay on *Comedy and the Uses of the Comic Spirit* takes a view very different from Lamb's in some things, but not irreconcilable with it. His essay, originally a lecture, is one of the most interesting, one of the most ample, as well as one of the most subtle, pieces of criticism that ever came from the studio of a working artist. There is a value attaching to such explanations and confessions, beyond what is found in the opinions of the unpractising philosopher. The man in the workshop— Ben Jonson or Corneille or Dryden—sees what the looker-on, even Aristotle or Hazlitt, cannot speak of in the same way.

The argument of Meredith's essay is to prove that Comedy requires the best society, a peculiarly favourable world of conversation, good manners, and intelligence, before it can begin to thrive. It is what Dryden was looking for when he complained of the low life in Ben Jonson: 'The poets of this age will be more wary than to imitate the meanness of his persons. Gentlemen will now be entertained with the follies of each other; and though they allow Cob and Tib to speak properly, yet they are not much pleased with their tankard, or with their rags.'[2] No unsophisticated spectators will do

---

[1] *Autobiography of Benjamin Robert Haydon* ('World's Classics' ed., 359 ff.).

[2] *Defence of the Epilogue: or An Essay on the Dramatic Poetry of the Last Age* (1672); *Essays*, ed. Ker, i. 177.

for comedy. Tragedy may appeal to them; the blunt audience, the rustic mind, may be affected by tragedy in some degree. *Hamlet* is a good acting play. As Charles Lamb says, they take *Othello* in the same way as they take *George Barnwell*.[1] But the irony of comedy is wasted on many a spectator who is thrilled by the sensational part of tragedy. And further, audiences far above the rustic level may be unfit for comedy— like John Knox at the ballet in Browning's fancy.[2] We know what Bossuet thought of Molière, *un infâme histrion*.[3] Preoccupation with solemn things may be an obstacle, even in the best society; though Pascal and William Law, to say nothing of Plato, show that the ironic spirit is not afraid of the company of mystics. Votaries of the grand style may possibly, some of them, be disqualified for the lighter art.

The difference in the views of Meredith and Lamb is that Meredith requires along with the vanity, the raillery, the artifice, something deeper and more philosophical. In *his* School for Scandal there would be the element which Lamb finds incongruous; only, of course, instead of being incongruous and intrusive, as when actors put the wrong emphasis on Sir Peter Teazle, this serious study of motive would be harmonized with the lighter play—would be what, in fact, it is in the books of Meredith which we know. But these are not dramas. Where are the comic dramas, the comedies proper, that fulfil the ideal? Spenser's lost comedies were most probably sage and serious. Thinking over Meredith's demonstration, one is inclined to adopt the sentence of Rasselas: 'Enough! Thou hast convinced me that no human being can ever be a poet.' It looks as if no one could write a comedy, and that, if he could, very few would appreciate it.[4] And when one considers the facts, it is indeed not easy to find the works that come up to Meredith's specifications.

[1] 'On the Tragedies of Shakspeare, considered with reference to their fitness for Stage Representation.'

[2]
       As if you had carried sour John Knox
         To the play-house at Paris, Vienna, or Munich,
       Fastened him into a front-row box,
         And danced off the Ballet with trousers and tunic!
                 (*Garden Fancies*, II—Sibrandus Schafnaburgensis.)

[3] In his *Maximes sur la comédie* (1694), pp. 5, 19.

[4] Cf. Ker, *The Art of Poetry*, p. 128.

Menander has been respected for centuries, in his absence, as a perfect master, as including Molière and Thackeray and Anthony Trollope all in one Greek mind. But Menander has been shaken since his work began to be discovered. Attenders on the Westminster Play are familiar with the machines of the New Comedy; the recognition of the missing daughter by means of the things found along with her in her helpless infancy, the bracelet that she wore when the kidnappers stole her. Now this machine is all very well, and Shakespeare and Molière need not be ashamed of using it. But it is overdone in the Latin comedies; and when Menander is brought to the surface, it is chilling to find that so much of the new fragmentary material is taken up with this old bag of tricks, the πηρίδιον γνωρισμάτων, 'the fardel' in which the documents are contained that prove the descent of Perdita.[1] One of the most considerable of the newly discovered fragments of Menander is a scene which gives its name to the play, *The Arbitrants*[2]—two rustics disputing which of them is to have the fardel, the bag found along with the female infant; they refer this to a gentleman passing by for him to decide. Menander seems to have been able to do little without a fardel of this sort.

Is it not true to say that one finds, very often, the conditions and even the ironic spirit of comedy without the proper comic results upon the stage? The society of good conversation, wit, good manners, is it well rendered or expressed dramatically even in Molière, except in one or two plays? Would not one go to Plato or to Pascal, rather than to Menander or Molière, for the finest conversational humour, the true comic irony? The people in the plays have so little to talk about in comparison, and, as for acting, one is always in danger of the bag of tricks.

On the other hand, the spectator at the Westminster Play looking on at the *Andria* or the *Phormio* may find himself relenting and be prepared to go up afterwards to the headmaster and confess that the old dramatists knew what they were about. With all the stock artifices, the conventional

---

1 Cf. Ker, *The Art of Poetry*, p. 23.
2 Ἐπιτρέποντες.

types, there is something like life. The commonplaces are somehow freshened up by the dramatic poets, without any very obvious spices of wit. In the theatrical contrast of youth and age, of the liberal spirit and the grumbler, of the ingenuous youth and the fortune-hunter, may be found an interest which is different from that of mere good dialogue, as in Plato, or of ironical argument, as in the *Provincial Letters*. These other things, the irony and wit, are of the nature of comedy, but they are not the same. The drama takes a larger, if a rougher, hold upon life, and puts the movement of life immediately before the mind, as the dialogue or the ironical essay by itself cannot do. This movement is comically quickened when it is directed by the knave of the piece—the inventive servant or the man about town who lives by his wits, as Phormio does. To make life appear as if it were directed all by a mischievous good-humoured elf, is always one of the great successes in comedy. Shakespeare knows this, not only in the operations of Puck and Oberon, but in *Twelfth Night*, where the Clown gives himself the air of a Robin Goodfellow and flits through the play as though everything were directed by his bauble. This of course is illusion, but it is part of the whole illusion planned by the author; the movement of the jester through the play is a sort of elvish accompaniment to all the errors and confusions and surprises. Feste really does invent a good deal of the business, and he is so active that he looks as if it all belonged to him; he has the last word, too.

The matter of comedy is the movement of life through the illusions and several partial views of different characters. The matter of tragedy might be described in the same terms. Some tragedies are hard to distinguish from comedy; the *Philoctetes* of Sophocles, for example, a simple play where the action is the generous recovery of a young man Neoptolemus from the political domination of a schemer Odysseus—just such a living growth of right ideas out of wrong judgements as Jane Austen understands. In comedy (and in narrative comedy, also, of course) it is essential that this movement should be taken lightly, and that the humour of the errors should not be sacrificed to the moral of the correcting process.

The prejudice of Elizabeth Bennet, the misjudgements of Emma Woodhouse, must have plenty of room to play before they are cleared up. In the comic drama, where there is less room than in narrative, it is found convenient to have formal patterns which help to bring the comic business within compass. The artificial comic frame is not to be despised even though it be what is roughly called farcical. I once had the good luck to see a comedy of Calderón beautifully acted in the Teatro Español in Madrid, *El escondido y la tapada* (*The Gentleman in Hiding*), a play whose title means concealments and disguises, and which keeps this promise well. It is full of the bustle of farce, as ridiculous in its business as *The Magistrate*,[1] yet at the same time a true comedy of good manners. The people engaged are gentlefolk and the motive is the point of honour.

It occurs to the mind that Meredith himself, though a great comic artist, is not, except accidentally or in an amateur way, a comic *dramatist*. Further, that for some purposes of criticism the difference between comic drama and the novel is unimportant. The Muse of Comedy presides over *The Egoist*, and it is easier to find pure comic genius in England among novelists than dramatists—among the authors of the comic epic poem in prose, as Fielding defines the novel. The reader does not trouble himself much about the difference so long as the ideas come into his mind. Falstaff, Don Quixote, Mr. Dugald Dalgetty, Sir Lucius O'Trigger—one does not stop to consider closely how they are presented, which come from plays and which from novels. For the reader of a play, the play is narrative, with the ordinary narrative padding cut out, or reduced to stage directions which in some cases may be swollen to compete with the narrative or description of the novelist. The Comic Genius is the same whether it works in chapters or in scenes. But it is in its proper dramatic form that it is properly known and tested. Some of the best things in narrative comedy gain by a suggestion of the artifices of the stage—of the dramatic proportions and symmetries. Wilfrid Pole the sentimentalist

---

[1] Pinero's farce *The Magistrate* was first performed at the Royal Court Theatre in 1885.

in *Sandra Belloni* is anatomized in the full, leisurely, philosophic manner which is only possible in narrative Comedy, and in narrative with reflections interspersed. But the two passages where the story is brought to a point—the scene with Lady Charlotte, where Emilia overhears, and the scene with Emilia where Lady Charlotte steps forward—these two scenes have the artificial symmetry of the drama, the same situation with the parties counterchanged, a symmetry and correspondence seemingly too neat and perfect for true history, were it not that the author here has solved the difficult problem and managed to give his story both the full substantial varied life which is proper for narrative, along with the suggestion, which is a considerable part in every comic drama, of a mischievous power behind the scenes, arranging detections and surprises. Here is the climax of the scene with Lady Charlotte.

'You never loved Emilia Belloni?—don't love her now?—do *not* love her now? If you have ever said that you love Emilia Belloni, recant, and you are forgiven. . . . The word, if you please, as you are a gentleman.' . . .

He put on his ever-ready other self.

'Categorically I reply: Have I loved Miss Emilia Belloni?—No. Do I?—No. Do I love Charlotte Chillingworth? Yes, ten thousand times!' . . .

Suddenly the fingers in his grasp twisted, and not being at once released, she turned round to him.

'For God's sake, spare the girl!'

Emilia stood in the doorway.[1]

And here is the conversation with Emilia later in the book.

'Then,' came the clear reply, 'you do not love Lady Charlotte?'

'Love her!' he shouted scornfully, and subdued his voice to add:

'She has a good heart, and whatever scandal is talked of her and Lord Eltham, she is a well-meaning friend. But, love her! You, you I love.'

'Theatrical business,' Lady Charlotte murmured, and imagined she had expected it when she promised Emilia she would step out into the night air, as possibly she had.

<hr>

[1] Chapter xxxvi.

The lady walked straight up to them.

'Well, little one!' she addressed Emilia; 'I am glad you have re-covered your voice. You play the game of tit-for-tat remarkably well. We will now sheath our battledores. There is my hand.'[1]

There is the same sort of repetition in *The Egoist*. To see the device worked simply and clearly for stage effect, one need only go to *The Merry Wives of Windsor*, or to Ibsen's *The League of Youth*. In *The Merry Wives of Windsor* it is used for elementary fun in the successive disgraces of Falstaff. In Ibsen's *The League of Youth*, his one true comedy, there is an old theatrical device, formal and ob-viously symmetrical, in the successive flights for refuge of the impostor, the super-bounder who finds himself betrayed in turn by all the strings of his bow. The last scene is very near farce, where the three ladies of whom Stensgaard has been thinking come forward one after the other with news of her engagement to someone else.

Devices of this sort may be used well or ill; they are con-venient in the ordinary well-made play. The trick may be learnt. Ibsen probably learnt it in his practical acquaintance with the French theatre. At its second best it is a mechanical thing. But it is a dramatic thing, far more effective on the stage than in narrative—except where it is exceptionally used, as by Meredith, an artist with a fresh policy of his own, availing himself of all the liberties and digressions allowable in epic along with the pointed conclusions that take effect in the theatre. Nothing, I think, shows the art of Meredith better than his use of these theatrical strokes, so as to get the utmost telling power on the minds of his audience, to bring the house down, with no sacrifice or relaxation of his more subtle purposes, his imagination or his thought. His strength in this way is like Shakespeare's. It is very feebly described in what I have said about it, for I have made too much opposition between the stage effects and the subtler purposes. Those dramatic scenes in *Sandra Belloni* and *The Egoist* are natural products of everything that has gone before; they come spontaneously in their right place. The artifice, the mischievous meaning in them, is that they give you Wilfrid

[1] Chapter lviii.

Pole and Sir Willoughby Patterne shown up like the dupes of the comic stage—only with Meredith's Imps of Comedy laughing all round, invisible, instead of Sir Toby and Maria, Feste and Fabian, instead of the Windsor fairies, to bait the poor discomfited victim.

Shakespeare uses this kind of dramatic device in various ways. He can do without it altogether. Sometimes he has the simplest sort of repetition in his pattern, as in the most effective scene of *Love's Labour's Lost*, the successive explosions ending in the conviction of Berowne himself when he has just promised castigation to Dumaine, Longaville, and the King of Navarre. The trick of the stage here is not very recondite or elaborate, but it is fully justified; it is pure comedy, and farce at the same time, and the successful artifice is thoroughly dramatic, and thoroughly unfit for narrative form. The pattern of *A Midsummer-Night's Dream* is one of the finest and most dexterous ever shown; but the intricacy of the web includes some very distinct and simple repetitions in the Lysander and Demetrius episodes. With Benedick and Beatrice the practical joke of the comic stage is worked out in a symmetrical figure, and again the effect of this sort of drama is found to be something quite different from narrative, and different from the drama of Hero and Claudio, which is drawn from a story, and may be turned back into a story, as the play of Benedick and Beatrice hardly can.

In those three examples from Shakespeare the results of the artificial comic symmetry may be clearly seen. It is a help, and not an unfair help, to the dramatic effect; it frames the action so as to fit into the spectator's mind. Beyond that, it gives just the touch of unreality, of vanity, which suits with comedy; it reminds you that these graceful personages are being made to dance to the piper's tune. The comic zest and interest lies in the contrast between Benedick and Beatrice regarded as puppets, being 'propertied' unconsciously by the practical jokers of the play: this on the one hand, and on the other the real freedom and originality of their minds. Lysander might be taken as representative of all the figures of comedy; the whole theatre has just seen him put under witchcraft, and he is so sure of his own lucidity. The magic juice is squeezed by Puck on his sleeping eyes and he is beside himself when he wakes up, as the spectators understand; and he chooses Helena in place of Hermia. But he is not content with his wooing until he has defined his position philosophically:

> The will of man is by his reason sway'd.

The opinion might have been held and uttered by Brutus, and Brutus might be as wrong as Lysander.[1] It is just to prevent the illusion of comedy from being taken too seriously and forced into inconvenient pathos that the artificial comic pattern is useful. Comedy is not the same thing as life; and the artificial symmetries are of use to give this partial imitation of life its own proper rhythm. They are part of the comic policy of taking the audience into the showman's confidence.

In the large narrative scale, where the interests are not so limited and defined, the pattern is unnecessary and inexpedient. Likewise where the interest is all in the character. Falstaff, it is recognized, is not fully himself when he is brought into the conventional well-made play of *The Merry Wives of Windsor*. Similarly, the full narrative of *Sandra Belloni* would seem the wrong place for symmetrical *coups de théâtre*, if the expression may be allowed; but (apart from their stunning effect in themselves) they are useful because they bring out in Wilfrid Pole the family likeness to Lysander and the other dupes of comedy.

The comic genius has an infinite width of range, beyond the formal garden of the well-bred comic drama. The lyric enthusiasm of the old Athenian Comedy of Aristophanes is too strong for the new comedy of Menander, Terence, and Molière. The new comedy does not pay enough attention to Dionysus, the original master of the feast. The tribe of Aristophanes is dispersed, and their work is not restricted to the comic drama, and is found there when the comic unities are disregarded, as in Falstaff (when not at Windsor).

But among the works of the more regular dramatists there

---

[1] Cf. *Collected Essays*, i. 271.

is one that seems to me to have a peculiar share of the original Dionysiac freedom. That is *Le Menteur* of Corneille.[1] Dryden did not think much of it.[2] It is a play that requires good acting. I saw it once, with Delaunay[3] as Dorante. That great artiste was near the end of his days, but still the perfection of irresponsible youth, the young man of fine comedy, without a flaw in the grace of his demeanour. *The Liar* is a very simple play with only one really important character. It may appear on reading like a simple exercise in conventional types and incidents. But indeed it is something more. Corneille, in this comedy, has given to the modern stage a scene or two which have something of the old Dionysiac enthusiasm. The beauty of them is that the lies of Dorante are pure uncontrollable imagination. He lies for the pleasure of invention, and his inventions are not like the ordinary clever tricks of the comic knave; they are mere luxuriant, lawless vainglory and revelry. For the moment you might think of him as himself the young god triumphant; you see the fresh irresponsible ideas springing up in his mind, like the miracle of the vine of Bacchus suddenly breaking out and entangling all the ship on which the god was travelling. When Dorante is left to himself on the front of the stage, the clever servant is deposed from his regular command. He can no longer control the plot. He is swept to the background, he can do nothing but hold up his hands in horror and amazement, as helpless as any ordinary, respectable man. All his traditional ingenuities are made dull, no better than respectability, compared with this irruption of the original comic flame.

[1] Cf. Ker, *The Art of Poetry*, p. 135.

[2] 'Corneille himself, their arch-poet, what has he produced except *The Liar*, and you know how it was cried up in France; but when it came upon the English stage, though well translated, and that part of Dorant acted to so much advantage by Mr. Hart as I am confident it never received in its own country, the most favourable to it would not put it in competition with many of Fletcher's or Ben Jonson's.' Neander in *Of Dramatick Poesie, An Essay* (*Essays of John Dryden*, ed. W. P. Ker, i. 68).

[3] Louis Arsène Delaunay (1826–1903); he retired in 1887.

III. LECTURE-TALK

(i) *The English Poets*

SIR PHILIP SIDNEY

OPINIONS differ about the poetry of Sidney; it was admired by Charles Lamb,[1] Wordsworth,[2] and Ruskin;[3] Hazlitt did not like it.[4] On the whole I think that Hazlitt was wrong.

Sidney had to make up his mind about the stream of tendency which we call the Renaissance, though that was not its name in his day. You find him wrestling with the Spirit of the Age in his *Apologie for Poetrie*, and the results are curious. There is the same sort of conflict in his poetry, and the results are curious there also, and often beautiful.

The worst of the revival of learning was that it encouraged a new kind of pedantry, for example, that of Scaliger in his *Poetice*. It also, though this is not so commonly understood, carried on a good deal of the pedantry of the Middle Ages and developed and strengthened it, particularly in the work of the Petrarchists. A number of the conceited fashions of Renaissance poetry are old conceits of the medieval poets. Petrarch followed the Provençal school. One instance will suffice. 'Sweet enemy' as addressed by the lover to his lady

---

[1] 'Some Sonnets of Sir Philip Sidney' in *The Last Essays of Elia*.

[2] Wordsworth ('Essay Supplementary to the Preface', 1815), writing of Johnson's *Lives of the Poets*, asked indignantly: 'Where is the bright Elizabethan constellation? . . . where is Spenser? where Sidney? . . . and, lastly, . . . where Shakespeare?' He used the two opening lines of 'With how sad steps, O Moon, thou climbst the skies . . .' for a sonnet of his own.

[3] 'I know no such lovely love-poems as his, since Dante's. . . . If you don't like these love-songs, you either have never been in love, or you don't know good writing from bad (and likely enough both the negatives, I'm sorry to say, in modern England).' Ruskin, *Fors Clavigera*, letter xxxv.

[4] 'His Sonnets . . . are jejune, far-fetched and frigid.' *Lectures on the Literature of the Age of Elizabeth*, Lecture VI; *Works*, ed. P. P. Howe (1930–4), vi. 326.

is a commonplace in Renaissance authors; it is already old
in the time of Chaucer:

> Far-wel, my swete fo, myn Emelye![1]

an example of the artificial contradictory figure which every
medieval court-poet knew how to employ, and which the
Renaissance poets used with that thoroughness and confidence which belonged to the spirit of their age. They could
not have too much of a good thing, even when the good
thing might seem to have been exhausted by repetition in
the course of centuries. Sidney makes a new thing of it, in
the well-known passage in the forty-first sonnet of *Astrophel
and Stella*:

> Having this day my horse, my hand, my launce,
> Guided so well, that I obtaind the prize,
> Both by the judgment of the English eyes,
> And of some sent from that sweet enmie Fraunce....

'That sweet enemy France' is a memorable phrase which
strikes those who hear it as a new invention. Great things
can be done by poets, turning commonplaces into miracles.

    The ordinary use of that figure and its position as a
securely established and conventional literary term may be
exemplified in a quotation from *Don Quixote* which shows
up at the same time some other regular, almost obligatory,
decorations of Renaissance poetry.

Here Don Quixote gave a great sigh and said 'I cannot say whether
my sweet enemy (*la dulce mi enemiga*) is pleased or not that all the
world should know me for her servant; only I can tell in answer to
this most courteous request that her name is Dulcinea del Toboso; her
home Toboso, a village of La Mancha; her quality not less than Prin-
cess, since she is my Queen and Lady; her beauty above human, for
in her are made real all the impossible and chimerical attributes of
fairness which the Poets assign to their mistresses: her hair of gold,
her forehead Elysian fields, her eyebrows rainbows, her eyes suns, her
cheeks roses, her lips coral, pearls her teeth, alabaster her neck, marble
her breast, ivory her hands, her whiteness snow, and the parts which
honesty veils from human sight are such (as I think and understand)
that discreet consideration can only prize and not compare them.'[2]

---

[1] *Knight's Tale*, 2780.   [2] *Don Quixote*, pt. I, chapter xiii.

Sidney and Shakespeare, older contemporaries of Cervantes, had already turned their critical sense upon this conventional Idea.

> You that doe search for every purling spring
> Which from the rybs of old Parnassus flowes,
> And every flower (not sweet perhaps) which growes
> Neere there about, into your poems wring;
> You that doe dictionary method bring
> Into your rymes, running in ratling rowes;
> You that old Petrarch's long-deceased woes
> With new-borne sighes and wit disguised sing;
> You take wrong wayes; those far-fet helps be such,
> As doe bewray a want of inward tutch,
> And sure at length stolne goods doe come to light. . . .[1]

Shakespeare's satirical vein is stronger.

> My mistress' eyes are nothing like the sun;
> Coral is far more red than her lips' red; . . .
> I love to hear her speak, yet well I know
> That music hath a far more pleasing sound;
> I grant I never saw a goddess go;
> My mistress, when she walks, treads on the ground:
>   And yet, by heaven, I think my love as rare
>   As any she belied by false compare.[2]

The point of Cervantes's criticism is the same as Sidney's and Shakespeare's. The strange thing is that Sidney is sometimes content to use the old formulas. Don Quixote's speech might have been founded on Sidney's ninth sonnet in *Astrophel and Stella*:

> Queene Vertue's Court, which some call Stella's face,
> Prepar'd by Nature's cheefest furniture,
> Hath his front built of alablaster pure;
> Golde is the covering of that statelie place.
> The doore, by which sometimes runnes forth her grace,
> Red porphir is, which locke of pearle makes sure,
> Whose porches rich, with name of chekes indure,
> Marble, mixt red and white, doe enterlace. . . .

[1] *Astrophel and Stella*, xv.

[2] Shakespeare's twenty-first sonnet ('So is it not with me as with that Muse . . .') is a treatment of the same theme.

DONNE

Donne has been misjudged by those who have ranked him among the Marinists. Donne's wit is of a different sort from Cowley's, though there is an outward resemblance. The quality of his soul was not wit which can play calmly and imperially with all sorts of ideas, remaining indifferent to their essential value. His soul was of quite different nature, so passionate, so fervid, that it consumed the prosiest, woodenest images, and delighted in this evidence of mastery. The mark of the conceited poet is that his cool hands toss about the fieriest things without the least sense of warmth. He can use all things in the earth beneath or in heaven above to illustrate any happy thought that may have arisen in his icy, curious brain. Donne's use of metaphor is quite different. It is extravagant, perverse, preposterous, and all the rest of it; but it is not frigid—it is not acrobatic poetry. The charm of his wild allegories is in the spirit that informs them; his far-fetched images are precious for the sake of the high adventurous spirit that wandered out in such strange seas of thought in search of them.

The compasses in 'A Valediction: forbidding mourning' have been ridiculed by all the guild of critics. Did none of them feel any misgiving? The compasses may be mere wit; but it is the critic, not the poet, who makes much of it. The poet describes in the language not of compasses but of souls. 'It leans and hearkens after it'—the soul of his wife being joined with his in some sublime space above space, out of the jurisdiction of ordinary geometries.

The virtue of Donne's poetry is not its metaphoric wealth but its intensity of passion, and of vision. The things his mind rests on turn into Platonic ideas and recur to be lifted above the sensual flux as unchangeable realities, beacons to the thought.

COWLEY

One may be surprised on turning to Cowley's Pindaric Odes to find so little real novelty in them. They are written in irregular verse, but so were many earlier poems—Milton's 'On Time', 'At a Solemn Music', and 'Lycidas', the odes of

Drummond of Hawthornden,[1] &c. Cowley was a great classical scholar, one of the best of his time outside the small number of philologists by profession. He knew more about Greek poetry than any of his contemporaries, except possibly Milton. His Pindaric Odes really have their origin in Pindar, and the name which later became a mere conventional term was well-earned by Cowley and was the right description for his work. Cowley chose irregular verse because he wished to imitate the manner of Pindar, and it was the traditional opinion that Pindar's verse was irregular, though in reality Pindar is more regular than Horace, the poet who no doubt influenced Cowley in his belief as to Pindar's freedom and irregularity.[2] But in choosing irregular verse Cowley could not choose anything that differed much from earlier English irregular measures, and so his Pindaric invention seems to coincide a good deal with what had been previously done.

In the earlier English irregular verse Dryden's instinctive rule whereby 'the cadency of one line' determines that of the next[3] was commonly observed. 'Irregular', indeed, is rather a misleading term; for the verse of, say, 'On Time' or 'At a Solemn Music' is not irregular, but merely unsymmetrical, with no passage exactly answering to any other. These poems seem irregular if compared as wholes with Spenser's 'Epithalamion'; but if one stanza of 'Epithalamion' is compared with one stanza of these poems of Milton's, it is hard to say which is the more irregular. The so-called irregular verse of 'On Time' and 'At a Solemn Music' is derived from the same school as the regular verse of 'Epithalamion', from the Italian school, from the great ode of Italian poetry, the *canzone*. This measure was suggested to English poets by the irregular lyric verse used by the Italian poets in the choruses of dramas (for example, in the pastoral plays, the *Aminta* of Tasso and *Il Pastor Fido* of Guarini), where probably there was some imitation of the Greek choruses. But

---

[1] e.g. the well-known 'Phoebus arise'.

[2] Horace, *Odes*, IV. ii (*numerisque fertur | lege solutis*).

[3] 'The cadency of one line must be a rule to that of the next.' Without 'the nicety of this, the harmony of Pindaric verse can never be complete'. (Preface to *The Second Part of Poetical Miscellanies*, 1685: *Essays of John Dryden*, ed. Ker, i. 268.)

it had nothing to do directly with Pindar. It was a verse that had come down from long tradition, with no express rules, but with unexpressed laws well understood by Milton and others.

The difference made by Cowley in his Pindarics is due to the fact that he is not exactly following the Italian tradition of Milton and Drummond. He uses the same lengths of line as they do, and he does not vary from the iambic, the regular measure of Milton and his companions. But he has a different idea in his mind. Instead of the poetic music or poetic musical impulse, instead of hearing the cadence of the next line before the line is actually invented, instead of feeling, say, that the ten-syllable line requires a six-syllable after it, he has probably a pictorial idea of the stanza. He is not thinking of the sound, the music, but of the pattern as it is seen on the page, the look of the verse of Pindar as it is read in a printed book. This means that he has no proper poetic rule at all. He builds his verse out of separate lengths of line, knowing, for he is a poet, that different lengths of line, different lengths of iambic verse, will all agree to some extent if put together. But he is generally without the 'singing impulse' that carries Milton or Dryden on through magnificent periods, that instinct of the poet that makes the cadency of one line determine that of the next.[1] Cowley's Pindarics unfortunately started really irregular verse in English, verse which looks outwardly like the verse of 'Lycidas', but which is really very different, being a mere heap of lines of different sizes, without any proper unity of spirit to keep them together and make them move. Cowley is not always or altogether to be blamed. He lived in rather a bad time for English lyric poetry.

◈

Cowley's *Essays* are among the first pieces of writing which follow the ideal of good conversation. It is, of course,

---

[1] One can see the elementary principles of cadency, of correspondence, in the Hymn in Milton's 'On the Morning of Christ's Nativity'. It is built up of six-, eight-, ten-, and twelve-syllable lines, and there is correspondence between the six and the ten, and between the eight and the twelve.—W.P.K.

a great mistake to speak of them as colloquial English: no good writing is ever colloquial in the strict sense. But there is a kind of good writing which has the excellencies of good talking. Right conversation must not tyrannize over, bully, or impose upon the hearers. Talk that is flashy is ill mannered. Good essay-writing in the colloquial style avoids blustering and excess of emphasis. The poems of Cowley represent one ideal of brilliance in composition, his prose another.

POPE

Very few of Pope's works have unity of effect, the true classical excellence. If there is anything in the superiority of classical poetry, it is that which is brought out in *An Essay on Criticism*, the subordination of the parts to the whole. You do not generally find that merit in Pope.

> In wit, as nature, what affects our hearts
> Is not th'exactness of peculiar parts;
> 'Tis not a lip, or eye, we beauty call,
> But the joint force and full result of all.
> Thus when we view some well-proportion'd dome,
> (The world's just wonder, and ev'n thine, O Rome!)
> No single parts unequally surprise,
> All comes united to th'admiring eyes;
> No monstrous height, or breadth, or length appear;
> The Whole at once is bold, and regular.   (243-52)

It is only in *The Rape of the Lock* that the unities of narrative are observed, and the effect is that of classical art, where the intellectual imagination holds things together without excess, digression, and loose ends. Pope comes short of this ideal in most of his poetry, simply because he does not choose subjects requiring it. His poems are not in any marked way irregular or incoherent, but in the satire or the moral essay the coherence is less strict; there is less need for it than in tragedy or epic or mock-heroic, or even in the ordinary novel. Quite apart from the Essays and Satires, Pope shows little talent for proportion. In *The Dunciad*, which might have come under the same rule as *The Rape of the Lock*, there is little coherence, and the poem suffers in consequence.

'Nature' is a name for the classical ideal of unity and proportion, for the right instinct that does not exaggerate or under-value anything, that gives a lower place to details and a higher to the more important things. The advice to 'follow Nature' comes to much the same thing as the advice to be a good poet. But in spite of the identity in the precepts, 'First follow Nature' has an effect, an originality and freshness, that one cannot define simply by an analysis of the proposition. It is like a cheer or applause given to people who are struggling to do their best. It reminds poets of what is due from them, that they owe a high duty to reason.

Pope had very strong beliefs about correctness, but he never intended that those beliefs should interfere with his productions. Like any great artist he had to work out for himself the balance between law and freedom (or impulse), and he worked out that problem in such a way as to give himself an immense amount of freedom. There are very few of Pope's works in which the form is anything like strict or clearly discernible. The strict form of *The Rape of the Lock* is, as we have seen, exceptional. Pope's chief poetical productions are discourses, 'essays', where he seems to be talking merely from association of ideas, rambling from one topic to another. He carefully studied the composition of his poems, but that study did not give definite form or proportion; his writing is free.

The 'correctness' of Pope, therefore, is not quite the same thing as the classic spirit, for the reason that the dignity, harmony, and proportion of 'the grand style' (as Reynolds expressed it with regard to painting) requires a habit of mind that can rise above merely discursive ways of thought. Pope does not rise above such ways except in a few of his poems, and those not the most considerable in scale. He leaves the satiric way in *Eloisa and Abelard*, but that is not one of his large poems, and his work as a poet must be judged with reference to his habitual method, the satiric discursive way, the mode of the prose essay, not the mode of imagination.

The mode of the imagination, as distinct from the discursive or reflective method, comes in with the great novelists. Richardson and Fielding do the kind of work in prose that the Augustan poets had neglected, owing to their satiric habit of mind. In Fielding there is plenty of essay stuff, but that is subordinate to the narrative, plot, and characters. Now, narrative, plot, and characters were what the poets had all along admired; that is what is meant by the epic ideal that Dryden and Pope so respected. But narrative, plot, and characters were generally beyond their attainment. Pope shows his 'correctness' in kinds of poetry that are not of the highest. Dryden ventures much further into the imaginative kinds of poetry than Pope, but without ever accomplishing anything really final, really wonderful, really original, in narrative or in drama.

∾

Pope is really the severest critic of his own followers to come. He partly anticipates Wordsworth[1] in his contempt of ordinary, hackneyed poetic diction, with its conventional commonplaces and traditional phrases and rhymes. His poetry is far more in accordance with Wordsworth's principles of poetic diction than Wordsworth's own. If one goes to Pope looking for examples of false diction, one finds it very difficult to get the right specimens. Almost everywhere he uses language, musical, of course, because in verse, but not unnatural, not obviously from the poetic dictionary, not like the poetic language of Anglo-Saxon poetry, not like the idea of the eighteenth-century diction that one gets from contemptuous critics of the beginning of the nineteenth century. One can test this by considering the passage on the Man of Ross in the *Moral Essays*.[2]

> Whose Cause-way parts the vale with shady rows?
> Whose Seats the weary Traveller repose?
> Who taught that heav'n-directed spire to rise?
> The Man of Ross, each lisping babe replies.
> Behold the Market-place with poor o'erspread!
> The Man of Ross divides the weekly bread:
> He feeds yon Alms-house, neat, but void of state,
> Where Age and Want sit smiling at the gate:

[1] Cf. p. 92 above.   [2] iii. 259–74 ('Epistle to Bathurst').

> Him portion'd maids, apprentic'd orphans blest,
> The young who labour, and the old who rest.
> Is any sick? the Man of Ross relieves,
> Prescribes, attends, the med'cine makes, and gives.
> Is there a variance? enter but his door,
> Balk'd are the Courts, and contest is no more.
> Despairing Quacks with curses fled the place,
> And vile Attornies, now an useless race.

There was no true classicism prevalent in English poetry in the middle of the eighteenth century. There was, it is true, a survival of Pope's belief in 'correctness', but this is a different thing from the classical doctrine of poetry. The 'correctness' of Pope is very much correctness of detail. In England there was no realization of the classic ideal corresponding to the classical triumphs of French poetry, nothing comparable with Racine.

◦•

The verse of the *Pastorals* is recognized by Johnson as being singular, exceptional, peculiarly beautiful. In these poems there is certainly great beauty of verse, though it is hard to find anything definitely new. The melody can be heard in the opening lines of 'Spring':

> First in these fields I try the sylvan strains,
> Now blush to sport on Windsor's blissful plains:
> Fair Thames, flow gently from thy sacred spring,
> While on thy bank Sicilian muses sing;
> Let vernal airs thro' trembling osiers play,
> And Albion's cliffs resound the rural lay.

One fact may be noted, and that is the preference for the old regular caesura, or pause after the fourth syllable. Later in Pope's works the pause is varied indefinitely, but in the *Pastorals* this old division of the line is much more frequent. This is why his verse in these poems is in some ways lyrical. It has not the spring and variety of the *Epistle to Dr. Arbuthnot* and the great later satiric, argumentative works, which have something like the variety of pause of Milton's work, 'the sense variously drawn out from one verse into another'. The

verse of the *Pastorals* is much more like the earlier Elizabethan heroic line, where this same division is commonest.
It is through this regular technical character in the verse
that it is fit for musical setting.

> O deign to visit our forsaken seats,
> The mossy fountains, and the green retreats!
> Where'er you walk, cool gales shall fan the glade;
> Trees, where you sit, shall crowd into a shade;
> Where'er you tread, the blushing flowers shall rise,
> And all things flourish where you turn your eyes.[1]

The pause is not kept monotonously at every fourth syllable;
but this caesura is the most frequent, and lends the necessary
regularity to the rhythm. This division is the original, being
found in the earliest French examples of the verse; and it
probably means that the four syllables at the beginning are
made equal to the six at the end. Apart from the tune, or the
musical recitation, one can hear that there is greater weight
in the first section of the line to make up for its shortness, to
make the four syllables nearly equal in value to the six
following. In these early poems, it is obvious that Pope was
thinking more of the verse than of the meaning or anything
else, and he seems to have chosen this type of line as his
favourite.

❦

The 'Ode for Music on St. Cecilia's Day, 1708', is an
imitation of Dryden, in the convention of his earlier 'A Song
for St. Cecilia's Day, 1687'. One might call it a Pindaric,
just as 'Alexander's Feast' is a Pindaric ode. It is interesting, partly as an exercise, as a display of technical skill which
finds out and manages some of the most important things
rightly. It is easy to depreciate it, but one must own that it
avoids the great obstacle, the great vice of the seventeenth-
century Pindaric. It is not simply a poem of different lengths
shuffled anyhow. It has music in itself, and obeys the laws
of irregular verse. It would be absurd to equate it with
Milton's irregular verse, but it is much nearer to Milton

[1] 'Summer', 71–76.

than to the ordinary Pindarics of Cowley, and very far
removed from the bad Pindarics of Swift. There are some
passages in it which might very easily be passed off, even on
well-read people, as the work of some other author. Take,
for example, the passage,

> He sung, and hell consented
>   To hear the Poet's prayer:
> Stern Proserpine relented,
>   And gave him back the fair.   (83–86)

This is not likely to be detected as Pope's verse by one who
simply has general reading to judge from.

❧

In *Othello* we have one of the greatest curiosities of poetry:
the passage which may be called Iago's essay on the characters of women, where he is 'nothing if not critical', where he
declaims a rhyming satire on womankind in couplets as
detached as those of Pope.

❧

The charge against Pope in the *Essay on Man*, the accusation of 'facile optimism', really tells, not against his theory,
but against his temper, his frame of mind, his demeanour,
his gesture. His theory does not ignore the evil or pain in
the world; but the habit of his mind, the dance of his verses,
the jingle of his rhymes, these are in discord, in disagreement with the solemnities of the doctrine that he tries to
expound. It is the jaunty manner, and not the lightness or
superficiality in argument, that has provoked the reaction
against the *Essay on Man*.

❧

Homer had been depreciated a good deal by the scholars
of the Renaissance, and Pope's praise of Homer in the Preface to the *Iliad* is an original thing of the same sort as his
praise of Shakespeare in the Preface to his edition of Shakespeare. The *Homer* is not merely a conventional or respectable
enterprise. Though Homer had, of course, a conventional

reputation, that reputation was not unchallenged, and Pope, bringing out in his Preface the excellences of Homer, the poet of a barbarous age, was, in some ways, doing what he did for Shakespeare, when he compared Shakespeare to a great Gothic building. He employs freedom of thought in dealing with Homer, taking Homer in an original, spirited way, and his work is not to be considered as a mere repetition of things held respectable by convention, as mere conformity to the traditions of the schools.

JAMES THOMSON

It is curious that *The Seasons*, so well known and recognized as an anticipation of Cowper and Wordsworth, is not generally understood as a satiric poem in the old sense. Like Cowper's *Task*, *The Seasons* is a medley, a poetic argument with no strict groove or scope, giving the author's views on all sorts of things. The satiric passages are not so well known as the passages descriptive of Nature, but they are an essential part of the poem.

MATTHEW GREEN

That there was room for true wit in eighteenth-century poetry Green has shown in *The Spleen* (1737)—in the form of fancies scarcely to be separated from the conceits of seventeenth-century poets. The difference is that by Green they are more lightly and neatly employed, although, when one takes the poems of Marvell and compares them with the much slighter work of Green, one may find it difficult to prefer the skill of the later poet.

OLIVER GOLDSMITH

One of the best sentences on Goldsmith is Masson's statement that 'all Goldsmith's phantasies are phantasies of what may be called reminiscence'.[1] The text may be expounded

---

[1] See David Masson's Memoir in the 'Globe' edition of Goldsmith's *Works*: 'All Goldsmith's phantasies, whether in verse or prose—his *Vicar of Wakefield*, his *Traveller*, his *Deserted Village*, his *Good-Natured Man* and *She Stoops to Conquer*, and even the humorous sketches that occur in his *Essays* and *Citizen of the World*— are phantasies of what may be called *reminiscence*. Less than even Smollett, did Goldsmith *invent*, if by invention we mean a projection of the imagination into vacant

more fully than Masson does in this place. It is not only that
Goldsmith gets the matter of his works from memory, but
that the memory of his own life had a peculiar value for him.
Like Lamb and Stevenson, Goldsmith has a great affection
for his past, and many reminiscences of his early days are
repeated in his writings. Thus his love of the old songs
referred to in *The Vicar of Wakefield*[1] and in an essay of *The
Bee*[2] is a recollection kept in mind and turned into a phrase
that repeats itself.

The difference between Goldsmith and Lamb is that
Goldsmith almost always turns those phantasies of reminiscence out of the personal frame. He takes things that are
valuable to himself, and, instead of dwelling on them as
Lamb and Stevenson do, makes them the matter for impersonal narrative, for work, at any rate, that has much
meaning apart from the author. This is what gives peculiar
value to *The Deserted Village*, what makes it noticeable among
eighteenth-century poems, separating it from others in the
regular measure. It has a great deal of personal reminiscence,
of the melancholy of recollection found in Lamb and
Stevenson, but this is not the predominant thing in the composition. For the personalities are turned into external
history, the history of something intended to be interesting
apart from the author. Goldsmith has charged and quickened
the narrative and moralizing out of his own life; yet his
personal interests are not the prevailing spirit of the poem.

It is noteworthy that Goldsmith had some acquaintance
with Rousseau, who had tried the other way, the mode of
literature in which the sensibility of the author is the main

---

space, and a filling of portion after portion of that space, as by sheer bold dreaming,
with scenery, events, and beings, never known before. He drew on the recollections
of his own life, on the history of his own family, on the characters of his relatives,
on whimsical incidents that had happened to him in his Irish youth or during his
continental wanderings, on his experience as a literary drudge in London. . . .'
(p. lix.)

[1] 'These harmless people had several ways of being good company; while one
played, the other would sing some soothing ballad, Johnny 'Armstrong's Last
Good-night, or the Cruelty of Barbara Allen.' (Chapter iv.)

[2] 'The music of Mattei is dissonance to what I felt when our old dairy-maid sang
me into tears with Johnny Armstrong's Last Good Night, or the Cruelty of Barbara
Allen.' (*The Bee*, No. ii, 'Happiness in a great measure dependent on constitution'.)

thing. Goldsmith had no conscious repulsion from Rousseau's method, but he certainly chose this way of his own.

◦◦

In the descriptions of *The Deserted Village* Goldsmith worked with something of the method of Pope, composing separate pieces and working them later into the regular literary frame. This is proved by the way in which some lines from a 'Description of an Author's Bedchamber', which occurs as a distinct poem, were translated and modified for *The Deserted Village:*

> There, in a lonely room, from bailiffs snug,
> The Muse found Scroggen stretch'd beneath a rug;
> A window, patch'd with paper, lent a ray,
> That dimly show'd the state in which he lay;
> The sanded floor that grits beneath the tread;
> The humid wall with paltry pictures spread:
> The royal Game of Goose was there in view,
> And the Twelve Rules the royal martyr drew;
> The Seasons, fram'd with listing, found a place,
> And brave Prince William show'd his lamp-black face . . .
> With beer and milk arrears the frieze was scor'd,
> And five crack'd tea-cups dress'd the chimney board. (5-18)

Here is the description of the village tavern in *The Deserted Village:*

> Imagination fondly stoops to trace
> The parlour splendours of that festive place;
> The white-wash'd wall, the nicely sanded floor,
> The varnish'd clock that click'd behind the door;
> The chest contriv'd a double debt to pay,
> A bed by night, a chest of drawers by day;
> The pictures plac'd for ornament and use,
> The twelve good rules, the royal game of goose; . . .
> While broken tea-cups, wisely kept for show,
> Rang'd o'er the chimney, glisten'd in a row. (225-36)

◦◦

In some of the best comedies much of the success is due to the abstract architecture of the play, to the correspondence of the different parts. Good comedy may be compared to a figured dance, in which one part of the figure corresponds to and contrasts with the other. Much of the effect of *A Midsummer-Night's Dream* and *Twelfth Night* comes from the pattern of the plot, all the various scenes being made to contribute to the single impression of the whole. Another example of this sort of thing is to be found in Congreve's best play, *The Way of the World*. But in Goldsmith the pattern is defective. His plays are not very characteristic of the eighteenth century, being in form more like the irregular Elizabethan comedies. There is some construction in *She Stoops to Conquer*, but the comic idea of the play is not quite strong enough—the comic idea being the contest between Marlow and Miss Hardcastle. Marlow is too feeble; and so the episodes and digressions, the whole business of Tony Lumpkin, get a disproportionate value and effect.

The Good Natur'd Man may be called a bad play without any disrespect to Goldsmith, being too old-fashioned, too simple in its idea. The good-natured man himself is a 'humour' in Ben Jonson's sense, an eccentricity, an oddity; and he is driven in the same way as Ben Jonson's exaggerated characters, impelled in his course of action into open absurdities and incredible things. When he sacrifices his love in order to be generous, he is really as ridiculous as Prince Volscius in *The Rehearsal*, as any character in Dryden's dramas. Goldsmith has put forward a character who acts on the point of honour as absurdly as anyone in the heroic plays. The impostor, Lofty, is a fairly good comic liar, and there is some effect in the scene where he is talking to Sir William Honeywood, the unknown father of the good-natured man, of his influence with this same Sir William. But 'humours' of this sort are not enough to cure the want of truth, of nature, in the play—at least, this is the conclusion arrived at of the play as read.

THOMAS GRAY

The Pindarics prove that Gray, who wrote very little because he could not write very much poetry, had thought steadily about poetic form and meant to do something more magnificent than had ever been done before. The great odes, particularly 'The Progress of Poesy', are a work of pure and sincere poetic ambition, quite as much as is *Paradise Lost*. What is most important for the study of Gray's Pindarics is not the history of the form, not the anticipations of Ben Jonson or Cowley or Congreve, not the system of verse, the strophe and antistrophe corresponding with each other and the epode with a form of its own, but the conduct of the poetic argument along with the poetical music. Gray, we may imagine, felt his earlier poems too slight, lacking in dignity and unity. He wished to 'build the lofty rhyme', to make a poetical thing of some magnitude, something which should be large and at the same time coherent, a work of fine poetic architecture. One must, of course, understand 'large', in thinking of the scale of lyric literature, as a comparative term for the lyric kind; it is hardly possible for lyric to come in mere size near the scale of drama. The Pindarics are 'great' lyric poems, 'great' in the ordinary sense of 'large' as well as otherwise. They are great in poetic thought and imagination that could not be brought out apart from the elaborate structure; the thought requires and fills out the structure, and the odes are poetical monuments far beyond the attainment of any of his contemporaries.

⌒

The *Elegy* has something of the unpoetic reasoning found in moralizing poetry generally, in satires and moral essays. It has something of the old poetic diction, of the smoothness, perfection, completeness, and obvious care in the phrasing that rather puts off the modern reader, that makes one think that this finished rhetoric is wanting in freedom and spirit. Something, however, must be allowed for the too familiar phrases and for the old fashion of the verse; that slow, stately, meditative verse is not the kind that is generally liked and appreciated in modern times. Of course, when one asks people to make allowances, to put themselves back into the fashion of those times, one is asking and conceding a great deal. One does not have to ask that sort of thing for Shakespeare. Where there is anything of this transposition to be done, it is done generally in an instinctive way; one feels oneself at home in *A Midsummer-Night's Dream* or *As You Like It*, and the differences of time and fashion are scarcely felt as an hindrance. If one has to think oneself back, as one has to with Pope frequently and with Gray's *Elegy*, one has to confess that poetry appreciated in this way is not of the very greatest. Still, it is better to take this trouble and to adopt this artifice than to be insensible of the real beauty and meaning of the older fashion.

It is undeniable that in the *Elegy* Gray has succeeded in keeping the mood throughout the poem, a poem of considerable length by lyric standards; that the mood is of value; and that the separate passages in this continuous music have a proper meaning of their own and are worth bearing in mind. The *Elegy* is not so ambitious as 'The Progress of Poesy' and 'The Bard', but it is beyond them in the steadiness of sentiment, and it is this truth of sentiment, a truth proved by its unity and its uninterrupted thought, that is the truth of an artist dealing with nature. If one takes a work of art as a contest between the artist and nature, in which the artist gets what he can out of nature and expresses it in a way that seems easy to those for whom the work is made, then Gray's *Elegy* is really the triumphant thing that his own generation said it was. What Gray has got from nature for his poem is not mainly the reflections, say, upon the life of the village, the 'village Hampden', the 'mute inglorious Milton', nor anything particular in the poem, such as the gem in the dark unfathomed caves of ocean, but the humane mode of thought, the temper shown in the reflection upon the mortality of the village churchyard. It is in the portrait he has given of his own mind, the reading of his own temper and sentiment, that he has succeeded.

The advice to poets to keep their eyes on the object is good enough advice, and the censure on the eighteenth-century poets to the effect that they have often not their eye on the object is well deserved. But the form of advice and censure is limited, and makes too much of the external world. It is, of course, only a rough rule, only an *obiter dictum*, not a principle, and it is apt to be misinterpreted.

One too easily forgets that the poet has other objects besides that on which he can keep or cannot keep his eye; he ought to keep his mind on the subject, and Gray has kept his mind on the subject without failure in the *Elegy*. Over against this success the remarks of censure on the old-fashioned diction fall away and become inept.

❧

The poem 'On the Death of a Favourite Cat', though disliked with good reason by many people, is not uninteresting. It is an imitation of the French lighter verse, of the French treatment of similar themes, not in a mock-heroic way, but in a lyric way corresponding to the mock-heroic travesty of the epic. The quality which Gray uses here in a very distinct and very clever way is the bright vision of particulars. Everything is clearly seen, and everything is translated out of its proper simple meaning. It is an elaborate paraphrase into affected fanciful language, and also affected fanciful vision. The artifice is thoroughly successful, but is spoilt by the obvious complacency of the author, by his much too obtrusive pleasure in the success of his fancies and his words, and the entire absence of any real interest in the subject, that sort of interest that one finds in Prior's later poetry. 'On the Death of a Favourite Cat' is one of the hardest and most unfeeling pieces of clever writing.

❧

The singular thing about the translations of Gray is that in the originals there are the very same qualities as in Gray's own poetry. There is a natural affinity between Gray and the old Northern poets he translated. Now the difference between old Northern and Anglo-Saxon poetry is very marked; it is a difference something like the difference between Gray and Spenser. Anglo-Saxon poetry is generally continuous; it likes to run on and avoids any pointed or staccato effect. The Northern poets, on the other hand, starting with the same kind of verse, regularly get quite a different sort of effect out of it by keeping the lines distinct, by working, in fact, on the principles of the school of Waller, the sense

being sharply concluded either in the line or in a small group
of lines. This sharp and detached kind of writing went along
with emphasis and compression and the love of very significant and telling words. 'The Descent of Odin' is a great
contrast to the Anglo-Saxon epics. It is on another ground
and in another language the very same thing as the difference
between Gray and any of the poets who move freely, as for
example Spenser and Dryden. Hence these translations from
the Icelandic are something more than curiosities; they are
the discovery by a poet of his own mind in a foreign language
and ages before his own time; and that is why these translations are particularly worth reading. Of course, the language
of Gray is not an exact rendering of the old Northern
diction, but it is in proportion to it, commensurable with it,
and Carlyle's criticism of Gray's renderings, his censure of
Gray's Icelandic versions for their regularity, is really off the
point.[1] The originals are as regular, as consistent, as clear,
as emphatic, as Gray's translations of them.

WILLIAM COLLINS

In the 'Ode to Evening' Collins has worked out a poetical
argument which, no doubt, has things like it elsewhere in
poetry, but with which there is hardly anything to compete
in fresh mythological imagination. In some things it is like
the Hyperion passage in Gray,[2] using personification and at
the same time not disguising the reality that is personified.
Evening is made into a sort of goddess, a divine being, but
the allegory is not worked out in the complete and regular
way of, say, an allegorical painting or statue of Evening. It
is treated poetically, so that the figure, the person, is never
definite and so that the evening itself is known along with
the mythology.

---

[1] 'Of the distinctive poetic character or merit of this Norse Mythology I have not
room to speak. . . . Gray's fragments of Norse Lore, at any rate, will give one no
notion of it;—any more than Pope will of Homer. It is no square-built gloomy
palace of black ashlar marble, shrouded in awe and horror, as Gray gives it us:
no; rough as the North rocks, as the Iceland deserts, it is; with a heartiness, homeli-
ness, even a tint of good humour and robust mirth in the middle of these fearful
things. The strong old Norse heart did not go upon theatrical sublimities; they had
not time to tremble.' (*Heroes and Hero-Worship*, Lecture 1.)

[2] *The Progress of Poesy*, II. i.

WILLIAM COWPER

There is no poet who trusts himself as fully as Cowper does to association of ideas, who lets his mind wander so freely. All his long poems are discourses, *sermones* (using a Latin name that included all kinds of essay in verse).

∾

Cowper's form of blank verse is original. It is a form of verse resembling his rhyming couplets in not putting the diction or phrase, the style of the author, emphatically and oppressively before the mind of the reader. It is a form of verse that escapes notice in order to bring out the meaning of the thought which it is a medium for conveying. Cowper's problem was partly the same as Wordsworth's: to find a poetic interpretation of reality that should bring ideas drawn from reality into the mind of the reader without any rhetorical interruption that might distract the reader's thoughts from the sense to the style of the poet.

∾

Landscape was, on the whole, better understood in the eighteenth century than it was after the appearance of the 'romantic' authors, because the 'romantic' authors took the mind away from pure landscape to other allied interests, such as the interests of historical association.

Cowper, like Wordsworth, is misjudged when thought of as a pure landscape poet. Both Cowper and Wordsworth tried to render life. Usually it is life from which the natural landscape is inseparable, life in which landscape has a large share; but what they are interested in is not the scene by itself, not the people by themselves, but the scene as animated by the people, the whole life in which the different elements are inextricable.

THOMAS CHATTERTON

The imaginative child lives happily in his imaginary world till the time comes when he has to strike out into the real and common-place. The likelihood is that the child's imaginative life is then ended utterly, that the creature will change his mind, take up some practical business, and sink into ordinary, average, practical utility and stupidity. Our great artists are those who can carry on their childhood's imaginative life into the maturer life, so as to keep up some of the early spirit of irresponsible dreaming when working definitely to shape some artistic work. In the life of Chatterton one can see the childish imagination passing away in two different modes, into the boyish mischief of the practical jokes on Bristol tradesmen, and, on the other hand, into the shaping, poetic mind, no longer content with dreams and fancies but desirous to make poetry, to create something.

Perhaps the most wonderful thing about Chatterton is the impersonality of his genius. In the conditions of his life there was every encouragement to romantic moodiness. But Chatterton never makes any literary profit out of his own soul. All his writings, both the *Rowley Poems* and the various pieces of prose and verse in the modern manner, written as a means of earning a living, all are impersonal, leaving the soul alone, in a double sense of the words. He had undoubtedly the shaping genius, as is seen in all his work, both good and bad, the mind that is not content with brooding over its own affairs, but goes out, either to study what is round about as in journalistic work, or to create, to frame something imaginative to be made permanent through some artistic medium.

The true poetry of Chatterton is in the *Rowley Poems*. It is a mistake, very often made, to consider these as medieval. There is hardly anything medieval in them, except the subjects and the old-fashioned words and spellings. The source and the model of the *Rowley Poems* is, far beyond any other, Spenser. Chatterton had really very little understanding of medieval literature; even of Chaucer he seems not to have known much beyond the glossary to his works. There is, on the other hand, ample proof of the influence of Spenser. Chatterton can hardly write a poem save in some Spenserian form, with an alexandrine at the end of the stanza. When he does take a form older than Spenser, nearer the Middle Ages, he uses that form in the eighteenth-century manner, with all the flatness of the other eighteenth-century imitations of ballad poetry.

BLAKE

Blake's imagination is of a kind very difficult to understand—to say 'of a kind', even, seems a misrepresentation: it is so very individual. In considering it, one must take into account the 'visions' and what he tells of them. He had a philosophical theory of the imagination something like Wordsworth's, but in many respects very different. The realm of the imagination is contrasted by Blake with what he calls 'the vegetable world' or ordinary consciousness, things as they appear to the dull, ordinary mind. It is imagination that discovers the 'real' world, that sees through and transforms 'the vegetable world'—how, it is impossible to tell, except by following the mind of Blake, which is hardly possible for an ordinary 'vegetable' mind. One great danger is pointed out by Blake himself. In a passage of *Jerusalem*[1] he speaks of the pitfalls of generalization, and, though he is not speaking particularly of theoretic generalization, we may apply what he says to the attempt to generalize about such mysteries as those where the mind of Blake dwells: in so doing one comes very near the danger of 'the scoundrel, hypocrite, and flatterer'.

Blake's theory of the imagination differs from Wordsworth's in that Wordsworth's does not alter the features of 'the vegetable world'. Wordsworth's imagination is not pictorial in any way that interferes with the ordinary vision; it does not add any mythological figures to the real world, as Blake's does. The 'vision' of Wordsworth leaves what one may call the physical outlines unchanged. The landscape he sees is the same as the photographic camera sees, as far as the main facts go. What is added in Wordsworth's imagination is something invisible, something intangible. Where his

---

[1] He who would do good to another must do it in Minute Particulars:
General Good is the plea of the scoundrel, hypocrite & flatterer,
For Art & Science cannot exist but in minutely organized Particulars
And not in generalizing Demonstrations of the Rational Power
(Folio 55; cf. also folio 91.)

mind is mythological, it is so in a vague way. Where he imagines presences or beings different from the human race, these are never seen definitely; they are merely felt vaguely. But Blake's imagination is so vividly pictorial that his mythological fancies come between him and 'the vegetable world'. His 'translation' of 'the vegetable world', of ordinary experience, into the higher imaginative view is always through figures like those of Greek mythology. His mind had in an extraordinary degree the power of imaginative vision, and this is shown in many ways, including a great number of comic ways. He could call up a picture before his mind so that it stood out away from him as vividly as anything seen with the bodily eye; and this power he often exercised in a light way, without any deep or prophetic meaning, and often with uncertainty as to what the 'visions' meant. In Gilchrist's *Life of William Blake* there are many pictures of what Blake saw, including 'The Man who built the Pyramids' and the 'Ghost of a Flea'.[1] There is no reason to doubt Blake's honesty when he speaks of these imaginary objects as changing places when he is looking at them; when drawing them he acts just as if he were taking the portrait of a bodily object, and he sees them moving just as clearly in front of him. It is clear that this habit of mind may have sometimes misled Blake. Living with these extraordinarily vivid day-dreams he may not have known when to take them seriously and when not.

The question of 'mysticism' and the application of the term 'mystic' to Blake deserves attention; very probably mystic in the right sense does not apply to him. Mysticism is properly that mode of thought or of intellectual life where the individual knows himself as nothing in comparison with the Deity, and knows the ordinary perceptible world as nothing in comparison with God. Mystics living in that kind of faith or 'vision' live with the notion of ecstasy continually in their minds—meaning by 'ecstasy' the getting out of oneself into rapture, into unity with God. In the lives of many famous mystical philosophers the ecstasies, the occasions on which they are rapt into direct communion with God, are

[1] Op. cit., 1880 ed. (2 vols.), i. 300, 303.

rare; but the mystic, in what for him is ordinary thought, is perpetually thinking of this communion, and judging his own life and the ordinary world as valueless in comparison with the Divine Unity. That is not the mysticism of Blake. Blake was a great student of the mystics, particularly of the German Jacob Boehme (generally called Behmen in English), who was very popular in England in the eighteenth century, and of Swedenborg. But the essence of his own theory of the universe was original, and the essence of it was utterly different from that of the true mystics, roughly and crudely described above. There seems to have been no swooning ecstasy in the life of Blake. His 'real world of imagination' is as clear, as definite, as coherent to his mind as the world of mathematical ideas. It is mythological rather than mystical.

Some writers on mysticism have got confused through not differentiating the various kinds of transcendental thought— of mystical religion, of philosophy, even of science. For philosophy without mysticism is a mode of life in communion with eternal things, and so is mathematics and other of the sciences. There is something common to religion, to philosophy, and to science, and that is the apprehension of ideas which are not affected by the contingent world of ordinary experience.

LANDOR

Landor is often spoken of as a classical poet, but this does not mean that he was an opponent of romance. He finds 'Roman' associations unromantic, and thinks 'romance' is required in poetry, which without it is blunted and flattened. In the volume entitled *The Last Fruit off an Old Tree* there is a letter to Philip James Bailey, the author of *Festus*. This epistle in blank verse clears up many of the difficulties and ambiguities of the terms 'classic' and 'romantic'.[1] Landor insists that the mere object does not cause any difference; any subject may be the subject of a classic writer, and any be used by a romantic one. The epistle is in lively, amusing blank verse, which yet dares the lofty, dignified mode proper to heroic poetry, along with quite familiar language. Blank

[1] Cf. Ker, *The Art of Poetry*, p. 147.

verse had, of course, been used for familiar discourses earlier, for example, in *The Task*; but Landor uses a form of his own.

As an example of Landor's consistency in his theories on the subject of 'classic' and 'romantic' one may take *Gebir*. *Gebir* is classic in the sense that it is written with great care and dignity, and yet, in its story, it is a romance of the most romantic. The plot is all imaginary, far back in the history of the world, with imaginary characters. It is quite unlike those classical poems that take recognized subjects, being as daring in exploration as *Thalaba* and *The Curse of Kehama*, and more remote from the generally accepted than *Endymion* or *Hyperion*. One should note also that Landor is one of the poets to take up Icelandic subjects. He writes a rhyming narrative poem on *Gunnlaug the Worm-tongue*, one of the shorter Icelandic sagas.[1] In his use of poetic forms Landor does not show anything like the pedantic classicism of the people who made a point of following classical examples at the time of the Renaissance. There is much variety of rhyming measure in him. One of his technical peculiarities is his refusal to use the eleventh syllable in blank verse.

In Landor's verse-letter to the author of *Festus* he seems to agree with the old classic prejudice which is expressed by Harvey, Spenser's friend, in his objection to *The Faerie Queene*. Landor apparently countenances the common distinction between the subjects of classic and romantic poetry, the fairies standing for Gothic, medieval, romantic imagination. But that opinion is contradicted later in the most significant part of the Epistle, where he speaks of 'the name being graven on the workmanship'; that is to say, we label a poem 'classic' or 'romantic', not on account of its subject, but of its style. This is borne out by Landor's own work. The subject of *Gebir* is romantic in the ordinary sense; the marvellous things in it are not indeed taken from the Gothic mythology of elves and fairies, but they are just as fanciful as anything popularly called 'romance'.

Where, then, is the limit of 'classic' and what is its mean-

---

[1] *Gunlaug and Helga*, printed in *Simonidea* (1806); *Poetical Works*, ed. S. Wheeler (3 vols., Oxford, 1937), i. 91. Also translated by William Morris in his *Three Northern Love-Stories* (1875).

ing? Landor recognizes that Shakespeare was 'romantic' and that his romantic art rose far above classic limitations:

> Shakespeare with majesty benign call'd up
> The obedient classicks from their marble seats,
> And led them thro dim glens and sheeny glades,
> And over precipices, over seas
> Unknown by mariners, to palaces
> High archt, to festival, to dance, to joust,
> And gave them golden spurs and vizors barred,
> And steeds that Pheidias had turn'd pale to see.[1]

Landor is a little hampered in judgement, a little prejudiced in taste, by his own skill in Latin verse. He is not altogether a good exponent of classic principles for English poets, because he was a good Latin poet. He had no doubt about his own skill in Latin poetry; he knew he was following classic examples; he knew he was in the literal sense 'classic' while he used the language of the Latins. Yet Latin poetry is not really a full representative of the classic idea; it is in Greek poetry only that the classic idea can be truly tested and judged. Landor's classic art in English is therefore somewhat too negative, too restricted. The classic character of it is found in the rejection of things many of his contemporaries would have employed. But a poet is not classic simply by refusing licences, by refusing to follow Shakespeare in the voyages Landor so nobly describes. Landor in his own poetry never attempts any close imitation of any one classic model, so he escapes from the difficulties Matthew Arnold gets into in his tragedy of *Merope*—a Greek tragedy in English, trying to imitate the outward form of Greek tragedy, attempting again what had been done in *Samson Agonistes*, but with closer attention to Greek form, and with a result utterly unlike the spirit of Greek tragedy, a spirit which always deals as closely as it can with life. Landor is not distracted, like Arnold, by close imitation of the classic form, but he is a good deal hindered by the ideal of restraint, exemplified in his blank verse by his avoidance (as already noted) of the eleventh syllable, a restriction cutting him off from the

[1] ll. 46–53; ed. cit. ii. 401.

flights of the English poets who are the real makers of English blank verse. Further, Landor's classic ideal leaves out what is noblest in Greek poetry, the wrestling with life. The beauty of the great classic tragedies is not in the formal observance of the unities, but in the evolution of the dramatic argument, in the process of thought through the tragedy, which tries to get at the meaning of life, just in the same way as a modern novelist, presenting the meaning in a poetic form which requires the highest poetic genius and the utmost poetic variety. For Greek tragedy is not the monstrous thing that imitations of Greek tragedy would have us believe. It is full of life and also full of poetic eloquence, of lyrical or musical beauty, through its variety of verse, through the lyric verses of the chorus. The fault of all pedantic modern poets, who try to be classic by setting themselves in opposition to romantic art, is that they do not see that the form of Greek tragedy is no more separable from the spirit and matter of the play than ripples on the surface are separable from the substance of water.

SHELLEY

Laon and Cythna is a poem of revolution, an attempt to put into poetry the moral ideas Shelley had in mind. The attempt in *Laon and Cythna* is a failure, partly at any rate because the poet was making up his story and thus exhausting himself in planning. But with *Prometheus Unbound* things are different. Here Shelley had the resources of Greek mythology, and he had in the Greek story things ready to hand. He did not need to interpret the allegorical myth of Prometheus, to work in the way of the medieval commentators of Ovid, or, what is the same thing in principle, in the way of the interpreters of *Orlando Furioso*. For the story of Prometheus is, from the time of its earliest literary use, a kind of allegory; and in the poetic treatment of it by Aeschylus the dramatic position was given in essentials as Shelley required it.

(ii) *The Novel*

The Greek romances, which had such a vogue in the sixteenth century, are in matter not very unlike the French and English medieval romances, not unlike the Old French *Amadas et Ydoine* (not *Amadis of Gaul*) or Chrestien de Troyes's *Cliges*, or, in some respects, the beautiful *Floris et Blanchefleur*. The Greek matter is the common matter of the true lovers separated and tried in a variety of ways and at last brought together—matter derived a good deal, no doubt, from classical poetry.

The difference between the Greek prose romances and the medieval western romances, between, say, Heliodorus' *Theagenes and Chariclea* on the one hand and *Amadis of Gaul* on the other, is that the Greek romances are rhetorical exercises in literature, not genuine in the same way as the Old French. The Old French romances are genuine because of their sincere interest in the theme, in the story and thoughts, the sentiment and characters. The Greek prose romances are exhibitions of literary skill, intended to be works of literary beauty, written in the best possible style.

Now for simple-minded readers it does not matter much what the motive of the author may have been, so long as the story is interesting. Such readers find no hindrance in the rhetoric of Spenser or Shakespeare, and probably see no difference in quality between, say, *Theagenes and Chariclea* and *Amadis of Gaul*. But the rhetoric of the Greek romances is important for the people who imitated them. The Greek romances were not known, because Greek was not known, until the Revival of Learning, until people were coming to be specially interested and careful in literary kinds and rules and style. The newly found treasures, with what may be termed their Euphuistic style, fell easily into and agreed with the taste of modern writers, who in other ways were learning to practise rhetoric.

∾

Most great writers begin with some sort of critical opposition to the follies, vanities, pedantries, and dullness of
their predecessors and their contemporaries. In the case of
Rabelais, as in the case of Cervantes, there has been some
exaggeration by commentators. Too much emphasis has
been laid on their hostility to the dullness of the past; too
little has been made, perhaps, of their sympathy with the
things they laughed at. That Cervantes was at heart and with
no small fervour a lover of romance, that Rabelais never
escaped, nor wished to escape, out of the comfortable
absurdity of the Middle Ages, will sound like paradox only
to people who have taken their opinions from the commentators.

Rabelais, Shakespeare, and Cervantes have the enormous
and unfair advantage over other writers that, in addition to
their 'abilities' (as the Scots student called them), they had
the whole abandoned region of medieval thought and
imagination to take over and appropriate. Of course they
saw the absurdity of it, but that was only one charm the more
in their inheritance. They had all the profusion and complexity, all the strength and all the wealth of the Middle
Ages to draw upon. The Reformers and the common
Humanists rejected it all, or drove their lean and blasted
cattle through the medieval fields and brought them out as
poor as when they went in. The Masters have another and
'more thriving and generous policy'. The Middle Age which,
as reality, was impossible and absurd, was restored by them
in a kind of *second intention*: as a humorous or poetical world
in idea. They were abstracters of quintessence.[1] The beauty
of *Don Quixote* is that it gets all the good of the adventures
of chivalry and of the pastoral idea while burlesquing them.

❧

Defoe was a great literary man, and one of the best
things he did for those coming after him was in respect to
style. One might profitably compare the style of *Robinson
Crusoe* with the style of the *Arcadia*. What was it that
hindered narrative fiction in the Elizabethan times? Very

[1] Cf. Rabelais, p. 132 above.

largely grammar and rhetoric. Novels were prevented by the rhetorical ambition of the Renaissance. This is what makes the pastoral romances so tiresome; it is not merely the insipidity of their characters and the monotony of their plots, but their fine writing. That is what spoils the Greek romances; they are rhetorical exercises rather than imagination. For narrative you do not want what is usually called 'fine writing' or 'show pieces', but a style that makes no display of its own art; and that is the style of Defoe, good vernacular language, not rowdy or slangy, like so much of the popular writing of the seventeenth century, and not rhetorical like so much of the Elizabethan romance and a good deal of the contemporary writing in Defoe's time.

THE EIGHTEENTH CENTURY

In studying the history of fiction in the eighteenth century it is worth while not to limit one's view to the actual prose stories, and to remember that, while the great novelists were writing their histories of modern life—*Tom Jones*, *Clarissa*, *The Vicar of Wakefield*—there were a number of practitioners of the drama who were imitating, as well as they could, Shakespeare and the Elizabethans, taking up historical subjects for the drama—the Earl of Essex in English history, Gustavus Vasa in foreign history, for example—and working up the sort of subjects that came to be popular with the nineteenth-century novelists.

All the old-fashioned concern with epic poetry, as long as there was the regular worship of the epic ideal, led to the same sort of research as you find among historical novelists; looking for subjects, ranging over old chronicles and such like. That may be said to last down to Southey's epics, to *Joan of Arc* and *Roderick*, *The Last of the Goths*. Southey might be thought of as one of the founders of historical fiction in the nineteenth century, through his narrative poems, his epics.

RICHARDSON AND FIELDING

Jonathan Wild is a work of fiction of a different kind from anything else of Fielding's. It is something like a species by itself. Outwardly it is a good deal like the rogue's romance, being a story of low life, of rascality, thieves, robbers, &c. But it is not the same as Defoe's novels of low life; it is Defoe overlooked by Swift. *Jonathan Wild* is really a moral romance with a definite satiric purpose, and this purpose is to show up the vanity of worldly greatness, particularly of conquerors and absolute princes. Of course, in the picaresque romances the element of satire is seldom absent, coming out very strongly in the *Gil Blas* of Le Sage, a sort of abstract of all the older Spanish picaresque romances. But the moral conclusion is very rarely insisted upon to such an extent as in *Jonathan Wild*. This book, though so different from *Tom Jones* or *Amelia*, is characteristic of Fielding in its simplicity and clearness, and also in its thinness or tenuity of argument. Fielding is fond of reasoning; but he is not careful to go deep, and he does not trouble himself as to whether his ideas are commonplace or not. Hence the moral of *Jonathan Wild* comes to be a little monotonous; one wishes to end it; the jury does not desire to hear more. The morality of it comes down from the classical moralists into Christendom; it is summed up by St. Austin in 'Great kings are great pirates'.[1] The nature of the absolute monarch and conqueror is brought out through the absolute life of the criminal.

◆

The difference between Richardson and Fielding is not so great as is usually believed, as may easily be proved by any-one taking the trouble to look at the works themselves. Much of Richardson is sentiment, but there is also much incident and conversation; on the other hand, in Fielding there is a great deal of talk and discussion that does not immediately help on the story. One can easily imagine Fielding's novels turned into the form of Richardson's and Richardson's into Fielding's.

Fielding had not the same widespread European reputa-tion as Richardson. What he did was, of course, within the comprehension of the reading public, and there was nothing

[1] 'Remota itaque justitia, quid sunt regna, nisi magna latrocinia? quia et ipsa latrocinia quid sunt, nisi parva regna?' *De Civitate Dei*, IV. iv.

difficult in it; but his art was not the sort that could produce much enthusiasm among people looking out for finer shades, searching for that sensibility they found so easily in Richardson. The people who took up Richardson were very like those who took up Ossian twenty years later than *Pamela*. They were often the same people, and the influence of Macpherson is very strong in *The Sorrows of Werther*. The European reputation was made by authors who could thrill, who touched the heart of sensibility. 'Any bungler can touch the heart of sensibility' is a phrase of Goethe's, the substance of one of his epigrams.[1] Though this does not prove Richardson a bungler, still, if true, it may prove that a number of foolish people were caught into the current of enthusiasm for sensibility; and Fielding was not so likely to touch or to thrill these.

·◇·

Fielding is not one of the reflective novelists who spend their time, as Dryden spent it, in reflecting on processes and drawing out rules. Flaubert and Henry James may be named with respect as artists of that sort, as workers talking over their problems and methods and rules of the workshop.[2] Fielding had not, as a definite idea in his mind, 'the English novel' as a thing to be realized, though in some of the essays in *Tom Jones* he comes very near that position. He was a scholar, at any rate he read Latin and Greek, and was rather fond of showing it off. He liked some of the things he had learned at school, and the analogy between the novel and epic poem pleased him, not only because of the truth in it, but because 'epic poem' had pleasant associations, something of that old religion of the epic found in Cervantes, Milton, Dryden, Pope, and all the seventeenth-century heroic romances. All the same, he does not allow the abstract pattern to divert him from his work; it is merely an occasional

---

[1] *Epigramme* (1790), No. lxxviii. 'Mit Botanik giebst du dich ab?....'
[2] Henry James's paper on 'The Novel in "The Ring and the Book"' is an interesting piece of literary 'shop' in which the documents on which Browning's poem is founded are taken and discussed, so as to see how they should be treated in order to get from them the best result as a novel. (*Transactions of the Royal Society of Literature*, xxxi (1912), 'Browning's Centenary', pp. 21–50).—W.P.K.

thing coming into his head while pausing. He is one of the writers who work freely, with no definite imperious sort of standard of the art of the novel. It is only now and again that he allows himself to reflect and discuss principles.

STERNE

Sterne had a great effect on succeeding literary men, and in the romantic schools later in the century his disorderly method was copied—particularly in Germany, and more particularly in Richter, from whom the irregular method comes back to Carlyle. Hence *Sartor Resartus* is the representative in the nineteenth century of the artistic policy of Sterne, of *Tristram Shandy*. Sterne was aiming at freedom. He must have seen it was not for him to write an 'epic poem in prose'. He did not wish to commit himself. He had many ideas and fancies and knew they would spring up when wanted or not wanted. He knew, if he let himself go, there was little danger of his vein failing him.

(iii) *Prose-Writers from Locke to Gibbon*

LOCKE AND POLITE LITERATURE

LOCKE is a great philosopher; but for literature and general culture his philosophical greatness is of less moment than his general vague encouragement of theorizing and argument. He undoubtedly authorized a great deal of ill-prepared, pretentious theorizing about all sorts of things. He seemed to set up a clear, simple philosophy within the reach of ordinary men, and many ordinary men were only too ready to accept his authority, and to consider themselves licensed to speak on any kind of topic in heaven or earth. Of course, before the time of Locke, there had been plenty of rash and random speculation by the ill educated, but Locke made hasty and superficial reasoning more respectable than before. Foolish, easy-going talk had been less reputable when it could be compared with learned and solemn writers, with Milton, with Jeremy Taylor, with Sir Thomas Browne, or with the Cambridge Platonists. But it was within the power of almost any man who had been at the grammar-school and university to write as good English as Locke, to deal in arguments which outwardly, from the look of the printed page, had as much appearance of serious knowledge as the work of the great philosopher, especially as Locke, in many of his opinions, actually did agree with such superficial disputants as the Deists.

As an essayist on the humanities or things in general, Locke is an inheritor of the Renaissance. He carries on that line of thought, or rather, that habit, that character, of Sir Thomas More, Bacon, and Hobbes—the opposition to the schoolmen, the dislike of 'superstitious language', that is, not the language of superstition, but the vague, quasi-philosophical language ('essences', 'entities', 'quiddities', and so forth) made current by a kind of superstition, by acceptance without criticism and reason. In Sir Thomas

More one finds this opposition to scholastic language. The people of Utopia are humanists, as More would like all men to be, and one peculiarity of their education is that they have no dealing with such terms and such philosophy; they are quite unable to comprehend them. This is one of the most humorous things in *Utopia*; it is put humorously and ironically as a defect in the Utopians, but More's real meaning, of course, is that the philosophy of the schoolmen is useless or worse.[1] In Bacon's *Advancement of Learning* there is much criticism of scholastic methods. In Hobbes's *Leviathan* there are many cheerful passages of satire upon meaningless language, very like the manner of Swift, for Swift was another inheritor of this tradition. Swift was true to this part of the doctrine and policy of the Revival of Learning, finding the work of human reason much impeded by the loading of difficult, half-understood terminology.

An historian of philosophy or thought might get something out of an inquiry into the attitude of men of letters, the attitude of the humanists, the men of culture, of no particular philosophical bent, towards the language of philosophy. It is easy to find examples like those quoted above of the widespread opposition to scholastic terms. It would be interesting to see how this opinion comes to be modified, how the war against scholasticism comes to slacken, how terms of the Aristotelian tradition come again into what may be called general literature. Coleridge was very fond both of inventing technical terms himself and of adopting terms from medieval technical scholasticism and the Aristotelian vocabulary. One remembers 'Pantisocracy', and the identifying of 'essence' with 'principle of individuation'.[2] 'Principle of individuation'

---

[1] 'But as they in all thinges be almoste equal to oure olde auncyente clerkes, so oure newe logiciens in subtyl inventions have farre passed and gone beyonde them. For they have not devysed one of all those rules of restrictions, amplifications and suppositions, verye wittelye invented in the small logicalles, whyche heare oure children in every place do learne. Furtheremore they were never yet hable to fynde out the seconde intentions: insomuche that none of them all coulde ever see man himselfe in commen, as they cal him, thoughe he be (as you kñowe) bygger than ever was annye gyaunte, yea and poynted to of us even wyth our fynger.' *Utopia*, book ii (ed. J. R. Lumby, Cambridge, 1879, p. 103).

[2] 'Essence, in its primary signification, means the principle of individuation, the inmost principle of the possibility of any thing, as that particular thing. It is equiva-

is an old-established scholastic term, and Coleridge's un-hesitating use of it is a very strange contrast in the history of literary manners to the manner of Hobbes and Locke, to the old humanist view of such a vocabulary.

◦

The style of Locke is something like the style of Dryden with most of the life taken out of the language. There is the informal manner, the half-colloquial frame of the sentences, but none of the spring, the liveliness, the fancy, that makes Dryden's arguments so delightful. There are point and sense and matter worth listening to in everything that Locke writes. His is good language for conveying instruction, but not the best. There is in it very little of what we admire in the seventeenth century; it is modern plain prose as com-pared with the seventeenth-century prose of Milton, Jeremy Taylor, or Sir Thomas Browne. But that it is not the best example of the modern style may be proved by comparing it with the brightness and clearness of Berkeley, with the clear-ness and sharpness of Hume. Beside these, Locke's style seems flat and tame.

◦

The chief characteristic of the polite literature of the late seventeenth century is not that it *is* shallow and superficial as compared with the literature of the middle of the century, but that it *appears* light and flimsy. The fashion of lightness, quickness, and ease was very general, and shared by minds of all varieties. This is not an inroad of jauntiness and ignorant self-sufficiency, an inroad of sciolism driving out true science, but a widespread and increasing fashion of easy writing, used by the lightest people and the gravest people, irrespective of the matter.

◦

Sermons may be taken in one way as a separate class of literature, but a division of that sort into, say, sermons, essays,

lent to the idea of a thing, whenever we use the word idea with philosophic pre-cision.' *Biographia Literaria*, chapter xviii.

&c., is not very valuable, for sermons and essays may have differences among them as great as differences between satire and comedy, or even between tragedy and comedy. The sermon is, in fact, a prose essay, and the subjects of sermons may be as various as the subjects of essays, the differences as great as the difference between Locke's *Essay concerning Human Understanding* and Lamb's 'All Fools' Day'. The sermon of those and of other times is used for many purposes besides the preaching of the Gospel—for ordinary morality and moralizing, for the discussion of interesting topics not belonging to the more difficult parts either of theology or of ethics. Barrow's sermon about foolish talking and jesting is an essay on comic literature, on the comic spirit, one might say, on the right place of wit in human life. Much of the sermon literature of the Augustan age deserves to be reckoned along with the essays of Cowley and Sir William Temple as part of the polite literature of the time, of the literature dealing with human life, society, and conduct in an informal unscientific way. Of course, one would have to exclude from this class the definitely theological sermons, the expositions of doctrine, and such careful and studied ethical treatises as Butler's sermons.

SWIFT

Where Swift's *Battle of the Books* brings out his own mind is in the hatred for useless learning, and in the belief that there are certain solid and profitable studies for mankind. In spite of its accidental origin, the book is a contribution to the literature of education and culture. It is an imperfect and unsystematic statement of one form of the great humanist ideal. The respect for the ancients is rather conventional; they are praised, not because Swift was really thinking of them carefully, definitely, particularly, but because the moderns were so definitely representative of the things he disliked—vanity, self-assertion, and kindred qualities. One cannot learn very much from the actual persons named; they seem to have been brought in merely to make up the army, and the mention of them does not mean that Swift knew much about their works, or thought much about their claims.

He had probably given very little serious attention to
Paracelsus, William Harvey, Hobbes, Descartes, Gassendi,
Boileau, the historians, and the rest. But his sympathies
generally are against their ways of thinking and studying;
he respects the ancients for their greater solidity.

The Fable of the Spider and the Bee teaches us much
more. The fable was a common one, and had often been used
by moralists before; the conceit was almost as well established as that of the moth and the candle, or that of the
phoenix. The useless industry of the spider contrasted with
the profitable work of the bee is a thing easy to understand,
and had become a favourite allegory. Swift's originality of
treatment comes out in the detail, in his use of the bee as the
representative of ancient learning, and of the spider to
illustrate the vanity and uselessness of the moderns. The
beauty of the whole thing is not in any relation, however, to
ancients and moderns, but in the noble expression of Swift's
mind, in his praise of 'sweetness and light' wherever it is to
be sought.

As for us, the Ancients, we are content, with the bee, to pretend to
nothing of our own, beyond our wings and our voice, that is to say, our
flights and our language. For the rest, whatever we have got has been
by infinite labour and search, and ranging through every corner of
nature; the difference is, that, instead of dirt and poison, we have rather
chosen to fill our hives with honey and wax, thus furnishing mankind
with the two noblest of things, which are sweetness and light.

Swift is not here alluding particularly to the ideals of the
ancients, but to his own times and what he hoped to do.
'Sweetness and light' is the aim of the humanists, the soul
of the Revival of Learning.

◦

Swift's low view of humanity is not exceptional. It agrees
with the common low tone of conversation and good society
in his time. Many people have remarked, and it can easily
be proved, that at the end of the seventeenth century and the
beginning of the eighteenth it was the fashion to depreciate
human nature. Hobbes is responsible for some of it, though

his opinions are not to be identified with those of the 'Hobbists'. The *Maximes* of La Rochefoucauld are another example of the same low view of the human race. One very trustworthy notice of this so-called misanthropy is in Bishop Butler,[1] the author of *The Analogy of Religion*, who mentions it distinctly as the characteristic of the age, the general tendency of good society not to believe in anything else but self-interest as the principle and motive of action. Swift gave more brilliant expression to this idea than most of his contemporaries, but it is not peculiar to him. It was part of the general sceptical judgement very widely spread among writers, and more widely spread among people who were not writers, of the age in which he lived.

❧

Swift aimed at being a poet, and his Pindaric Odes, though recognized as failures, deserve some attention. They are very good examples of the wrongness of the Pindaric convention, to be contrasted with Milton's 'Lycidas' or the splendid opening of Dryden's 'Ode to Mrs. Anne Killigrew'. They are pompous things, made in different lengths of line, without any sense of harmony and melody, and without the poetic music that makes the irregular lines and rhymes of 'Lycidas' always fall as if expected, as if one knew the recurring pattern in them.

Yet there are some good thoughts in the early poems. The passage beginning

> For this inferior world is but Heaven's dusky shade,
> By dark reverted rays from its reflection made;
>   Whence the weak shapes wild and imperfect pass,
> Like sun-beams shot at too far distance from a glass.[2]

is an ingenious thing in the metaphysical tradition, and well fulfils the rules of that particular kind of fancy.

One of the odes addressed to Sir William Temple (1689) may be marked as historically interesting:

> The wily Shafts of State, those Juggler's Tricks
> Which we call deep Designs and Politicks

[1] In his sermon, 'On Loving one's Neighbour'.
[2] *Ode to Dr William Sancroft*, 21 ff.

> (As in a Theatre the Ignorant Fry,
>   Because the Cords escape their Eye
>   Wonder to see the Motions fly)
>   Methinks, when you expose the Scene,
>   Down the ill-organ'd Engines fall;
> Off fly the Vizards and discover all,
>   How plain I see thro' the Deceit!
>   How shallow! and how gross the Cheat!
>
> (92–101)

One inference to be drawn from the Odes is that Swift at first was not afraid of the enthusiastic mode of thinking. Instead of irony, and instead of the light conversational manner adopted later, there is the ambition of poetic eloquence, of imagery, of the noblest kind of verse. For it should be remembered that Swift's failures are failures in no mean, trivial sort of poetry, but failures in the highest, in the grand ideal realized so nobly in 'Lycidas'. Swift gave up this kind in which he had rashly adventured himself, but his checked ambitions still remained as part of his being, and, although he adopted other ways to express his mind, his old poetic ideals were not expelled or abandoned.

◈

The great difference between the ideals of Swift and those of his contemporaries, Steele and Addison, is that Swift has a much more consistent practical aim and view of life. He is more of an intellectual fighting man than the others. He has almost always present in his mind the view of what is possible and desirable for the human race, particularly with regard to ideas, and to ideas as bearing on practice. This ideal is frequently neglected by writers on Swift, but is quite clearly expressed in *Gulliver's Travels*, in the opinions of the King of Brobdingnag, and in the fourth voyage. The last voyage, with its account of the Yahoos, has generally been taken as an extreme expression of Swift's incurable hatred of the whole human race. This is but a shallow judgement. Swift seldom tries to make himself agreeable. He exaggerates everything he dislikes, and, when he is attacking, he puts things strongly, in extreme terms. It is strange that Swift, who is a clear writer, and not very profound except in his feelings, is so often misunderstood. People have accepted literally Swift's childish fable—for the fable of the wise horses and the disgusting human beasts is really very childish—and not seen that Swift is trying to bring out what is possible for a community of reasonable creatures. People are childishly misled by the outward allegory, as if Swift were really trying to prove horses more reasonable than men. The fourth voyage is a simple contrast between reasonable and irrational, but somehow a large part of humanity has taken the story on the one side and not on the other.

A great deal of Swift's literary wickedness is really very innocent, and does not imply the deep-seated misanthropy often attributed to him. There *was* deeply rooted in him a passionate resentment of many things in his own life and in the condition of humanity generally, but instead of feeling hatred towards his fellow creatures, he is constantly filled with the motive of benevolence and beneficence. He is always trying to make things better, and he did this, partly through satire on existing evils, partly through such statements of what he thought desirable as are found in the second book of *Gulliver*. There is nothing in Swift's advice that is particularly new or original. It is a rehearsing of old profound morality, and most of it may be placed under the heads of the limitation of desires, the clearing-up of the understanding, or similar commonplaces.

ADDISON

The essence of Addison's criticism, and that which makes the papers on *Chevy Chase*[1] better as criticism than the papers on *Paradise Lost*, is the attention he pays to the narrative unities of the ballad, the detection of classical virtues in this old poem. There is nothing here of pretence or irony visible. It is not a literary joke meant to humble the proud and self-satisfied poets or critics of the time. Addison is quite honestly discovering what he thinks the best kind of poetry in an unpretentious, homely form. He contrasts *Chevy Chase* with the conceited poetry that loses its strength in small points,

[1] *The Spectator*, Nos. lxx and lxxiv.

frittering its fancy away in details. As against this conceited poetry, which Addison calls 'Gothic', he sets the sane poetry of the ballad, of the poet who knows what he is aiming at, and who puts the chief things in the chief place, filling in the details in proportion, so that the details contribute to, instead of detracting from, the whole effect. Throughout, Addison gives similar or parallel passages from Virgil, showing how, in the most perfect of the ancient poets, the main theme and details are managed in the same way as in *Chevy Chase*. This is a good example of 'ratio' in criticism. The *Aeneid* and *Chevy Chase* are very unlike in magnitude, but they are, as mathematicians say, 'similar magnitudes', and can be brought into comparison, with allowance for the difference in scope.

The papers on *Chevy Chase* are closely related to those on false wit. The latter seem to have been begun without any distinct plan. It is some time before Addison gets to the really interesting subject—the conceits of Cowley—but when he is once there he knows what he means. And he continues to mean the same thing through his papers on *Chevy Chase*. The moral of the papers on *Chevy Chase* is that all true and noble poetry is simple, attending to the main theme, not going off into false wit, into mere ornament and beauties of detail. Here is the true statement of the classical doctrine of unity, harmony, and proportion.

᳭

Addison had praised in *Chevy Chase* the beauty and dignity of the narrative unity of action. Yet in *Cato* he is unable really to hold things together, though the dramatic unities are mechanically observed. In the action and plot there is as much variety and inconsistency as in any so-called 'romantic' play. Addison has written what is really an old-fashioned 'heroic' drama in the form of a regular tragedy observing the unities. Love and valour are the important things, as much as they were in the heroic plays of fifty years or so before.

Worst of all, there is never in *Cato* any real strain upon the mind, either of the characters in the play or of the audience. Addison has not grasped the dramatic meaning, method, and scope of French classical tragedy. He has not understood the secret of the impressive way in which Racine keeps the spectator's attention on the characters—their sentiments, passions, and conflicts, out of which the action naturally and necessarily develops. Addison's characters give way to argument, waver, and change purposes, as right characters never do. The rhetoric of the good characters is not very different from the rhetoric of the bad. The eloquence of Sempronius is almost as good as that of Cato himself. And, at the end, the death of Cato, the sacrifice of his life for the public weal, is not made to seem right through the greatness of the stress on Cato's mind. Addison has so faultily arranged his action and developed his sentiments that there still seems hope for the republic when Cato kills himself. The beauties of *Cato* are all in the separate passages, and the excellences of true classicism that Addison found in *Chevy Chase* are not found in the tragedy.

Part of the difference between Dryden and Addison, and the part to the great advantage of Dryden, is that Dryden is much more of a working man, and, most important of all, much more of a working dramatist, than Addison. It was as a writer for the theatre that Dryden first came to deal with the abstract principles of drama, with the unities. Addison came to these doctrines before he himself was a dramatist, and he wrote his one tragedy, *Cato*, after he had 'passed', so to speak, in the abstract theory or science of drama. He adopted the conventional classic theory as a student and critic before he actually set to work to write a play. Dryden had much more natural energy than Addison; he was a much busier man. That irrepressible, tremendous energy led him to the theatre first, and so brought him into situations and circumstances where he could judge the unities as he did, where he was obliged to be sceptical, to overhaul his catechism,[1] if he wished to succeed as a working dramatist.

On the epic poem Dryden is more conventional than he is with regard to drama, or with regard to Chaucer and Ovid in his Preface to the *Fables*. The theory of epic poetry seems

[1] 'Overhaul your catechism till you find that passage, and when found turn the leaf down.' Captain Cuttle in *Dombey and Son*, chapter iv.

to have been imposed on English poets by the French writer, 'the reverend father' Bossu.[1] This is rather strange, for Bossu is a simple-minded, commonplace sort of man, who says obvious things in a simple-minded, commonplace, clear, and not too dull way, with nothing like the intellect and power of Dryden or Pope. Yet both Dryden and Pope refer to him with respect. 'Spenser wanted only to have read the rules of Bossu',[2] says Dryden, and Pope acknowledges Bossu's authority in his discussion of the *Iliad*.[3] Addison refers to him in the papers on *Paradise Lost*, and Bossu's recipes are everywhere respected.

One reason for this opinion about the French abstract theorist, about the doctrines of epic poetry, is that the epic is much less necessary in everyday life than the drama. It is therefore much easier to take in block, and accept as simple rules, the doctrines of epic poetry than the doctrines of drama. The unities were a practical trouble to the playwrights, who had to make plays for their living. There was a great demand for dramatists, and they could not allow themselves to be bound by any abstract theory that would spoil their living. But there was no real demand for the epic, though there was a great deal of traditional respect for it, and the principles of epic poetry could not be tested in the same quick and decisive way as the principles of drama. A play failed or succeeded by the taste of 'pit, box, and gallery', and there was very little use in trying to prove to pit, box, and gallery that a play they damned was right and proper according to the rules. But an epic might have a conventional sort of life and repute for a long time before it was discovered that 'the brains were out' and that it had to die.

The description of the epic in Bossu is very far from nonsense, and those who are wearied by Addison's regular discussion of 'those four great Heads of the Fable, the

---

[1] René le Bossu, *Traité du poème épique* (Paris, 1675); translated into English by W.J. as *Monsieur Bossu's Treatise of the Epick Poem* (1695); a summary ('*A General View of the Epic Poem*') was prefixed to Pope's *Odyssey* (1725); cf. p. 157 above.

[2] Dedication of the *Aeneis*; *Essays of John Dryden*, ed. Ker, ii. 220.

[3] 'The Archbishop of *Cambray's Telemachus* may give [a translator] the truest Idea of the Spirit and Turn of our Author, and *Bossu's* admirable Treatise of the Epic Poem the justest Notion of his Design and Conduct.' Preface to the *Iliad*.

Characters, the Sentiments, and the Language',[1] are un-reasonable. If one thinks of the epic, one can scarcely avoid using the heads or topics of Bossu and Addison. They are the categories that one almost necessarily and naturally uses in reviewing, or simply thinking over, any sort of story. In reading Dickens or Thackeray or George Meredith one cannot help paying special attention to one or more of these epic topics. For example, in reading *Vanity Fair*, or *Pendennis*, or, still more, *Martin Chuzzlewit*, one finds one is not thinking so much of the 'fable' or plot as of the 'characters'. There is nothing wrong in Addison's arrangement, save that it does not suit the taste of later times as well as it did the taste of his day.

'Fable' means the design of the story, and it is in the design of the story that the essence of the epic lies. It was through attention to the 'fable' that eighteenth-century critics understood the *Iliad* in many ways better than some modern critics, who know far more about the Homeric age and the early history of heroic poetry. Some later critics take the *Iliad* as a sort of working-up of a chronicle, as a slab taken out of a long-continued history, as a section of the Troy Book executed in more detail, and worked up into poetic beauty. Addison and the people who attended to the 'fable' saw that the *Iliad* was what it professes to be, the story of the wrath of Achilles. It has the same kind of plot as a tragedy, and it is in the plot that the essence of the story lies. The difference between the two sorts of view has been brought out in a fine piece of criticism by Joseph Bédier on the *Chanson de Roland*.[2] The critic shows how the unities are preserved, how the episodes are all relevant to the principal tragic theme, the lasting conflict between Ganelon the traitor and Roland, and the principal tragic motive, the refusal of Roland to call for help when he and the rear-guard of Charlemagne are beset in the pass of Roncesvaux. In this essay by a great modern scholar and critic there is the same point of view as in the old-fashioned regard for the 'fable'. Only, instead of the old, conventional, separate treatment of 'fable'

[1] *The Spectator*, No. ccxci.
[2] 'L'art et le métier dans la "Chanson de Roland" ', in the *Revue des deux mondes*, 1913, pp. 292–321.

and 'characters', the writer applies his judgement to the individual thing, to the poem before him, so as to bring out, simply by careful, intelligent reading of the story, how thoroughly all things contribute to the single effect, to the climax of the narrative, and so as to show how impossible it is for such a thing to have been cobbled together out of mere historic particulars and separate passages relating to the wars of Charlemagne against the Moors.

The weakness of Addison's systematic criticism of the epic ·is that he treats it too much as a continuous web of story. He does not bring out the dramatic part of the epic. He very curiously fails to explain how essentially dramatic the true epic always is. He repeats what Aristotle says about the drama in epic:

It is finely observed by *Aristotle*, that the Author of an Heroic Poem should seldom speak himself, but throw as much of his Work as he can into the Mouths of those who are his Principal Actors.[1]

Aristotle does not use these terms ('drama in epic') but it is obvious what he means. Aristotle says that the great excellence of Homer is that he does not tell the story about the people, but makes them interpret themselves by dialogue. Addison notes this, but does not dwell on it; he does not see that it is this that makes all the difference between flat narration and true dramatic epic. Although he knew this passage of Aristotle and admired the speeches in Virgil, Homer, and Milton, he was not really much interested in the opposition of character. He thought of the speeches, not as the opposition of characters dramatically interpreted, but as varieties in the narrative. He seems to have construed the different speeches of Satan and Beelzebub, Adam and Raphael, as narrative variations, like descriptive passages, episodes, and similes. The truth is, surely, in the *Iliad* and *Odyssey* at any rate, that the speeches *are* the characters; it is the speeches that make one interested in the characters, and this constitutes all the difference between a dramatic epic, which allows the characters to speak for themselves, and a mere romantic poem which simply tells how things happen.

[1] The *Spectator*, No. ccxcvii.

Possibly Addison's criticism may have suffered from the want of good novels in his time, for the rule of epic poetry is the same as the rule of novel-writing. The novel is the prose epic, and it is not pedantry but the merest common sense to say that the novel that succeeds best is that which tells as little as possible by narration, and as much as possible by dialogue. Aristotle, in speaking of the epic, prophetically included the novel. He spoke before its time, but he spoke truth. In Addison's day, people had not our advantage of being acquainted with good novels, with good examples of the 'comic epic poem in prose', and this may account for Addison's failure to grasp the dramatic nature of the true epic.

JOHNSON

Dr. Johnson's greatest work is *A Journey to the Western Islands of Scotland*, if one is to judge greatness by the amount of the author's varied powers which the work produces. Here there is something more than literary reminiscence, much more than mere literary form. There is the result of scientific experiment, of exploration among realities, of direct observation, of the study of unfamiliar conditions of life—all so expressed as to bring out for political historians and economists the true meaning of things seen. The book is a remarkable piece of contemporary history done very nearly at the right time, and so getting facts and interpretation of facts in a strange time of transition in the Highlands of Scotland between rather early and old-fashioned medieval society and modern life. Generally, in thinking of Johnson's studies and compositions, one has the impression that there is very much in his mind of which he does not make use, that his faculties are not fully employed; but this is not apparent in the *Journey*.

As a moral essay *Rasselas* is monotonous and weak, through the repetition in different forms of the same situation. We have over and over again the man or the woman trying a certain experiment in a certain mode of life and discovering that it is unsatisfactory. The fault of Johnson's morality is that he keeps his moral experimenters always in the same kind of relation to life, as external observers or experimenters. In spite of the difficulties of travel and all the various impediments, Rasselas, Nekayah, and Imlac seem always able to move freely, to put themselves in different places for a little time, to taste, to speculate, and then to pass on to something else. This is not really a deep examination of life, because it hardly ever allows any of the personages to be involved in life. They are hardly ever caught up with anything greater than themselves, being always left, as essayists, free to change the subject, to go from one subject to another.

◦

Dr. Johnson's political tracts, though commonly neglected, as is a great deal of his original writing, are interesting both from matter and style. Johnson, though not an active politician, had a great deal of knowledge of parliamentary debates as a journalist and reporter. When he dealt with politics, as in *The False Alarm, Thoughts on the Late Transactions respecting Falkland's Islands, The Patriot*, and *Taxation no Tyranny*, his style changed in movement from that of the slower reflective essays into the more brisk debating method. Consider, for example, the following from *Taxation no Tyranny*:

But hear, ye sons and daughters of liberty, the sounds which the winds are wafting from the Western Continent. The Americans are telling one another, what, if we may judge from their noisy triumph, they have but lately discovered, and what yet is a very important truth: That they are entitled to life, liberty, and property, and that they have never ceded to any sovereign power whatever a right to dispose of either without their consent.

While this resolution stands alone, the Americans are free from singularity of opinion; their wit has not yet betrayed them to heresy. While they speak as the naked sons of nature, they claim but what is claimed by other men, and have withheld nothing but what all withhold. They are here upon firm ground, behind entrenchments which never can be forced.

Humanity is very uniform. The Americans have this resemblance to Europeans, that they do not always know when they are well. They soon quit the fortress that could neither have been mined by sophistry, nor battered by declamation. Their next resolution declares, that their ancestors, who first settled the Colonies, were, at the time of their emigration from the Mother-country, entitled to all the rights, liberties, and immunities of free and natural-born subjects within the realm of England.

This likewise is true; but when this is granted, their boast of original rights is at an end; they are no longer in a state of nature. These lords of themselves, these kings of *me*, these demigods of independence, sink down to Colonists, governed by a charter.

◦�〇◦

Sometimes we may be inclined to think of Johnson in his own writings as dignified and majestic, generalizing his own experiences and keeping out of his work those private sentiments and confessions found so frequently in Lamb, Hazlitt, and Stevenson. This is a mistaken view, a view of part of his work only. It may do for *The Vanity of Human Wishes*, perhaps for *Rasselas*; but even in the Preface to the *Dictionary* Johnson speaks of himself with feeling, not putting on at all the stoic air and demeanour. *A Journey to the Western Islands* is autobiography, and in the *Lives of the Poets* again and again he speaks of himself, as, for example, in the Life of 'Rag' Smith, one of the most curious of all the biographies, where he digresses to speak of Walmsley, a gentleman who had furnished him with some particulars.

For the power of communicating these minute memorials I am indebted to my conversation with Gilbert Walmsley, later register of the ecclesiastical court of Litchfield. . . .

Of Gilbert Walmsley, thus presented to my mind, let me indulge myself in the remembrance. I knew him very early; he was one of the first friends that literature procured me, and I hope that at least my gratitude made me worthy of his notice.

He was of an advanced age, and I was only not a boy; yet he never received my notions with contempt. He was a Whig, with all the virulence and malevolence of his party; yet difference of opinion did not keep us apart. I honoured him, and he endured me. . . .

At this man's table I enjoyed many chearful and instructive hours, with companions such as are not often found: with one who has lengthened and one who has gladdened life; with Dr James, whose skill in physick will be long remembered; and with David Garrick, whom I hoped to have gratified with this character of our common friend: but what are the hopes of man! I am disappointed by that stroke of death, which has eclipsed the gaiety of nations and impoverished the publick stock of harmless pleasure.[1]

JAMES MACPHERSON

In James Macpherson's translation of the *Iliad* (1773) the study of rhythmic prose is curiously exhibited. The book was not a success; Johnson speaks very contemptuously of it.[2] But the failure was not altogether deserved. There is originality in it, and it was a good attempt to do what the well-known prose translators, Lang, Leaf, and Myers, have done: to translate the *Iliad* into prose which should have a definite cadence of its own, a more metrical cadence than even oratorical prose. Macpherson's real enjoyment of prose writing, his fondness for experiments in prose style, comes out not only in the *Iliad*, but also in the *History of Great Britain* (1775), which covers roughly the same ground as Macaulay's, from the Restoration downwards. In this work Macpherson's style is remarkably like Macaulay's. Macpherson had discovered the device of the broken-up period, which is not a trick of short, separate sentences, but a trick of dividing up a longer period into short sentences with capital letters and full stops so that the sentences are not really separate but parts of a whole.

EDWARD GIBBON

Gibbon knew quite well how impossible it is to exhaust history, but his work produces quite a different impression of finality, which it is not his intention to give, for he would not impose upon historical students. His full notes, and allusions in the notes directing people to inquire for themselves, are proof enough of that. But, as a story, as a book to be read, Gibbon's history is satisfying, and makes things clear at every point. One naturally contrasts his work with Carlyle's. There is nothing more unlike Carlyle's groaning and agony than Gibbon's pleasure in his work. He was thoroughly happy, as happy as a man of letters can be, at

---

[1] *Lives of the English Poets*, ed. G. Birkbeck Hill (3 vols., Oxford, 1905), ii. 20–21.

[2] 'Your abilities, since your Homer, are not so formidable', Johnson wrote in his famous reply to Macpherson's 'foolish and impudent letter' (Boswell's *Life of Johnson*, ed. Birkbeck Hill, rev. Powell, ii. 298).

every stage of his book, and the enormous labour of reading never seems to have depressed him, or to have destroyed his delight in the success of his art. He sent off to the printers his rough copy as soon as it was finished; no one read his proofs; the whole work was done by his own hand. And all this with a style that is regular throughout, full of life, but not with the life of Burke—varied through the subject, not varied through the rhetoric as in Burke.

In style Gibbon is one of the most correct and consistently rhetorical of English writers. By 'rhetorical' here one does not, of course, mean 'showy', but 'governed by rules of rhetoric'. When young, Gibbon read chiefly Latin and French, and did exercises in composition in these languages. The French he had read was the French of nearly his own time, and French as written by people who had gone through a training themselves in rhetoric, and who belonged to a very old rhetorical tradition, a tradition which attended to the sort of things that are attended to in *Euphues*, but with more skill and intelligence. Latin is not the ultimate source of modern prose; but the Latin authors, Cicero especially, had learnt all the special rules taught by Greek writers and theorists, and it is from Cicero that all modern good prose is descended, except good prose of the medieval tradition of modern languages.

Gibbon's remarks on earlier literary artists are interesting. He praises Fielding[1] and Spenser[2]—authors with

---

[1] 'Our immortal Fielding was of the younger branch of the Earls of Denbigh, who draw their origin from the Counts of Habsburg, the lineal descendants of Ethico, in the seventh century Duke of Alsace. Far different have been the fortunes of the English and German divisions of the family of Habsburg: the former, the knights and sheriffs of Leicestershire, have slowly risen to the dignity of a peerage; the latter, the Emperors of Germany and Kings of Spain, have threatened the liberty of the old, and invaded the treasures of the new world. The successors of Charles the Fifth may disdain their brethren of England; but the romance of *Tom Jones*, that exquisite picture of human manners, will outlive the palace of the Escurial, and the imperial eagle of the house of Austria.' *Memoirs of My Life and Writings*, ed. G. Birkbeck Hill (1900), pp. 4–5. Later (p. 243) he praised *Tom Jones* as 'the first of ancient and modern romances', and in *The Decline and Fall of the Roman Empire* he had spoken of it as 'the romance of a great master, which may be considered as the history of human nature' (ed. J. B. Bury (7 vols., 1897 ff.), iii. 363).

[2] 'The nobility of the Spencers has been illustrated and enriched by the trophies of Marlborough; but I exhort them to consider the *Fairy Queen* as the most precious jewel of their coronet.' *Memoirs*, ed. cit., p. 4.

whom he seems at first to have nothing congenial. It is certain that he learned a good deal from Johnson, for in general the rules of his prose are the same. There is the same regular construction, the same dislike of colloquial qualifications, second thoughts, additions, hanging clauses, and the like. The difference which makes the individuality of Gibbon's style not easy to seize comes partly through the cadence. Gibbon is so fond of ending his sentences with the genitive construction, for example, '. . . the imperial eagle of the house of Austria', that that comes to be a true, an habitual cadence. In almost every page there are examples, as '. . . the imperious or respectful invitation of the Senate'; or, '. . . whose effects are still visible to the eyes of superstition'.

Gibbon is fond of an ending which may be possibly scanned as two dactyls and a trochee, the end word, especially the word governed by 'of', being more often a trochee than anything else—for example, '. . . that they had not descended from the Carthaginian hero', '. . . the misfortune and courage of the captive tyrant', '. . . the eternal basis of the marble column' (trochaic endings). The dactyllic phrase before the ending might be well represented by '. . . the imperial eagle of . . .', though this does not come immediately before the trochee. This sort of thing must have been in Gibbon's mind, because this sort of thing is discussed by Cicero, and Gibbon tells us he had read Cicero's rhetorical works. It may become very tiresome, but the strange thing about Gibbon's style is that, in spite of its monotony, it is always lively. It is more regular and therefore more monotonous than Johnson's style. Johnson has many colloquial passages and a good deal of variety, at any rate in the later works, *A Journey to the Western Islands* and the *Lives of the Poets*. But Gibbon, even when talking colloquially in his notes, always minds the proportions of his phrases.

Much of the interest of Gibbon belongs, of course, to his subject. He has a great story to tell and he manages it most wonderfully, picking out the important events, and explaining from time to time the more abstract things, such as the faith of Christendom and Roman Law, necessary for the understanding of the story. This, however, is not enough to explain the freedom from monotony, page after page. Gibbon is interesting because he makes his readers feel that he himself is interested. He never writes for the sake of writing. If you felt he was merely writing for the sake of becoming a good writer, you would drop him at once. But he holds you throughout by his own interested and lively spirit.

(iv) *On Literary History*

A HISTORY of literature does not need to be closely knit. If a political history is written in bad proportion, with sudden changes of focus, abstract reasoning followed by gossip and memoirs, then it is unlikely to be of much value. But a history of literature may be ill planned and disorderly, and yet be useful and interesting, as Warton's is, because it gives valuable long extracts.[1] Literary history is like a museum, and a museum may be of use, even if ill arranged; the separate specimens may be studied by themselves. Thomas Warton's *History of English Poetry* is an excellent book to dip into, because, through its long extracts, it brings one into actual contact with the things themselves, and that, after all, is the main thing. Warton's book is much more interesting than the *Cambridge History of English Literature*, because the latter is constantly talking about things at a distance, while Warton makes distant things present.

Warton's *History*, however, was severely criticized; not only, as by Joseph Ritson,[2] for inaccuracy, but even more, as by Scott, for incoherence. Scott is merciless.

As for the late laureate, it is well known that he could never follow a clue of any kind. With a head abounding in multifarious lore, and a mind unquestionably imbued with true poetic fire, he wielded that most fatal of all implements to its possessor, a pen so scaturient and unretentive, that we think he himself must have been often astonished, not only at the extent of his lucubrations, but at their total and absolute want of connexion with the subject he had assigned to himself.[3]

This does not make allowance enough either for the difficulties of Warton's explorations or for the various purposes

---

[1] Cf. Ker, *Collected Essays*, i. 99 ff.

[2] *Observations on the three first Volumes of the History of English Poetry, in a Letter to the Author* (1782).

[3] From a review of H. J. Todd's edition of Spenser in the *Edinburgh Review*, October 1805 (*The Miscellaneous Works of Sir Walter Scott* (Edinburgh, 1861), xvii. 96).

of literary history. The relation of book to book is not like
the relation of one battle to another in the same war, or of
one political act to the other events of a king's reign.
Desultory reading and writing in literary history need not
be senseless or useless; and Warton's work retains our
interest and has a value which will outlast many ingenious
writings of critics more thoroughly disciplined. Further, his
biographer Richard Mant has ground for his opinion (contrary to Scott's) that Warton 'can trace the progress of the
mind, not merely as exemplified in the confined exertions of
an individual, but in a succession of ages, and in the pursuits
and acquirements of a people'.[1] There is more reasoning and
more coherence in Warton's history than Scott allows. The
following sentences (on Leo X and the revival of learning)
are not an unfair sample of his skill:

> It is remarkable that the court of Rome, whose sole design and
> interest it had been for so many centuries to enslave the minds of men,
> should be the first to restore the religious and intellectual liberties of
> Europe. The apostolical fathers, aiming at a fatal and ill-timed popu-
> larity, did not reflect, that they were shaking the throne, which they
> thus adorned.[2]

CLASSICAL AND ROMANTIC

In dealing with the contrast between 'classical' and
'romantic' one ought to remember that the classical ideal
produced in England hardly anything with the full classical
virtue in it. There is, of course, Milton, the great English
example of a classic poet, a poet by whom the classical ideal
was thoroughly understood and obeyed. But then Milton
was not recognized in this way; he was admired by everyone
of taste, but his wonderful classical art was not appreciated.
    The classicism of the eighteenth century is a very partial,
limited classicism; it consists a good deal in the following of
classic diction. The models for classic poetry were the satires
and epistles of Horace, the satires of Juvenal, and the works
of the elegiac poets. Those English writers who knew most

---

[1] 'Memoirs' by Richard Mant in *The Poetical Works of the Late Thomas Warton*
(2 vols., Oxford, 1802), i, p. cxxix.
[2] Ed. W. C. Hazlitt (4 vols., 1871), iii. 326.

of the classics knew generally much more Latin than Greek, and had spent much of their school time on the elegies of Ovid and in doing Latin verses in imitation of Ovid. They had little understanding of the great classics, particularly of the drama. Gray is exceptional in his Greek scholarship, and Gray had not the genius for great constructive work in the larger kinds. He could 'build the lofty rhyme' in the fashion of the Pindaric ode, but only with great labour and study, and he completed only two 'buildings' of this sort.

One of the strange things about the false classicism of the seventeenth and eighteenth centuries is that it should have been practised by people brought up on the Bible; for the English Bible, partly through its Hebrew origin, and partly through its sixteenth-century translations, afforded all sorts of contrasts to the restricted classical ideal. The metaphorical language, for instance, was often difficult for the correct classic taste to admire—as may be seen in Bossu's well-known treatise on the epic. James Macpherson was wise enough to understand the value of the Bible as a literary model, and began that tradition of solemn, impressive language which is so strong in much greater men than Macpherson—in Carlyle, for example.

Burns's poetry is no more 'romantic' than Cowper's; its attraction is not like that of *Ossian* or the *Rowley Poems*, unless you are to make 'romantic' mean everything that is lively and sensitive, in contrast with everything that is stiff and conventional. You might argue that Burns *is* 'romantic', because his poetry is full of emotion, of life and energy, and is very often rebellious. But are you then to confine the name 'classical' to literature which is merely correct, cold, wanting in spirit and sensibility? Surely that is absurd, and a hindrance to right criticism and appreciation. If the term 'romantic' is to have any value, it must be contrasted with something of a different positive value, not with something utterly frozen. 'Classical' must be kept as a term not only to

denote the false classicism of the eighteenth century, but also
the classicism of the classics themselves. When you think of
'classicism' you must think not only of the imitators of Pope
or, in France, the late imitators of the classical drama dispersed by Victor Hugo and *Hernani*, but also of Sophocles
and Virgil, of Matthew Arnold's quotation from Pindar in
his essay on Gray.[1]

> A secure time fell to the lot neither of Peleus the son of Aeacus, nor
> of the godlike Cadmus; howbeit these are said to have had, of all mor-
> tals, the supreme of happiness, who heard the golden-snooded Muses
> sing,—on the mountain the one heard them, the other in seven-gated
> Thebes.

This passage from Pindar[2] translated by Arnold is of the
most elaborate, 'classical' Greek art, and yet there is life in it
resembling that of 'romantic' poetry, simply because such
life must be found in all true poetry, the life of imaginative
thought. This passage of Greek allusive poetry moves in the
same sort of world as romantic poetry, flashing upon regions
of memory, dwelling on associations. The allusions to
'Cadmus' and 'seven-gated Thebes' have the same imaginative life as Shakespeare's 'romantic' allusions in the moon-
light scene of *The Merchant of Venice*.

> *Jessica*   In such a night
>   Did Thisbe fearfully o'ertrip the dew
>   And saw the lion's shadow ere himself
>   And ran dismay'd away.
> *Lorenzo*   In such a night
>   Stood Dido with a willow in her hand
>   Upon the wild sea banks, and waft her love
>   To come again to Carthage.
> *Jessica*   In such a night
>   Medea gather'd the enchanted herbs
>   That did renew old Aeson.[3]

✧

Where classical education, more particularly classical
education of poets and men of letters, went wrong in the

---

[1] Ward's *English Poets*, iii. 315; reprinted in *Essays in Criticism*, Second Series.
[2] *Pyth.* iii. 86.   [3] v. i. 6–14.

eighteenth century was in not appreciating the greater kinds of poetry. The epic was studied; Homer was not neglected. But Homer and Virgil, unhappily, had come to be rather bad examples for poets, through the pedantic discussions on the nature of the heroic poem. All that could be got out of the ancient epic was got by Milton; but he is an exception. There was little study of the drama till towards the end of the eighteenth century, when there appears a remarkable set of Greek scholars, Porson being the chief; and they, being scholars, had no immediate effect upon the production of English poetry. It was not till well on in the nineteenth century that the study of Greek drama began to tell upon the minds of original English writers.

The history of poetry in France is very different. Racine had got from the Greek drama something like what Milton had got from the Greek and Latin epic. Racine did what no Englishman did in the dramatic form, and no English poet, except Milton, in the epic. Racine kept the external rule or pattern of the ancients in rather too pedantic and obedient a way, but he filled that abstract plan with fresh and original life. In the tragedies of Racine the pedantry does not prevent the welling of fresh poetic energy. This new French classical tragedy has not the perfect freshness of Greek tragedy; for there is a certain externally-applied, fixed frame which the artist has to fill. But it is filled with life. There is nothing near Racine in English classic drama. Addison's *Cato* is dead, utterly dead, as a dramatic poem, and the experiment was not imitated by other poets.

༚

The spring or motive of most changes of fashion in art is not a definite taste for any one kind of fancy, but a desire to range freely, a vague hope of discovery and invention. This is as true of the change of taste in Dryden's time as of the change of taste that followed the tradition of Dryden and Pope. Dryden and his contemporaries wished to escape from the bondage of the later Elizabethans, and to strike out for fresh things, such as Dryden found in his experiments in the heroic drama, in the warfare and victories of his satiric time,

Absalom and Achitophel, and the rest. In the second half of the eighteenth century, while it is true that medieval studies help a great deal in adding new interests to literary work, it is not in any definite taste for the Middle Ages that relief and deliverance come. The most successful 'new poets', Cowper and Burns, have very few distinctly literary romantic ideas in their minds. There is hardly anything distinctive in their genius except the freedom of it, the way in which in their best work they take up any subject coming into their minds. The desire of novelty and freshness explains much more in the new literature than any particular liking for any particular source of plots and decorations.

∾

It may be observed in modern medieval art (that is, in modern literature using medieval subjects or suggestions) that very little comes from medieval literary form. The romantic authors who have made most of the Middle Ages have either not been particular students of medieval literature, or have not paid much attention to medieval forms. Victor Hugo, an example of the one sort, deals much in medieval literature, yet does not know anything particular about it. Walter Scott, an example of the other, is deeply read and widely interested in medieval literature, but what occupies his mind is the medieval business, the history and fashions of the times, not really the medieval forms. There are, of course, some interesting exceptions to this general statement, particularly Scott's conclusion to *Sir Tristrem*, his imitation of the language and stanza of the old romance. It is not till you come to Morris and Rossetti that you find the fascination of the medieval poetic forms. There are in these two romanticists very interesting oppositions and contrasts. The most medieval thing of Morris, the volume called *The Defence of Guinevere and other Poems*, is made up of all sorts of poetic forms, many of which are not strictly medieval, but applied to medieval subjects and matter. But there is undoubtedly in Morris's poetry the influence of the medieval tunes, the tunes of the metrical romances especially. In

Rossetti the chief inspiration is that of the old Italian lyric-poetry of the thirteenth century.

When medieval subjects begin to be popular in the eighteenth century, they do not come chiefly from the ages of chivalry or the ages of Gothic architecture, but from times further back in the dim, unhistorical past, and from among nations outside the well-known European system. For instance, Gray read the authors of the age of chivalry, Ville-hardouin, Joinville, and Froissart, but he did not use them much in his own literature; he went further back, and translated from Icelandic poetry. Ossian, the most successful medieval poet, belongs to the time before the Middle Ages in the common, narrow sense of the term. So, in the romantic literature of the eighteenth century, one may distinguish between literature associated with chivalry and Gothic archi-tecture (literature, say, in the region of *Ivanhoe*) and litera-ture dating for its inspiration further afield and still further back. The Scandinavians, of course, are the ancestors of a civilised people, but they are on the edge of Europe, not in the lands of the Empire. The same thing may be said of the ancient Caledonians made popular by Macpherson under the name of Ossian.

This fact may be related to what has been said already of the meagre influence of medieval poetic form. If medieval poetic form had been the spiritual power at work, it would have shown itself in imitations of Provençal verse, of old medieval lyric measures. But the existing medieval things in modern literature come either from places where the poetic form is too difficult to adapt, as in the case of Gray's Icelandic poems; or from places where the poetic form is practically non-existent, as in the case of Ossian—for, though there is a great deal of Gaelic poetry extant, this was exactly what was despised by Macpherson and refused as a model for literary form.

LITERATURE AND PHILOSOPHY

Philosophy was weak in England at the time of the great imaginative poets, weak in comparison with German philo-sophy at the same time, with German philosophy which accompanied imaginative work not less remarkable than that of English authors. After Hume philosophy in England comes to be a secondary thing; it falls out of the main road, and the succession is taken up not in England but in Germany. The most distinguished British philosopher contemporary with Wordsworth and the rest is Dugald Stewart in Edinburgh, a fine writer and an estimable man, but not comparable with Hume or his own predecessor Thomas Reid, the founder of the Scottish school of the philosophy of common sense.

Philosophy is a science, dealing with the nature of things in general, and where there is no serious philosophy, where philosophy is not the main interest, there is likely to be a reign of anarchy, of mere opinion, of guesses at truth, and a great chance for false rhetoric. One may note in the prose literature of the time of Scott, Wordsworth, and Coleridge a growth of flowery reflection and of ornamental rhetoric. Sentiment there had been before in the eighteenth century; but the early nineteenth century, while it changed the form, did not diminish the amount of sentimental literature, so that there is in nineteenth-century prose a mixed kind of composition, which pronounces, like philosophy, judgement on things in general, but without any carefully sought foundations as found in Hume, and with a good deal of vanity and caprice and unsatisfactory showy work such as can be turned out without much trouble by people who would gladly be poets, but who have not the genius or time. This look of caprice and self-will is found in some of the greatest writers: in Coleridge, who was a student of philosophy, but who never studied enough, who never really set his mind to secure himself against fallacy; in Carlyle, whose imagination was greatly influenced by German philosophy, particularly by Fichte, but rather by results, and the more popular expression of the author's meaning than by the scientific process. Coleridge and Carlyle both take short cuts and the easy way; hence the value of their philosophy is below what Wordsworth calls 'imagination, which . . . is but another name for . . . Reason in her most exalted mood',[1] and near the danger of mere preaching.

[1] *The Prelude,* xiv. 190.

Some of the essayists, particularly those who are critics of poetry, are saved from this danger; for the critics of poetry had something to discover, and, when explaining the beauties of the older poetry or of contemporary poetry (as when Coleridge explained Wordsworth in *Biographia Literaria*), they were in contact with the real world and had something definite to say. One may note that among the essayists Hazlitt began with serious application to moral philosophy, far more close than any philosophical work ever done by Coleridge.

◆

Historical students of literature are compelled to work with philosophical notions. It is one of the difficulties of the business. They cannot get along without 'the spirit of the age' in one shape or another. They talk of 'general tendencies'; they read 'the history of thought'. Further, they have to study authors who are not philosophers but full of philosophy—Goethe, Burke, Wordsworth. What are they to do? They generally have to get on as well as they can with a kind of more or less respectable sophistry. They live in a region of opinion, where debaters can play with any number of plausible commonplaces—progress, reaction, tendency, development, and so forth. They are exposed to many cruel hazards especially in dealing with those authors who are both philosophical and imaginative in genius, and chiefly imaginative in their mode of speech. It is so easy to translate them into summaries that have a noble sound about them and yet are worthless, because they try to give the poet's meaning without the poet's eye or voice. One thing may be as good as another to the prophet or the poet; the plausible summarist reads in his own way and is edified; he finds Ezekiel[1] or Wordsworth prophesying about a tile and an iron pan, handfuls of barley and pieces of bread, and then he goes telling his friends complacently that 'nothing is ignoble', that the real world is wonderful in its meanest capacity. Then that is fulfilled which was spoken of by Tennyson in *The Holy Grail*—'But one hath seen, and all

---

[1] Chapter 4.

the blind will see.' The poet or the painter has a right to speak of what he sees.

And when the evening mist clothes the riverside with poetry as with a veil, and the poor buildings lose themselves in the dim sky, and the tall chimneys become campanili, and the warehouses are palaces in the night, and the whole city hangs in the heavens, and fairyland is before us—then the wayfarer hastens home; the working man and the cultured one, the wise man and the one of pleasure, cease to understand, as they have ceased to see, and Nature, who, for once, has sung in tune, sings her exquisite song to the artist alone, her son and her master—her son in that he loves her, her master in that he knows her.[1]

The worst of it is that Formalist and Hypocrisy are waiting, on the look-out for an easy way[2]—and it is so easy to repeat 'Nothing is ignoble' or 'Every common bush afire with God'[3] when the real meaning of the plausible doctrine is that the edifier is unable to tell the difference. The dangers of plausible popular moralizing are frequent in the history of literature; philology, on the whole, is exempt and consequently at times refreshing.

There is one part of philosophy where the student of literature may be better off than his philosophical neighbour. He is protected against some of the common fallacies of ethics. He will not say that conduct is three parts of life. He knows, if he has properly attended to his novels and his comedies, that conduct is four parts of life. That is because he knows something about characters and humours, and sees nothing in the demeanour and conversation of any man that may not be called conduct, nothing that does not come under the moral law, whatever laws may be. He is also generally indifferent to ethics. What is commonly called ethics is apt to strike him as moralizing carried on by moralists who know less about humanity than Mrs. Oliphant or Anthony Trollope. For a metaphysic of ethics he may

---

[1] J. A. McNeill Whistler, 'Mr. Whistler's "Ten o'Clock" ', *The Gentle Art of Making Enemies*, 1890, p. 144.

[2] 'They said, That to go to the Gate for entrance, was by all their Countrey-men counted too far about; and that therefore their usual way was to make a short cut of it, and to climb over as they had done.' *The Pilgrim's Progress.*

[3] *Aurora Leigh*, book vii.

have some respect, because it is out of his element; and he ought not to speak irreverently of Aristotle, but he cannot help wishing that the author of the *Nicomachean Ethics* had read a few novels. The ordinary consciousness, when it belongs to a novel-reader, is sometimes ready to exclaim against the philosopher for taking human beings too much in the lump. The novel-reader is not only a casuist, who likes to take each case as it occurs, he is a thorough-going nominalist, for whom each individual is separately valuable and irreplaceable. Some of the poets who have attempted moralizing have been strong on the value of particulars as against generalizations—Blake[1] and Shelley agree in this. Shelley says (it is the title of a chapter in his *Speculations on Morals*)— 'Moral Science consists in considering the difference, not the resemblance, of persons';—and again: 'In truth, no one action has, when considered in its whole extent, any essential resemblance with any other.' This may seem a little exaggerated, or at any rate open to misconstruction. The novel-reader in his experience finds too many actions which resemble one another. But the opinion of Shelley, as a poet's criticism of moral philosophy, is significant. I do not know whether philosophers have any value for the poet's contribution; it expresses the mind of many who touch the outskirts of philosophy in the debatable land between imagination and pure reason—a dangerous enchanted ground.

[1] See p. 233 above.

I. INDEX OF NAMES

II. INDEX OF CHIEF TOPICS